1/24

Sources Of American Spirituality

Devotion to the Holy Spirit in American Catholicism

Edited by Joseph P. Chinnici, O.F.M.

PAULIST PRESS
New York ◆ Mahwah

Library of Congress
Catalog Card Number: 85-60950

ISBN: 0-8091-0366-4

Published by Paulist Press
997 Macarthur Boulevard
Mahwah, N.J. 07430

Printed and bound in the United States of America

CONTENTS

PREFACE

Imagine the "people of God" gathered together. Some, dressed impeccably, have left their downtown businesses on Market Street to spend an hour in prayer; others, reflecting the hungry eyes and ragged lives of more permanent residents, have pushed and crowded for their places inside the spacious, gilded interior of the Church. They are all present in one body: the rich and the poor; old and young; male and female; cleric and lay; Protestant and Catholic; White, Black, Hispanic, and Asian. Ringed by cross and candle acolytes winding their way around the nave's dark edges and pausing fourteen times to commemorate some place in the world where the Lord is daily tortured, these people rise and fall together, exchanging "misereres" for their sins. Later in the service, they abandon their pews and jostle each other in a slow, pained procession of humanity prostrating itself before the image of the crucified Christ. It is Good Friday at St. Boniface Church, San Francisco.

I believe that on this Good Friday in 1983 the traditional Catholic devotion of the "Way of the Cross" came to a new and fuller expression in a Church laboring to find a spiritual identity almost twenty years after the Second Vatican Council. Many of us grew up with the "piety void" of the 1960s, and so this scene at St. Boniface was not an ordinary one. In the space of one hour, the service integrated, for those of us who were there, our Catholic heritage, the commitment to reform and renewal in the Church, a sensitivity to Christian unity, and the demand for justice in the world. Led by the laity in a paraliturgical service traditionally presided over by the clergy and reciting prayers rooted in the Scriptures, we had finally crossed the gulf separating our vision and experience of the Church and the world from the vision and experience of the Catholic immigrant community. A pattern for a new devotionalism had at last been discovered; key elements in a contemporary spirituality had found expression.

This book is written from the perspective of this experience. In trying to open in a scholarly way the field of the history of American Catholic spirituality, I have presupposed some of the issues posed by the changes in Catholicism in the 1960s: What is American Catholic spirituality? What is the relationship among particular devotions, a single expression of spirituality, and Catholic identity? What do devotions imply about ecumenical relationships? Do they embody a particular ecclesiology? Why has the traditional structure of devotional Catholicism excluded the concerns of social justice?

Of course, such broad questions would completely submerge any historian in a never-ending study of the diverse forms of religious experience and expression in the Catholic community. The questions could be answered differently depending on the region of the country, the ethnic background, and the popular base of the materials consulted. Partially to remedy these problems, to limit the topic, and to acknowledge the fact that Catholic spirituality in the United States has been predominantly focused around particular devotions, I decided to examine the history of one devotion. I accidentally discovered the topic of the Holy Ghost in post-Civil War Catholicism. To distract myself during a session of our provincial council meeting, I perused the library shelves and found Thomas Hopkins' *Novena of Sermons on the Holy Ghost*. That was five years ago. *Spiritus ubi vult spirat*. The choice of this particular topic was also influenced by the belief that an historical discussion of the Holy Ghost might be especially important for a contemporary American Church influenced in so many ways, from the Pentecostal movement to the bishops' latest pastoral on economics, by Pope John XXIII's "New Pentecost."

Finally, the concerns of this book carry implications for what I believe is one of the most pressing challenges of our time: How can we express the experience of God's Spirit which has been mediated to us through our own history? How can we give our spiritual identity flesh? How can spirituality—simply put, life in the Spirit—take contemporary shape? These questions can only be addressed by a coordinated social, pastoral, institutional and theological approach, and I have tried to take into account these various perspectives and their relationship to each other in my historical narrative. I have not attempted to make specific contemporary applications, which would be out of place in a work of this nature; nor have I defined ''spiritual identity.'' Both identity and its expression are part of the person's and community's dialogue, an experience before God, born through the Word, and enlivened by the Holy Ghost. It is my hope that as a volume of historical scholarship with accompanying texts, the following pages will help shape that identity and practice. May they provide a firm base for contemporary renewal, raise some key issues, and reveal some of the vast resources which we have in the heritage of our American Catholic spirituality.

The research for this book could not have been completed without the help of numerous people. I would like to thank the following archivists: Sister M. Teresa Brady, R.D.C., Sisters of the Divine Compassion, White Plains, New York; the Rev. William C. Burn, Diocese of Charleston, South Carolina; the Rev. Louis J. Delahoyde, Diocese of Sioux Falls; James A. Donohue, Diocese of Richmond; Brother Philip Hurley, O.S.B., St. Vincent Archabbey, Latrobe, Pennsylvania; Sister M. Felicitas Powers, R.S.M., Archdiocese of Baltimore; Sister Marguerita Smith, O.P., Archdiocese of New York; Anthony Zito, Catholic University of America, Washington, D.C. Special thanks to John Farina, archivist for the Paulist Fathers, New York City, and editor for the Sources of American Spirituality series, who opened the Hecker and McSorley papers to me and provided helpful comments and valued encouragement. The Rev. Steven Avella sent me information on devotion to the Holy Ghost at St. Francis Seminary, Milwaukee. Jay Dolan, Philip Gleason, and the Rev. Gerald Fogarty, S.J., commented on the project when it was first being researched. Meg Ashcroft deciphered my scrawl for a preliminary draft, and the community at St. Francis Retreat, San Juan Bautista, provided gracious atmosphere and hospitality. Mary E. Lyons suggested stylistic and critical changes in the final manuscript. I will always be grateful to Monsignor John Tracy Ellis, scholar and friend, who has given me advice and inspiration all along the way. I owe my deepest thanks to my colleagues at the Franciscan School of Theology and my brothers in the Province of Saint Barbara. This work is dedicated to a Franciscan friar who bridged pre-Vatican II religious experience and post-Vatican II life in the Spirit. The Holy Ghost gave him a heart of flesh and through his love of the Scriptures inspired many. May Friar John Altman, O.F.M., now enjoy the expansive geography of the Spirit's own good life.

Introduction

I

POST-CIVIL WAR CATHOLICISM AND
THE HISTORY OF SPIRITUALITY

By almost any account the prevailing mood of the Catholic community from the close of the Civil War until the beginning of the twentieth century may be described as one of expectation and expansion. On October 7, 1866, thousands of onlookers gathered outside the cathedral in Baltimore as archbishops, bishops, abbots, and theologians marched in procession to open the Second Plenary Council of the Catholic Church in the United States. The ceremony reflected the fact that the Catholic population now numbered over three million, and the Church was the largest single denomination in the land. Isaac Hecker, the founder of the Paulists and one of the council's theologians, captured the mood of the day in a letter to a confrere: "The opening yesterday was *grand,* imposing and solemn. It seemed to me like a vision of Pentecost Day. The procession was admirably managed. The weather was all one could desire. It was the grandest day for all concerned, Baltimore, and the Church in the U.S. in the way of ecclesiastical expression." Here was a Church of unity, a supernatural society undamaged by the fratricidal divisions of the Civil War, a militant Body of Christ ready to take its place as the rightful heir of the American dream.[1]

The priest and literary critic in New York City, John Talbot Smith (1855–1923), wrote forty years later that the Civil War had

---

1. Isaac Thomas Hecker to Fr. [Tillotson], October [8], 1886, Paulist Fathers Archives (PFA).

weakened Puritanism as a public force and paved the way for the
growth of Catholicism as an urban social phenomenon. As a result,
succeeding years witnessed numerous parades, religious ceremonies, gigantic bazaars, and public lectures; parochial life manifested
a similar flurry of activity in the building of churches and the growth
of religious devotions. Richard H. Clarke, a prominent New York
lawyer, reflected a parallel mood in a statistical analysis of the Catholic body. He noted that in the decade from 1860 to 1870 the value
of the Church's property increased 128 percent; hospitals, colleges,
female academies, and other ecclesiastical institutions multiplied.
The Catholic community experienced a significant middle class for
the first time. The same period saw the emergence of a literary establishment, a publication industry, and a small but influential number of millionaires. By 1900 the Catholic population had quadrupled,
as German, Italian, Irish, and Eastern European immigrants arrived
to claim their inheritance. Although any generalizations must be approached with caution, it is clear that for many of the participants,
the years from 1866 to 1900 were ones of great growth and expansion.[2]

Historians have noted that this emergence of the Catholic community from its pre-Civil War defensiveness brought with it a reevaluation and critical examination of almost every aspect of the
Church's life. What Arthur Schlesinger wrote of American Protestantism equally applied to Catholicism during the period: "Perhaps
at no time in its American development has the path of Christianity
been so sorely beset with pitfalls and perils as in the last quarter of

---

2. John Talbot Smith, *The Catholic Church in New York* (New York & Boston: Hall and Locke Company, 1905), I:312–28; Clarke, "What Catholics Have
Done in the Last Hundred Years," in *Official Report of the Proceedings of the Cath-
olic Congress, Held at Baltimore Md., November 11th and 12th, 1889* (Detroit,
Michigan: William H. Hughes, 1889), 164–77. On socioeconomic status, confer
Jay P. Dolan, *The Immigrant Church, New York's Irish and German Catholics,
1815–1865* (Baltimore: The Johns Hopkins University Press, 1975); Andrew Gree-
ley, *The American Catholic, A Social Portrait* (New York: Basic Books, 1977),
Chapter 2; Paul R. Messbarger, *Fiction with a Parochial Purpose* (Boston: Boston
University Press, 1971), Chapter 2, where he correlates the emerging literature with
a middle-class social base.

the nineteenth century."[3] Such diverse phenomena as the Church and the labor movement, the development of the laity, the problems of ethnic rivalries, the establishment of colleges, the controversies over secular and parochial schooling, the intellectual encounters with Darwinism and higher criticism, and the ecumenical dialogue with Protestantism have already received scholarly treatment.[4] The bulk of the historiography has concentrated on the specific crisis known as "Americanism," which culminated in Leo XIII's encyclical *Testem Benevolentiae* in 1899. The Catholic community itself has been broken down into its various traditional and progressive factions as social, institutional, political, biographical, and most recently, theological themes have each received treatment.[5] Still, there has been

---

3. Arthur Meier Schlesinger, "A Critical Period in American Religion 1875–1900," *Massachusetts Historical Society Proceedings* 64 (June 1932):523–24.

4. Some representative titles are: H.J. Browne, *The Catholic Church and the Knights of Labor* (Washington, D.C.: Catholic University of America Press, 1949); Colman J. Barry, O.S.B., *The Catholic Church and German Americans* (Milwaukee: Bruce Publishing Co., 1953); John Richard Betts, "Darwinism, Evolution, and American Catholic Thought 1860–1900," *Catholic Historical Review* 45 (July 1959):161–85; "The Laity and the Ecumenical Spirit, 1889–1893," *Review of Politics* 26 (Jan. 1964):3–19; James F. Cleary, "Catholic Participation in the World's Parliament of Religions, Chicago, 1893," *Catholic Historical Review* 55 (Jan. 1970):585–609; Joseph F. Gower, "A 'Test Question' for Religious Liberty: Isaac Hecker on Education," *Notre Dame Journal for Education* (Spring 1976):28–43; Christa Ressmeyer Klein, "The Jesuits and Catholic Boyhood in Nineteenth Century New York City: A Study of St. John's College and the College of St. Francis Xavier, 1846–1912" (Ph.D. diss., University of Pennsylvania, 1976).

5. The literature on Americanism is vast. A good survey of the term and its religious meanings can be found in Philip Gleason, "Coming to Terms with American Catholic History," *Societas—A Review of Social History* 3 (Autumn 1973):283–313. The standard account is Thomas T. McAvoy, C.S.C., *The Great Crisis in American Catholic History* (Chicago: Henry Regnery Co., 1957). More recent perspectives are offered by Gerald P. Fogarty, S.J., *The Vatican and the Americanist Crisis: Denis J. O'Connell, American Agent in Rome, 1885–1903* (Rome: Universita Gregoriana Editrice, 1974); Robert Emmett Curran, "Prelude to 'Americanism': The New York Academia and Clerical Radicalism in the Late Nineteenth Century," *Church History* 47 (March 1978):48–65; David Killen, "Americanism Revisited: John Spalding and Testem Benevolentiae," *Harvard Theological Review* 66 (Oct. 1973):413–54; Margaret Mary Reher, "The Church and the Kingdom of God in America: The Ecclesiology of the Americanists" (Ph.D.

no attempt to interrelate many of the different dimensions of the Catholic experience during the period nor to approach the period from the viewpoint of the history of spirituality. In this context, it is important to note one minor but perhaps very significant theme in the source material which may help toward that goal. This theme was a concern for the Catholic community's spiritual experience and its religious expression in the United States.

SPIRITUALITY, POLITICS, AND COMMUNITY IDENTITY.

In a series of articles in the 1860s and early 1870s, Orestes A. Brownson, the leading Catholic intellectual of the time, analyzed what he believed were some of the interconnections between political theory, ecclesiology, the role of the Christian in society, and devotional expression. The convert-apologist argued that the Church's traditional link with Christendom, its reliance on the legal and institutional structures of the state to protect its position of social preeminence, had led in the post-Reformation period to an emphasis on the external supports and manifestations of religion: law, customs, devotions, ecclesiastical authority. This tendency was further encouraged by the acceptance of a bureaucratic system of government in Catholic countries, a type of government which affected the Church's own administration. The fear of heresy and schism and the struggle with Protestantism solidified the defensive approach. In this

---

diss., Fordham University, 1972); "Pope Leo XIII and 'Americanism,' " *Theological Studies* 34 (Dec. 1973):679–89; Thomas P. Wangler, "The Ecclesiology of Archbishop John Ireland, Its Nature, Development and Influence" (Ph.D. dissertation, Marquette University, 1968); "John Ireland's Emergence as a Liberal Catholic and Americanist: 1875–1887," *Records of the American Catholic Historical Society of Philadelphia* 81 (June 1970):67–82; "John Ireland and the Origins of Liberal Catholicism in the United States," *Catholic Historical Review* 56 (Jan. 1971):617–29; "Emergence of John J. Keane as a Liberal Catholic and Americanist (1878–1887)," *American Ecclesiastical Review* 166 (Sept. 1972):457–78; "The Birth of Americanism: Westward the Apocalyptic Candlestick," *Harvard Theological Review* 65 (July 1972):415–36; "The Americanism of J. St. Clair Etheridge," *Records of the American Catholic Historical Society* 85 (March–June 1974):88–105; "American Catholic Expansionism: 1886–1894," *Harvard Theological Review* 75 (March 1982):369–93.

way the alliance with the temporal power encouraged absolutism in state and in Church. The *oscurantisti,* those who desired "a civil government which establishes the church as the law of the land, and uses its whole force, if needed, to protect her, and to suppress error or dissent," still supported this position.[6]

Brownson continued his critique by noting the disastrous effects that this traditional type of government had on the laity. "Excessive government and over-direction of the faithful" rendered them weak and timid, a conquered people, subordinate to the clergy in matters of Church property, political responsibility, attitudes toward the civil rights of wives, and parental rights in determining educational standards. An emphasis on the monastic virtue of obedience and an apolitical asceticism completed the picture, which received its concrete expression in a mechanistic devotionalism.[7] This approach presupposed, Brownson wrote, that the laity "must be kept in leading-strings, and in no respect be trusted to their own reason and conscience." He further declared:

> They are to be treated with all gentleness, with all a father's and all a mother's love; to have plenty of dolls, toys, hobby-horses, wooden swords, and wooden guns, miniature drums and flags, plenty of play-things and amusements, pictures, statues, music, processions; but never to be treated as free agents, or to be allowed to speak for themselves. In church and state they are to be cherished and tenderly cared for, but held to be *infantes,* or mutes, incapable of speech. They cannot think or speak for themselves, and are not to assume the responsibility of their acts.[8]

---

6. Cf. Orestes A. Brownson, "Rights of the Temporal," *Brownson's Quarterly Review* 22 (Oct. 1860):462–96; "Civil and Religious Freedom," in *Brownson's Quarterly Review* (July 1864), reprinted in *The Works of Orestes A. Brownson,* collected and arranged by Henry F. Brownson (Detroit: Thorndike Nourse, 1885), 20:308–42, quotation from 323; "Recent Events in France," *Brownson's Quarterly Review* 18 (Dec. 1871):481–502.

7. Brownson, "Civil and Religious Freedom," 327; "Rights of the Temporal," 490–92.

8. Brownson, "Civil and Religious Freedom," 324.

Brownson considered this type of piety weak, effeminate, and sentimental.

In contrast to this approach, the apologist painted another picture more compatible, he felt, with modern civilization and the situation of the Catholic community in the United States. The traditional distinction in education and intelligence between the clergy and laity no longer existed; the whole population was now taken up into the governing class. In the United States, a Church's status was no longer supported by legal establishment. Instead, the law guaranteed equal protection to all religious beliefs. As a result, the Church was "thrown back on its naked rights and resources, as the spiritual kingdom of God on earth." Such a situation emancipated the faithful, restored them to political responsibility, and ushered in a regime of liberty. Brownson believed that within the Church the laity must "work under their spiritual chiefs, but that is not saying they may not work at all, or that it is not lawful for them to work with intelligence of their own, and with free will, as free moral agents."

Within this context of the "autonomy of the temporal," Brownson called for a new spiritual discipline that would train people in interior habits and "robust virtues": self-reliance, courage, individual initiative, and intellectual development. Such a spirituality could include particular devotions, pilgrimages, and loyalty to the hierarchy, but its distinctive characteristic was that it based such actions on interior dispositions and an awareness of the mystery of Christ.[9]

Although Brownson's analysis of political and religious history was tendentious, his underlying purpose was clear. He wished to provoke "thought and free discussion" on a much deeper preoccupation of the Catholic consciousness of the period: How could the experience of the Catholic in the United States, someone who was at the same time both believer and citizen, best be expressed not only in the Church and society, but also in specifically religious activity? Brownson, in contemporary language, was concerned with the relationship between history and the concrete expression of life in the Spirit.

---

9. Brownson, "Rights of the Temporal," 496, 470; "Recent Events in France," 499.

Numerous Church leaders of the late nineteenth century testified with Brownson to the fact that the devotional expression of social and religious experience was a significant component of Catholic self-definition, one which was intimately connected with other dimensions of life. In 1866, one year after the Paulists began publication of the *Catholic World,* the Jesuits started *The Messenger of the Sacred Heart.* It was not accidental that both magazines carried long commentaries on the social, political, and intellectual trends of the day while at the same time presenting sharply different attitudes toward religious expression. Three years later, in a sermon on St. Patrick's Day, Isaac Hecker asked his Irish listeners how it was possible for them to maintain religious fervor in a country where there were no monuments and battlefields comparable to those in Ireland, no social protections for the religious life of the family and neighborhood. He argued for a stronger intellectual understanding cultivated through reading, home catechism, Catholic schooling, publication societies, and libraries. The Paulist founder consistently placed his reflections on devotion within the context of contemporary society; he consciously sought for new models of holiness.[10] John Talbot Smith recognized that the celebration of the Forty Hours devotion in New York City in the 1870s became an event which concretized Catholic political and religious identity. It combined social commentary, apologetics, preaching, and a clear definition of the relationship between clergy and laity.[11] John J. Keane, the Bishop of Richmond, followed the lead of Brownson and Hecker in arguing that the religious experience of Catholics in the United States needed new forms of expression. "But the spirit of Christianity," he preached before a St. Cecilia Society in 1876,

> was not meant only for the monastic ages and the monastic orders. It was meant for every age of the world and for every situation in life. It was meant to mold and sanctify

---

10. Cf. Isaac T. Hecker, "Sermon on St. Patrick's Day," 1869, PFA; "The Saint of Our Day," *Paulist Sermons, 1863* (New York: D. & J. Sadlier, 1864), 90–102; "St. Catherine of Genoa," *The Church and the Age, An Exposition of the Catholic Church in View of the Needs and Aspirations of the Present Age* (New York: Office of the Catholic World, 1887), 170–80.

11. Smith, *The Catholic Church in New York,* 316.

every phase of advancing civilization, and to avail itself of
every improvement in the arts and sciences, for the greater
glory of God and the greater good of souls.[12]

At the Third Plenary Council in 1884 the Bishop of Dubuque,
John Hennessy, took a more polemical stance toward the position of
Catholics in a pluralistic society. He did so by emphasizing sanctity
as a mark of the Church, a "supernatural society instituted and organized by Christ," and relating it strongly to the priesthood and sacramental structure of Catholicism. Lastly, James Cardinal Gibbons
attempted to make religious expression a relevant feature of Catholic
life by removing it from the cloister and relating it to faithfulness in
the ordinary duties of one's state.[13] Whatever their approaches, these
churchmen recognized that in some way their experiences of being
Catholics in the United States needed to be related to their concrete
expressions of life in the Spirit.

SPIRITUALITY AND CONTROVERSY.

The felt need for a religious expression which in some way reflected one's experience of the Catholic community's social and religious identity also surfaced either directly or indirectly in almost
every major controversy of the time. The debate over parochial education was a good example. On November 15, 1873, the fourteen
bishops of the ecclesiastical Province of New York published a pastoral letter on the Sacred Heart. In the letter, they argued that the
devotion would provide strength and courage in the midst of
"gloomy and perilous times." Basically following the standard European explanation, the bishops emphasized the need for a public
profession of faith, and an act of reparation "for the daily outrages

---

12. Keane, "Sermon," August 23, 1876, John J. Keane Papers, Clippings,
Archives of the Catholic University of America (ACUA).
13. Hennessy, "The Sanctity of the Church," *The Memorial Volume, A History of the Third Plenary Council of Baltimore* (Baltimore: The Baltimore Publishing Company, 1885), 224–44; Gibbons, "What Is a Saint," *A Retrospect of Fifty
Years* (Baltimore: John Murphy Company, 1916) I:249–61.

and insults, the sacrileges and impieties, the indifference and unbelief, which so grievously afflict and wound the Divine Heart.'' They
also made one explicit application of the devotion to the American
religious and social situation. The people were to take the Heart of
Jesus as their model, especially the scene in the Gospel where Jesus
''suffered the little children to come to him.'' The parents could per-
form this duty toward their children only ''by giving or securing to
them a sound Catholic education.''[14]

In Advent of the same year, Thomas Scott Preston, convert pastor of St. Ann's in New York City, preached a series of sermons
further expanding the significance of devotion to the Sacred Heart.
He believed it was the antidote to the decline in faith, lack of docility
to ecclesiastical authority, and compromising attitudes especially
manifest among ''Liberal Catholics.'' These latter, he argued, were
those who

> would seek to accommodate the verities which God has re-
> vealed to the tastes and dispositions of the age; who are
> willing to hide what God has spoken, as if it were possible
> thus to be liberal in keeping from man the glorious gift of
> truth, and leaving him in the darkness of sins, where the
> bright rays of the Sun of righteousness that shine in the
> temple of Emmanuel cannot reach him.

Preston wanted to remove religion from the cloister; so did Hecker,
Brownson, Keane, and Gibbons. But the New York pastor also
wanted to do this by reestablishing Catholicism as the basis of social
order, especially in the field of education. The public act of consecration to the Sacred Heart, a religious act, conveyed for him and for
the bishops of New York a very specific political, ecclesiological,
and social meaning. It was not by chance that Preston was a major
force behind the ''shaping of conservative Catholicism.''[15]

---

14. The bishops' Pastoral is printed in Thomas Scott Preston, *Lectures Upon
the Devotion to the Sacred Heart of Jesus Christ* (New York: Robert Coddington,
1874), 165–174, quotations from 171.

15. Ibid., 159. For Preston's role in the Church in New York see Robert Em-
met Curran, S.J., *Michael Augustine Corrigan and the Shaping of Conservative Catholicism in America, 1878–1902* (New York: Arno Press, 1978).

A second more subtle but perhaps more significant example of the connection experienced between political, ecclesiological, and devotional approaches could be seen in the 1887 Memorial on the Knights of Labor. The document dealt almost exclusively with the Church in its relationship to the working classes. Still, quoting the Cardinal Archbishop of Westminster, Henry Edward Manning, the Memorial noted that a new task was before the Church. In aligning itself with the people, it needed "a new spirit and a new law of life," one which would hold the "affections" and "heart" as much as the understanding of the multitudes. Thomas Wangler has indicated that John J. Keane wrote this section of the Memorial.[16] The language is extremely significant. Keane's terminology in the Memorial could not be divorced from his language when he spoke to the St. Cecilia Society in 1876, his 1883 pastoral, or his address on Catholic societies before the 1884 Plenary Council of Baltimore. For Keane "heart" carried connotations of interiority and spirituality; it was explicitly related to religious sentiments, often as these were expressed in people's devotional attitudes and practices. If the Spirit of Truth enlightened the mind, the Spirit of Love touched the "heart." People needed to make their "hearts" conformable to the Sacred Heart, so that they could be "warm and tender and faithful towards our Saviour and God." Confraternities existed in the Church in order to give the cravings for Christian perfection external shape, to ensure "time and heart for God." Keane's advocacy of the Knights of Labor in the social sphere thus connected at a deeper level with his reflections on holiness of life in the religious sphere: the object of both was the Catholic person and the desires of the heart. Just as churchmen needed to align themselves with the desires of the worker, so they needed to give "a new spirit and a new law of life" to religious aspirations. As will be indicated, Keane attempted to do this very thing. In a very subtle way, on the anthropological level, his view

---

16. The Memorial is reprinted in Gibbons, *A Retrospect,* I:190–209, with the relevant section found on p. 201. For Wangler's opinion see Thomas Wangler, "Emergence of John J. Keane as a Liberal Catholic and Americanist (1878–1887)," 468.

of society, understanding of the role of the hierarchy, and his spirituality were interconnected.[17]

Speeches at the Columbian Catholic Congress and the World's Parliament of Religions in 1893 continued this same search to give social and religious experience concrete form in symbolism. Richard Clarke portrayed Columbus as the new model of holiness for the United States. He argued that the discoverer of America, a child of the Church, linked the Middle Ages with the present, came "in the fullness of time," united science and faith, and fought every popular superstition. Marked by "religious devotion and contemplativeness," Columbus was a true mystic, "one who saw in the fall of the sparrow, the raiment of the lily and the rose, the mystic and ever provident hand of God. . . ." "Christopher," Clarke romanticized, "means Christ-Bearer—not the ordained eucharistic priest, but, in another and exceptional sense, one who carries the living and teaching Christ, the brother, Redeemer, and Savior of men in his human, divine, and missionary personality, across continents and over oceans to other continents and oceans to the utmost boundaries of the earth."[18] Walter Elliott followed Clarke at the Congress and pursued the same theme. At the Parliament of Religions, Keane and Gibbons attempted to appeal to the universally shared desires of humanity by presenting Christ as a living symbol uniting all people and the Church as a perfect society embodying multiplicity in unity.[19]

---

17. This analysis of Keane is based on a close reading of the following texts: "Sermon," August 23, 1876, John J. Keane Papers, Clippings, ACUA; "In Spiritu et Veritate," 1879, ibid.; "Pastoral Letter, Feb. 2, 1883," (Richmond: Catholic Visitor Press), 15–22, ibid.; "Catholic Societies," in *The Memorial Volume: A History of the Third Plenary Council of Baltimore,* 190–208; John J. Keane to Cardinal Manning, April 23, 1887, Manning Papers, ACUA.

18. Clarke, "Columbus: His Mission and Character," *The World's Columbian Catholic Congresses with an Epitome of Church Progress* (Chicago: J.S. Hyland & Company, n.d.), 21–28, quotations from 22, 24–26.

19. Elliott, "Walter Elliott on Catholic Missionary Work," ibid., 55–61; John Joseph Keane, "The Ultimate Religion," and "The Incarnation Idea in History and in Jesus Christ," in Rev. John Henry Barrows, D.D., ed., *The World's Parliament of Religions, The Columbian Exposition of 1893* (Chicago: The Parliament Publishing Company, 1893), II:1331–38, 882–88; James Gibbons, "The Needs of Humanity Supplied by the Catholic Religion," ibid. I:485–93.

Lastly, the specific debates over "Americanism" at the end of the century testified that part of the controversy involved the ways in which distinct experiences took outward shape in religious practices. Charles Maignen in his work *Le Père Hecker: Est-il un Saint?* touched the issue directly. He addressed at length the issue of sanctity and its social dimensions. A large portion of Maignen's work was devoted to asceticism, the monastic life, the evangelical counsels, preaching of the Gospel and homiletic content, the revival of mysticism, devotional life, and the role of the virtue of obedience in the life of the Church. He correctly related traditional religious practices to the politics of the 1864 *Syllabus of Errors*. *Testem Benevolentiae* itself linked American customs and political views with opinions "de ratione christiane vivendi." John Ireland, writing as J. St. Clair Etheridge, Félix Klein, A. J. Delattre, and P. L. Péchenard, presented ample testimony that part of the disagreement between the two sides involved expressions of spiritual life.[20]

All these sources indicate that a struggle to fashion a religious expression reflective of experience took place in an unprecedented way in the post-Civil War Catholic community. Bishops, intellectuals, and lay commentators sought to give the social and spiritual experience of the people concrete embodiment. Devotions, prayer forms, and examples of holiness thus symbolized for many their views of politics, society, the Church, and themselves. Otto Zardetti, a professor of theology, consultor to bishops, and Bishop of Saint Cloud, Minnesota, described part of the process in this way:

> Devotion, as well as Religion, is at first something internal, spiritual, and as such is the universal source or origin of all external worship. But, though internal, it cannot long conceal itself; for the nature of the operations of the Soul

---

20. Charles Maignen, *Le Père Hecker. Est-il un Saint?* (Rome: Desclée, Lefebvre et Cie, 1898); Wangler, "The Americanism of J. St. Clair Etheridge"; Félix Klein, "Catholicisme Americain," *Revue francaise d'Edembourg* (Sept.–Oct. 1897):305–14; A.-J. Delattre, S.J., *Un Catholicisme Américain* (Namur: Auguste Godenne, 1898); P.L. Péchenard, "The End of 'Americanism' in France," *The North American Review* 170 (March 1900):420–32; for the Latin Text of *Testem Benevolentiae* see *Lettres Apostoliques de S.S. Léon XIII* (Paris: A. Roger et F. Chernoiz, 1903), V:182–201.

is such that they speedily make themselves felt for good or for evil outwardly. Hence devotion no sooner takes firm root in a soul than it breaks forth into outward acts of worship, takes shape and form in various ways, and gradually develops into a corresponding external organization in the Church. By a certain law of crystallization working in the Church of God, every internal religious event soon becomes externally perceptible, soon binds together by a spiritual bond of common feelings and views the minds of pious people already impressed and influenced alike by the same internal devotion.[21]

Today, the historian of spirituality would note that this internal reality was inextricably connected with the space and time in which the subjects stood who experienced it: the life of the Spirit was always historically rooted.

In summary, what I have tried to describe is a Catholic community in the process of self-consciously articulating its own religious experiences. When examined from this perspective of the history of spirituality, the post-Civil War Church seems to have been plagued by several significant questions: What is the relationship in a person's experience between politics and religious expression? What does it mean to represent devotionally one's Catholic experience within the context of a disestablished Church and a pluralistic society? How do certain religious practices express, shape, and, in turn, determine a community's religious identity? It is clear that these questions were at times spoken; at other times, they simply lay beneath the surface of events. Still, they formed at least one of the strains in the Church's consciousness and determined the shape of some of its controversies. It is in the context of this struggle to shape a Catholic spirituality in the United States that it now becomes possible to examine one of the most creative, widespread, and indicative religious expressions of the era, devotion to the Holy Ghost.

---

21. Otto Zardetti, *Special Devotion to the Holy Ghost, A Manual* (Milwaukee: Hoffman Brothers, 1888), 135–36.

II

THE SEARCH FOR A SPIRITUAL IDENTITY:
EUROPEAN AND AMERICAN ORIGINS OF
DEVOTION TO THE HOLY GHOST

The Third Person of the Trinity has always represented one of the most interior, personal, and mysterious aspects of Catholicism; in the nineteenth century, as a sign of transcendence, the Spirit also embodied the desire for universal reconciliation or synthesis. Perhaps precisely because of this all-embracing character, close association with personality (i.e., identity), and inability to be pictured, the Holy Ghost became the dominant symbol of a Catholic community searching for ways to express its emotional experience. Margaret Mary Reher has argued the importance of the Holy Spirit in the ecclesiologies of the Americanists, but the Spirit's role went quite beyond the confines of a theological difference among bishops.[1] A concern to describe the meaning of the Spirit in the community, and therefore the identity of the community itself, surfaced on the elite and popular levels, in juridical, institutional, and intellectual ways. This concern cut across geographical, economic, social, political, ethnic, and educational lines. At least five different but interacting historical sources witnessed to this interest in the Spirit:

(1) Institutional directives: Papal decrees; conciliar and synodal legislation.

---

1. Reher, "The Ecclesiology of the Americanists," 80–91.

16

(2) Communal representations: sodalities, confraternities, immigrant societies, particular devotions of religious orders.

(3) Personal interaction: private journals, correspondence, conversation, and spiritual direction.

(4) Popular literary compositions: sermons, novena cards, theology texts, prayer books, periodical articles, pamphlets.

(5) Artistic expression: images and pictures.

The origin of this devotion to the Holy Ghost and its significance for the Catholic community can be seen first in the activities of two leading churchmen between 1865 and 1884.

HENRY EDWARD MANNING:

EUROPEAN ROOTS OF DEVOTION TO THE HOLY GHOST.

The example and writings of Henry Edward Manning provided the major European source for devotion to the Holy Ghost in the United States. The Archbishop of Westminster corresponded about the devotion with Isaac Hecker, John Keane, Otto Zardetti, and Denis O'Connell, the last when he was rector of the North American College in Rome. Manning's *The Temporal Mission of the Holy Ghost* went through at least seven American editions between 1865 and 1890; its counterpart, *The Internal Mission of the Holy Ghost,* saw five reprintings from 1875 to 1890. These essays inspired four major works on the Spirit: Keane's *Pastoral Letter* and *Sodality Manual* (1879); Thomas Scott Preston's *Divine Paraclete* (1879); Zardetti's *Devotion to the Holy Ghost* (1888); and *Novena of Sermons on the Holy Ghost* by Thomas F. Hopkins (1901). In 1883 the cardinal personally spoke with Keane about the ''efforts to spread abroad our blessed devotion to the Holy Ghost, but also to arouse a more Apostolic spirit among the clergy, and a more solidly Catholic spirit among the faithful at large.'' In addition, the Americanists heavily relied on Manning for their ideas on the importance of the local hierarchy, support of the labor movement, and the inevitable tendency toward democracy. No clear picture can be given of the significance of devotion to the Holy Ghost in the United States without first examining Manning's understanding of the relationships among the Spirit and the Church, the state, history, and the person.[2]

The Church. In an autobiographical memoir written late in life Manning described the origin of his own devotion to the Holy Ghost. He noted that after he had published a series of sermons, someone castigated him because he had not included any reflections on the Third Person of the Trinity. As a result, Manning purchased every book he could find on the subject and soon realized that an appreciation of the Holy Ghost was at the heart of the Church's infallibility. The "perpetual presence and office of the Holy Ghost," he wrote, "raises the witness of the Church from a human to a Divine certainty." Manning's interest in the devotion was thus rooted in his own conversion experience from the Anglican to the Roman Church. The Holy Spirit represented that principle of life which supported the unity, perpetuity, and visibility of the Body of Christ.[3]

The convert's writings on the Spirit reflected his apologetic and ecclesiological interests. In *Temporal Mission,* Manning argued that the Spirit supported a truth which was "one, harmonious, indivisible; a structure in perfect symmetry, the finite but true reflex of truth as it reposes in the Divine Intelligence." The Spirit of Unity meant one which was organic "in succession, hierarchy, and valid sacraments"; moral, "in the communion of charity among all members of the particular churches." Manning summarized his thinking in these words:

> One principle of life cannot animate two bodies, or energise in two organizations. One mind and one will fuses and holds in perfect unity the whole multitude of the faithful throughout the ages, and throughout the world. The unity

---

2. John J. Keane to your Eminence [Manning], August 1, 1885, Manning Papers, ACUA. For other examples of correspondence see Cardinal Manning to Denis J. O'Connell, Whitsunday, 1887, ibid.; Otto Zardetti to Your Eminence, October 14, 1889, ibid. The relationship between Hecker and Manning will be treated later as will the major works on the Holy Spirit printed in the United States. For Manning's impact on the Americanists confer Thomas Wangler, "The Birth of Americanism, Westward the Apocalyptic Candlestick."

3. Confer Edmund Sheridan Purcell, *Life of Cardinal Manning, Archbishop of Westminster* (New York: The Macmillan Company, 1896), II:795.

of faith, hope and charity—the unity of the one common Teacher—renders impossible all discrepancies of belief and of worship, and renders unity of communion, not a constitutional or an external rule of discipline, but an intrinsic necessity and an inseparable property and expression of the internal and supernatural unity of the mystical body under one Head and animated by one Spirit.[4]

It was not surprising that he could conclude in *Internal Mission:* "The test of the spiritual man is his conformity to the mind of the Church. *Sentire cum Ecclesia* in dogma, discipline, traditions, devotions, customs, opinions, sympathies . . ."[5]

When reflecting on the relationship between the Spirit and the Church, the English cardinal also consistently defined the Body of Christ as a moral person existing in a visible, hierarchical organization. Manning interpreted the article in the Creed, "I believe in the Holy Ghost, the Holy Catholic Church," to mean that the indissoluble union between the Spirit and the Church was personal and substantial. It took place in the *"visible incorporation* of His presence." "The Holy Spirit, through the Church," he wrote,

enunciates to this day the original revelation with an articulate voice, which never varies or falters . . .

And this office of enunciating and proposing the faith is accomplished through the human lips of the pastors of the Church. The pastoral authority, or the episcopate, together with the priesthood and the other orders, constitute an organized body, divinely ordained to guard the deposit of the Faith.[6]

---

4. Manning, *The Temporal Mission of the Holy Ghost: Or Reason and Revelation.* (New York: D. & J. Sadlier & Co., 1890), 34, 43, 87–88.

5. Manning, *The Internal Mission of the Holy Ghost* (New York: D. & J. Sadlier & Co., third edition, 1885), vi.

6. Manning, *Temporal Mission,* 51, 77, 91. Confer his essay "Christianity and Antichristianism," in Henry Edward, Cardinal Archbishop of Westminster, *Miscellanies* (New York: The Catholic Publication Society, third American edition, 1880), especially 610–17.

Manning argued that this "temporal office" of teaching had been given on Pentecost "emphatically to the Apostles, and inclusively to the faithful." The people, "listening for a voice to guide them in the midst of contradictory teachers," would hear the Holy Spirit primarily in "Pontiffs, Councils, Traditions, Scripture, and universal consent." Although individuals could exercise their reason and private judgment, those human faculties could not really be considered "principles of faith." The English churchman's work definitely stood out among the theologians of the nineteenth century as giving a spiritual foundation to an apologetics of hierarchical authority.[7]

State. Just as Manning's discourses on the Holy Spirit in *Temporal Mission* were framed within the context of his conversion from Anglicanism, so his work *Internal Mission* cannot be understood outside of his battle with the nineteenth century laicist state. In 1873 the cardinal wrote a series of essays on "Caesarism and Ultramontanism." At that time the Prussian government had passed the Falk laws curtailing the Church's liberty in the German Empire to communicate with Rome, educate the clergy, and appoint priests to parishes. Manning referred to these policies as manifestations of a "modern Caesarism," or the union of the spiritual and temporal powers in one person. To counteract it he outlined the principles of "Ultramontanism." This latter, he wrote, consists (1) in the separation of the two powers, and the vesting them in different persons; (2) in claiming for the Church the sole right to define doctrines of faith and morals; and (3) to fix the limits of its own jurisdiction in that sphere; (4) in the indissoluble union of the Church with, and submission to, the universal jurisdiction of the Holy See.[8]

Manning believed that only the Church with its doctrine, discipline, faith, and jurisdiction *rooted in the Holy Spirit* was capable of limiting the state's encroachment on the modern liberties of conscience, religion, family life, and citizenship. Only the strength of the Spirit could withstand the assaults of the absolute state. The *Internal Mission* repeated this position in its discussions of the virtue of faith. Referring specifically to the attempts in England "to interfere with the Christian education of your children," Manning argued

---

7. Manning, *Temporal Mission*, 92, 6, 98.
8. Manning, "Caesarism and Ultramontanism," *Miscellanies*, 536.

that the test of the Spirit dwelling in the hearts of the faithful would be their obedience and loyalty to the institutional Church. That meant that the people would not suffer their children to go to "any school whatsoever where they will be exposed to the remotest danger of losing their faith."[9]

History. Manning's understanding of the historical course of Christendom supported his interpretation of devotion to the Holy Ghost in Church and state. In 1849 he addressed the clergy of the archdeaconry of Chichester in words which would become familiar to his followers in the United States:

> The foundations of Christendom—not of the Church—are disappearing, and modern legislation has removed itself from the basis of revealed truth to the state of natural society. What is then our duty?—not to lament the past nor to dream of the future, but to accept the present. Dreams and lamentations weaken the sinews of action: and it is by action alone that the state of the world can be maintained. . . . A new task, then, is before us. The Church has not [sic] longer to deal with parliaments and princes, but with the masses and with the people. Whether we will or no, this is our work. And for this work we need *a new spirit and a new law of life*. The refined, gentle, shrinking character of calm and sheltered days will not stand the brunt of modern democracy.[10]

The apologist expanded on this view in *The Fourfold Sovereignty of God*. He argued that the persecution by the modern state had forced the strongest alliance possible between pope and bishops, pastors and people. It had also forced the Church to identify itself as

---

9. Manning, *Internal Mission,* 79–80. For Manning's understanding of the Church as a corporation with powers of legislation, government, and judicial authority, see "Inaugural Address, Academia of the Catholic Religion, Session 1868–69," *Miscellanies,* 267–91, especially 268.

10. As quoted in Zardetti, *Special Devotion to the Holy Ghost,* 53–54. It was this passage from Manning that was quoted in the Memorial on the Knights of Labor.

a spiritual society. History, then, was providential. Free of the state, the Church could now become "once more, what it was in the beginning, a society of individuals, vigorous, pure, living, and life-giving." The opportunity had indeed come for "a new spirit and a new law of life," for the spread of a supernatural society "requiring of all men—from its highest pastor, the supreme Pontiff, who sits on the throne as Vicar of Jesus Christ, down to the little Catholic child in the school—the same act of faith, the same submission of the intellect and of the will to the sovereignty of God."[11]

Person. When Manning analyzed how the Holy Ghost worked in the life of the individual, he emphasized both the Spirit as an antidote to rationalism and the Spirit as the source of personal dignity. He addressed the relationship between reason and faith first in *Temporal Mission,* where he argued that the corroding tendency to accept reason as the "supreme and spontaneous source of religious knowledge" could only be met by strict adherence to the infallible teaching authority of the Church. His presentation particularly rejected the critical interpretation of biblical inspiration in the Anglican *Essays and Reviews.* The consequences of his position for the individual were more clearly presented in *Internal Mission.* There Manning argued that although the prelude to the act of faith rested upon reason, once a person professed belief, the Holy Spirit entered, "illuminating the reason, moving the will, and kindling in the heart a love of the truth." Thus, once baptized, a person remained in this supernatural order or new dispensation by practicing loyalty, obedience, docility, and submission to the Church. It was characteristic of Manning's approach that he saw three evils threatening faith as a gift of the Spirit: infidelity, "an intellectual denial of the truth" and "an

---

11. Henry Edward Manning, *The Fourfold Sovereignty of God* (London: Burns & Oates, n.d.), 159, 171. The first passage was quoted in Zardetti, *Special Devotion to the Holy Ghost,* 48. Manning's interpretation of an alliance between pastors and people should be read within the context of the popular Anglican interest in Catholic ritual and the struggle of the Irish people against an established church. Confer "Inaugural Address, Academia of the Catholic Religion, Session 1866–7," *Miscellanies,* 173–92, especially 186; "A Letter to His Grace the Archbishop of Armagh, Primate of All Ireland," ibid., 361–87; "Ireland, A Letter to Earl Grey, 1868," ibid., 213–55, especially 222. The context was completely different from that of republicanism in the United States.

indolent refusal to correspond to the light of the Holy Ghost''; a contentious spirit marked by pride, indocility, prejudice, controversy, animosity, and perversity; and immorality. Here the Spirit functioned as the supernatural prevention of the criticism of authority.[12]

This concentration on the Spirit as a principle of obedience to institutional authority was in large measure balanced by Manning's understanding of devotion in the life of the individual. He divided theology into dogmatic, moral, ascetical, and mystical categories. In this system, although dogmatic theology, ''a correct verbal expression of the truth correctly conceived and known,'' ruled over all of life, it also generated and quickened devotion or mystical theology. Correct devotion, in turn, preserved dogma in the life of the person by making it vivid, tender, intimate, interior, and personal. For Manning, the maturity of the Christian message was most fully represented in particular devotional practices, especially those focusing on the Incarnation: devotion to the Blessed Sacrament, Sacred Heart, Holy Name of Jesus, Passion, and Blessed Mother. It was in these activities that the abstract and the concrete, the communal and the individual, truth and affection, the Church and the person combined into one whole. Running throughout his works on the Holy Ghost were heartfelt prayers, encouragements to devotion, and reflections on the beauty of the indwelling Spirit in the souls of the just. What great dignity this Spirit conferred on people, making them creatures of God, children of the Church, possessors of truth, providential agents of the Incarnation.[13]

Given this understanding of the role of devotions, it is not surprising that Manning's interpretation of the Holy Ghost in Church, state, history, and the person took concrete form in the foundation of a religious association. During Lent of 1877, Father Henry Augustus Rawes, superior of the Oblates of St. Charles, founded the

---

12. Manning, *Temporal Mission*, 24; *Internal Mission*, 63, 26, 74–75. For a similar interpretation see his sermon, ''The Disciples of the Holy Ghost,'' *Sermons on Ecclesiastical Subjects* (New York: Christian Press Association Pub. Co., 1899), 310–41.

13. See Henry Manning, *The Glories of the Sacred Heart* (New York: D. & J. Sadlier & Co., 1876), 75–99; p. 80 for the definition of dogma; and *Temporal Mission*, 242–47.

Confraternity of the Servants of the Holy Ghost in the Church of St. Mary of the Angels, Bayswater, London. Upon Manning's request, Leo XIII formally erected the Confraternity on March 10, 1878, and it was elevated into an archconfraternity in June 1879. The object of the new association was "to arouse the Catholic clergy and laity to greater devotion in the practice of that faith, which the Church professes concerning the Third Person of the Godhead." Although the members undertook no obligations other than enrollment and the intention to promote the glory of the Holy Ghost, Rawes composed a handbook or manual of prayers which reflected many of Manning's ideas. The cardinal himself later elaborated the significance of the devotion in a letter to Denis O'Connell:

> Our Lord ordained and commissioned His Apostles, and yet commanded them to wait till they should receive the Holy Ghost coming upon them. Is not this, then, the devotion for bishops and priests? Are not Christians the anointed, and is not the devotion for all Christians? How can we be spiritually minded or supernatural without it? Are not men spiritual and supernatural in the measure in which they have fellowship or communion with Him? But I am writing truisms. Is not the peril of the day the unspirituality of men and the revival of naturalism in the world? And how can this be met by a diametrical and supreme antagonism if not met by preaching the Holy Ghost and making our priests His disciples? Lastly, it is this devotion that illuminates and infuses the light of all dogmas of the faith. All things are visible in the light of the sun, so all truths from the Holy Spirit to Extreme Unction are made manifest by devotion to the Holy Ghost. If we were to *pleni Spiritu sancto,* we should understand the divine tradition of the Church and the Summa of St. Thomas by a kindred intuition.[14]

---

14. Manning to Denis J. O'Connell, Whitsunday, 1887, as quoted in Zardetti, *Special Devotion to the Holy Ghost,* 178. On the foundations of the Confraternity, see ibid., 141–50.

It is clear that for Manning the particular devotion to the Holy Ghost symbolized in a religious form many of his other opinions on the person, the Church, and the state. It was a symbol that both shaped and was shaped by the Catholic Church's own identity in the modern world. The Englishman's contemporaries in the United States would not be slow to recognize this fact.

ISAAC THOMAS HECKER:

ORIGINS OF THE DEVOTION IN THE UNITED STATES.

Isaac Hecker, a convert and founder of the Missionary Priests of St. Paul the Apostle, was the most important indigenous source for devotion to the Holy Ghost in the United States. His early years have been well studied, and the full significance of his activities and thought for Catholicism need not be repeated here.[15] Suffice it to say that the New England Transcendentalism of the 1840s was the seed ground for his beliefs about the Spirit. Personally in contact with George Ripley, Orestes Brownson, and Bronson Alcott, and intellectually conversant with the German romantics, Hecker fashioned from them a theological base for his own preoccupation with the inner life. His writings testify that the "earnest seeker" grew to identify his own inner yearnings and aspirations first by the name "spirit" and then by the more traditional concept of the "Holy Spirit." "Spirit" in its personal and intimate dimensions represented for him the fullness of Christian perfection, union, and communion, for which he longed. Present in the deepest part of himself, the Spirit was also a transcendental principle of synthesis, the reality of God's life in which action and contemplation, the person and the world, the individual and society, faith and reason, authority and liberty were united.

---

15. Major works on Hecker include Walter Elliott, C.S.P., *The Life of Father Hecker* (New York: Columbus Press, 1891); John Farina, *An American Experience of God: The Spirituality of Isaac Hecker* (New York: Paulist Press, 1981); Farina, ed., *Hecker Studies, Essays on the Thought of Isaac Hecker* (New York: Paulist Press, 1983); Joseph McSorley, C.S.P., *Father Hecker and His Friends* (New York: B. Herder, 1952).

This life of the Holy Spirit, Hecker came to believe, was symbolized in an historical way in the institutional structures, intellectual tradition, and mystical sacramentalism of the Roman Catholic Church. Describing his conversion experience in a letter to Brownson four months before his entrance into the Church, he wrote: ''all outward reforms presuppose an inward regeneration of the heart as their cause and foundation and no institution but the Church has the power to effect this nor has this aim [in] view. Therefore I would yield myself up wholly to the Church as the only means of Redeeming the Race from the innumerable evils under which we now suffer.''[16] Just as the argument with Anglicanism had shaped Henry Edward Manning's understanding of the Holy Spirit, so Hecker's own conversion experience provided the foundation on which he would build his views. He would always make a close correlation between the Spirit as the interior life of the soul, the Spirit as a higher agent of reconciliation, and the Spirit as embodied in the historical reality of Roman Catholicism.

In addition to the Transcendental emphasis on synthesis, the focus on the personal experience of the Spirit in the depths of the soul revealed Hecker's background in Jacksonian politics and his ''new apologetics'' in religion. From his earliest exposure to the Locofoco Party in the 1830s until his death, Hecker was committed to the tenets of Jacksonian democracy: The acceptance of a fundamental moral and natural law as the basis of constitutionalism; the exaltation of the free and responsible individual; confidence in the divine destiny and special mission of America. In the 1840s he developed his own correlative formulation of the ''theological anthropology that discerned within human consciousness the traces of an orientation towards a supernatural destiny.'' As a Catholic, Hecker combined these two positions into a unique blend of politics and religious apologetics which emphasized the convergence in the person between republican

---

16. Hecker to Brownson, March 15, 1844, in Joseph F. Gower and Richard M. Leliaert, eds., *The Brownson-Hecker Correspondence* (Notre Dame: University of Notre Dame Press, 1979), 86. Especially helpful on the Transcendentalist notion of synthesis is Farina, *An American Experience,* chapters 4–6; Mary E. Lyons, *A Rhetoric for American Catholicism: The Transcendental Voice of Isaac T. Hecker* (Ph.D. diss., University of California, Berkeley, 1983).

political institutions and ecclesiastical structures. The synthesis came to clear expression in his "Future Triumph of the Church" speech before the Second Plenary Council of Baltimore in 1866. Throughout his life Hecker reflected out of this experience of the unity between political and religious beliefs. Theologically, he translated it to mean that the "Creative Spirit" was one both inwardly and outwardly; one in reason, nature, society, and Church.[17]

Hecker's mature reflections on the Spirit in the person, the Church, and the world fully evolved only after Vatican Council I in 1870. The definition of papal infallibility and the European reaction to it forced him to rethink the theological synthesis he had implicitly accepted since the 1840s. Given his own personal experience and his encounter with Transcendentalism, it is not surprising that he turned to the Holy Spirit as both the agent and symbol of his new synthesis. He clearly expressed this understanding in his programmatic essay of 1875, *An Exposition of the Church in View of Recent Difficulties and Controversies, and the Present Needs of the Age.* Fortunately Hecker has left some correspondence and a series of "Notes on the Holy Spirit" which indicate the key principles of his thinking and clarify the significance of devotion to the Third Person of the Trinity in his experience during this time.

From June 1873 to October 1875, Hecker traveled extensively in Europe, Egypt, and the Holy Land. In his notes taken during that time he presented some observations on the contrary tendencies of the age. On the one hand, the Church had just proclaimed the dogma of papal infallibility. This declaration was the providential culmination of three centuries of emphasis on external organization and the Latin-Celtic virtues of authority, tradition, loyalty, and obedience. Yet, precisely because of this, Hecker noted, the Church was

---

17. Confer Edward J. Langlois, C.S.P., "Isaac Hecker's Political Thought," in Farina, *Hecker Studies,* 49–86; on the theological anthropology see Joseph Gower, "Democracy as a Theological Problem in Isaac Hecker's Apologetics," in Thomas M. McFadden, ed., *America in Theological Perspective* (New York: Seabury Press, 1976), 37–55; Gower, "The 'New Apologetics' of Isaac Thomas Hecker (1819–1888)," (Ph.D. diss., University of Notre Dame, 1978), 117 for quotation. For the speech before the Second Plenary Council see *Sermons Delivered During the Second Plenary Council of Baltimore* (Baltimore: Kelly & Piet, 1866), 66–86.

weak: The Dollingerites and Old Catholics had separated from
Rome; the Catholics in France, Italy, and Spain, enfeebled by the
emphasis on passive obedience, were allowing themselves to be governed by a handful of atheists; in Germany the Church suffered from
state persecution. On the other hand, he wrote, there were signs of
life: some republican tendencies in the Latin-Celtic races; the great
drive to national unification in the German Empire; the dominance
of the Teutonic and Saxon races with their emphasis on individual
rights, science, reason, conscience, the dignity of the person. The
question posed itself: In such a world, how could the Church be restored to its normal state, "when she is led by the Holy Ghost in the
peaceful work of the conversion of the world and salvation of souls,
and the advancement of Christian civilization"? To answer the question, Hecker looked for a transcendental principle of synthesis between the Church and culture: "We must elevate our minds to the
higher region, where all truth is found in unity exclusive of all di-
vergency, to bring about an entire union which will be lasting."
Once again, as in the 1840s, the Holy Spirit seemed to be leading
him. His own personal experience in Egypt and the encounter with
Eastern culture confirmed this belief.[18]

Hecker believed that the most important step in the "restoration
of the Church to its normal position" would be "to turn the attention
of the souls of the faithful to the Holy Spirit within their souls as their
immediate guide." The Holy Ghost working in the interior of the
person would then enable individuals to break from the excesses of
external authority and mechanical devotionalism. This direct contact
with God would give rise to new and enlarged hopes, spontaneous
life, increased sanctity, enlightened intellects, intense activity, great
deeds, and heroic action. In addition, such an emphasis on the part
of the Church would align it with the modern political movements
of republicanism and the "longing of every soul to be united with
God." A focus on the Holy Spirit would reinstate the Church in the
intellectual and moral conscience of the age as the source of supreme
truth and highest good for humanity. A new phase of the Church's

---

18. Isaac T. Hecker, "Notes on the Holy Spirit," 22, 87, and passim., PFA.
For background see Farina, *An American Experience,* 137–57; Langlois, "Isaac
Hecker's Political Thought."

history had begun, Hecker argued. The coming age would be one of the Spirit. He summarized his positions in these words from the *Exposition:*

> The renewal of the age depends on the renewal of religion. The renewal of religion depends upon a greater effusion of the creative and renewing power of the Holy Spirit. The greater effusion of the Holy Spirit depends on the giving of increased attention to His movements and inspirations in the soul. The radical and adequate remedy for all the evils of our age, and the source of all true progress, consist in increased attention and fidelity to the action of the Holy Spirit in the soul.[19]

It was clear that for Isaac Hecker the Spirit was the agent and symbol of reconciliation between the person, the Church, and the world.

The significance of this experience and understanding of the Spirit comes into sharp relief in an examination of the extant correspondence between Hecker and Henry Edward Manning. In a letter to the English churchman in the early 1870s, the American outlined the basic principles of his approach:

1. The Church on its human side consists of those souls who are united to God through Christ.
2. The divine external authority of the Church is the criterion of supernatural truth.
3. The interior inspirations of the Holy Spirit are the immediate guide and proximate means of the sanctification of the soul.
4. The immediate aim of the authority of the Church is to teach supernatural truth and the paths of the Holy Spirit, and to keep men from going astray.

---

19. Isaac T. Hecker, "Notes on the Holy Spirit," 84–85, 47; *An Exposition of the Church in View of the Recent Difficulties and Controversies, and the Present Needs of the Age* (1875) was reprinted as "The Church in View of the Needs of the Age," in *The Church and the Age,* 7–63; quotation from 26.

5. The papal authority having been defined and fixed forever by the Church in the Vatican Council, her work now is to turn the attention of souls primarily to the interior operations of the Holy Spirit.
6. This will give rise to the increase of the Holy Spirit in the hearts of the faithful, the renewal of the face of the earth, and the regeneration of society.[20]

These beliefs about the Holy Spirit summarized the principles of Hecker's *Exposition of the Church in View of Recent Difficulties.*

Before he published the *Exposition,* Hecker again wrote to Manning for his impressions. The archbishop was highly complimentary. He agreed that the "low state of mind in respect to the office of the Holy Ghost in the Church has caused much of our modern errors; and forgetfulness of His presence in us had made us unspiritual and merely natural." The Englishman apparently also interpreted Hecker to be arguing for a new outpouring of the Spirit, on which, he noted, he had "no light." Manning continued in these words:

> But that we ought to revive the two-fold office of the Holy Ghost in our intellect and our soul is clear. . . .
> I fully believe either that we are near the end or that a vaster reign of the Catholic Church is near to come. The reconciliation of science and faith also does not seem to me to be so far off or so difficult, as the reconciliation of society to that divine authority[,] to the Church.[21]

Hecker commented to his Paulist confrere, Augustine Hewit, on Manning's letter. He basically appreciated the archbishop's response and agreed that there would be a "vaster reign of the Church." He denied that he anticipated any special outpouring of the Holy Spirit: the Holy Spirit was present enough now. What he could emphatically

---

20. Isaac T. Hecker, "Notes on the Holy Spirit," 58, "Statements sent to Dr. Vaughan to show to Archbishop Manning."

21. Henry E. Manning to Revd. and dear Father, Feb. 1, 1875, PFA.

not accept in Manning's response was the statement about "the low state of mind in the Church" or the need to revive the twofold office. "The Church is God," Hecker answered, "and Dr. M. does not appear to sufficiently apprehend her divine action."[22]

This exchange of views indicated both the common ground and the distinction between Manning's and Hecker's appreciation of the Holy Spirit. It is clear that both men agreed on the divine institution and teaching authority of the Church. Manning's position had always been known. The American's conversion experience had also convinced him of the truth that the Roman Catholic Church embodied the fullness of the life of the Spirit in its magisterium and hierarchical organization, and he had never questioned this position. Second, both agreed that the Church could be the only effective agent in the regeneration of society. "The life of the Church," Hecker argued in his notes,

> is the indwelling Holy Spirit, who is the guide and Initiator of all her actions.
> 2. The Holy Spirit as a saving grace acts in and through the Church only, and is the sole immediate and direct divine action in the world.
> 3. It is only through the divine action of the Holy Spirit in the Church that the soul is regenerated, saved, and sanctified, society ameliorated, and progress possible, attainable, and attained.[23]

Manning's *Temporal Mission* and *Fourfold Sovereignty* were in hearty agreement. What then could account for the vehemence of Hecker's comment that Manning did not sufficiently apprehend the Church's divine action?

The differences between the two men lay in their unique political and religious backgrounds. Manning confronted the laicist state. To counteract it, he emphasized the Church as a corporate, visible, hierarchical organization, a perfect society. His conversion from An-

---

22. Hecker to Dear Father Hewit, Feb. 13, 1875, PFA.
23. Isaac T. Hecker, "Notes on the Holy Spirit," 117.

glicanism supported this approach. The archbishop thought in terms of institutional and structural relationships. Hecker's experience was different. First, he grew up in a world where the legal separation of Church and state broke with the juridical and structural categories of post-Reformation Europe. Second, and more important, his own intense inner experience taught him that there was a strong convergence between conscience, self-reliance, republican political responsibility, and Christian perfection; that the origin and goal of all of the dimensions of life was personal union with God. Hecker converted to Catholicism because he believed that the Church was the place where that purpose was and could be accomplished. In contrast to Manning, his reflections were founded on the experience that the Spirit led him, revealed these truths to him, and served as the agent and symbol of synthesis.

It is significant that when Hecker toured the continent in 1873, he realized not only that the Church could not regain its position in the modern world through an alliance with the state, but also, in contrast to Manning, that it could not rely on a tight hierarchical authority. The Church's hope lay in strengthening the individual actions of Christians. Hecker stated the heart of their disagreement in "Notes on the Holy Spirit": "The hierarchy," he wrote, "is not God, the Sacraments are not God, the whole Church is not God, but [only] the means instituted by God to bring this divine action into the soul, to increase it, and to perfect it. To bring souls to God"; "The Church is that body authorized by Christ to convey to souls the grace, the divine actions, which He came down from heaven to convey to man"; "The Church is for man."[24] With such an understanding Hecker naturally felt Manning had a poor comprehension of "divine action." After all, to experience the Spirit was to long for reconciliation; it was to unite the inward and the outward, to live personally in that higher realm "where all truth is found in unity."

One other element separated Hecker's devotion to the Holy Spirit from that of the Archbishop of Westminster. Manning concretized his doctrine into symbolic form: The Confraternity of the Servants of the Holy Ghost, with its recommended prayers and de-

---

24. Isaac T. Hecker, "Notes on the Holy Spirit," 24a, 24d, 73.

votional practices. The Paulist founder, with his more intuitive bent, focused attention on the interior formation of the "men the age demands." There were two major reasons for this. First, unlike Manning in his experience with Anglican ritualism, Hecker reacted strongly to American Protestant accusations of excessive Catholic devotionalism. He followed Brownson's analysis of the role of pious practices in the post-Reformation Church. For example, Hecker narrated to his brother how an intelligent author approached him and asked: "Can the soul communicate with God otherwise than through the priesthood?" He answered: "God is the center of the soul as the Author of Nature. God dwells supernaturally and substantially in the soul after Baptism. This being so, it puzzles me to find out or see how you can get the priesthood in between God and the soul."[25] In his later years, Hecker would argue that this stress on the direct action of the Holy Spirit in the soul came not so much as a reaction to excessive Catholic devotionalism, but as a positive principle of rapprochement with Protestantism. His teaching on the Holy Spirit then received a less polemical and more ecumenical interpretation.[26]

Second, Manning argued that devotional practices should externally manifest a loyalty to the institutional Church. The cardinal's view of loyalty emphasized ritual action and hierarchical mediation. In his attempt to reconcile the person, the Church, and society, Hecker argued for a piety which could be practiced anyplace, not just in churches or private corners of the home. "Our age lives," he wrote in one of his most famous passages, "in its busy marts, in counting rooms, in workshops, in homes, and in the varied relations that form human society, and it is to these that sanctity is to be introduced." Thus, although he did not reject the efficacy of devotional practices, Hecker presented an alternate way to be guided by the Holy Spirit: recollection and purity of heart, attention to interior

---

25. Isaac T. Hecker to George and Josephine, March 4, 1875, PFA. For Hecker's reaction to formalism in Catholic devotional life see "St. Catherine of Genoa," in *Church and the Age;* "Notes on the Holy Spirit," 12–13.

26. For Hecker's ecumenical attitude see Isaac T. Hecker, "The Things that Make for Unity," *Catholic World* 47 (April 1888):102–9; Farina, *An American Experience,* 168–70; "Nineteenth-Century American Interest in Saint Catherine of Genoa," *Catholic Historical Review* 70 (April 1984):251–62.

inspirations, meditation, silent prayer, spiritual direction, fidelity to conscience, attentiveness to the ordinary duties of life.[27] His vision correlated well with the Catholic emergence into society after the Civil War.

In conclusion, Hecker and Manning were two churchmen whose language, self-understanding, and prayer forms, although sharing a great deal, reflected two distinct definitions of Catholic identity, two different experiences of "life in the spirit." For each one devotion to the Holy Ghost symbolized a unique approach to the relationship between Catholicism and the modern world. Their different approaches, sometimes in dialogue, sometimes in conflict, would surface throughout the post-Civil War period as the Catholic community in the United States struggled to discover a religious form expressive of its own experience.

---

27. Isaac T. Hecker, "The Saint of Our Day," *Paulist Sermons, 1863*, 102; "Notes on the Holy Spirit," 1–2; and Hecker's three articles, "The Guidance of the Holy Spirit," *Catholic World* 45 (Aug. 1887), 710–12; *Catholic World* (Sept. 1887), 846–47; "Spiritual Guidance," *Catholic World* 46 (Feb. 1888), 715–16.

III

DEVOTION TO THE HOLY GHOST
AND PASTORAL PRACTICE

The struggle for identity in the post-Civil War Catholic community took popular form in part in the various pastoral practices surrounding devotion to the Holy Ghost. The Confraternity of the Servants of the Holy Ghost first spread to the United States in 1879 through a Dominican priest who worked in Washington, D.C. On Pentecost Day of the same year James Frederic Wood, Archbishop of Philadelphia, sent the names of 3000 new Confraternity members to Manning. On August 26, Thomas Scott Preston, with the approbation of Cardinal John McCloskey, Archbishop of New York, introduced the devotion to St. Ann's Parish, New York City. Preston later preached a series of Advent sermons on the Divine Paraclete which explained the devotion to the people. John Joseph Keane wrote a pastoral letter in October 1879, in which he requested all the pastors in the Diocese of Richmond to promote the confraternity in their parishes. The 1880s saw a concerted effort to spread the devotion in the Catholic community through parishes, seminaries, and religious orders.[1] Although the confraternity derived from Manning, these various devotional expressions reflected the conflicting expe-

---

1. For background information on the devotion to the Holy Ghost confer Zardetti, *Special Devotion to the Holy Ghost,* 168–69. The only reference that could be found to the Dominican priest in Washington, D.C., was the *Catholic Mirror* 30 (Oct. 18, 1979): 4.

riences and interpretations of both the English cardinal and Hecker.
It is that struggle for identity on the pastoral level which will now be
examined.

JOHN JOSEPH KEANE:

DEVOTION IN THE DIOCESE OF RICHMOND.

John Joseph Keane was one of Isaac Hecker's "men the age
demands," someone endowed, Hecker thought, with the seven gifts
of the Spirit to counteract the superficiality, materialism, and im-
piety of the period. Born in Ireland, Keane immigrated with his family to Newfoundland, Canada, in 1846, and then to Baltimore,
Maryland, in 1848. He was ordained in 1866 and assigned to work
at St. Patrick's Church, Washington, D.C. While there, Keane met
Hecker who was to have a lasting impact on his personal and intellectual formation. Keane served as Bishop of Richmond from 1878
to 1888, when he was commissioned as the first rector to establish
the Catholic University of America. He finished his years as Archbishop of Dubuque, Iowa. He resigned his see in April 1911, and
died in June 1918. From the very beginning of his work in Washington, Keane's life was dominated by pastoral concerns. A man of
the people, he was especially interested in temperance, education,
and the formation of young adults. As a young priest, Keane was
instrumental in the foundation of the Catholic Total Abstinence
Union (1872) and the Catholic Young Men's National Union (1875).
As bishop, one of his primary concerns was the spiritual formation
of priests and people through advocacy of devotion to the Holy
Ghost. For the purposes of this essay, it was Keane's combination
of the spirituality of Isaac Hecker with his own pastoral dedication
and genius for concrete organization that made his contribution to
the devotional life of the post-Civil War Catholic community especially significant.[2]

---

2. The most complete work on Keane is Patrick Henry Ahern, *The Life of
John Keane, Educator and Archbishop, 1839–1918* (Milwaukee: Bruce Publishing
Co., 1955). Confer Thomas E. Wangler, "Emergence of John J. Keane as a Liberal

In 1872 Keane requested permission to join the Missionary Priests of St. Paul the Apostle, or Paulists, as they were popularly known. Although he was denied permission, the request itself indicated his deep indebtedness to Isaac Hecker. In the 1860s the latter introduced Keane to the *Spiritual Doctrine* of Louis Lallemant with its emphasis on sanctification and the indwelling of God in the soul. Denis O'Connell and Walter Elliott would later testify that Hecker also inspired Keane in devotion to the Holy Ghost and reliance on the guiding hand of providence in history. The bishop himself acknowledged his spiritual and intellectual indebtedness. This dependence was symbolized in a prayer Keane offered for Hecker in a letter of 1886:

> The matter of our conversation when I was last with you
> has been in my mind ever since, and often and often have
> I begged the Paraclete to be to you indeed a Comforter;—
> to make you ever *rejoice* in the holy will of God, and exult
> in your perfect abandonment to Him and your perfect trust
> in Him—to mould you more and more perfectly into the
> image and spirit of our Divine Lord, and to use you to
> mould others in like manner, even when you have least of
> the consolation of seeing the moulding accomplished.
> During the blessed Pentecost days, may the Holy Spirit indeed fill you with His own Fruits of Peace and Joy.[3]

The interdependence of Hecker's vision and Keane's pastoral program can be most easily seen in the bishop's understanding of holiness and his view of the relationship between the Church and modern civilization.

Keane's understanding of holiness converged with Hecker's in two ways. Like the Paulist, the bishop severely criticized the ex-

---

Catholic and Americanist''; ''A Bibliography of the Writings of Archbishop John J. Keane,'' *Records of the American Catholic Historical Society of Philadelphia* 89 (Mar.–Dec. 1978): 60–73.

    3. For the Keane-Hecker relationship see John J. Keane, ''Father Hecker,'' *Catholic World* 49 (April 1889): 1–9; Walter Elliott, C.S.P., ''Personal Reminiscences of Archbishop Keane,'' *Catholic World* 107 (August 1918): 641–46; Ahern, *The Life of John J. Keane,* 28–29, especially footnote 66. For Keane's prayer see John J. Keane to Isaac T. Hecker, July 4, 1886, PFA.

cesses of Catholic devotionalism. He consistently alluded to the
"risk of making our spiritual life a mere collection of forms and ex-
ternals, without internal meaning and life and soul." Keane especially responded to Protestants who viewed Catholic practices as a
set of contrivances to take the place of our Lord; the Church's authority as a substitute for guidance; her sacraments as a substitute for
direct contact between God and the soul. To counteract the Catholic
tendency toward formalism, Keane emphasized God's grace as the
sole source of all life, truth, blessing, thought, word, and deed. He
also argued that the Church existed not for itself but to advance
souls in interior perfection and to direct human action in channels
which would be most helpful to humanity and give greatest glory to
God.[4]

In his fullest statement on "Holiness of Life," Keane emphasized the fact that the pursuit of moral perfection, the duties associated with Christian education and marriage, the exhortations to
avoid intemperance, dangerous literature and amusements, the
administration of the sacraments, in short, everything in the Church
and life, existed for the one great end of sanctification. Echoing
Hecker, the bishop wrote: "To bring one's whole being and life more
and more completely under this control of grace, more and more intimately into this union with God, is the chief object of our vocation
as Christians."[5] He definitely framed his understanding of holiness
within the context of Brownson's and Hecker's criticism of post-Reformation spirituality.

Second, as Hecker had done so before him, Keane broke from
the institutional and polemical developments which had described
sanctity primarily as a mark of the institutional Church. The bishop
instead began with the classical notion of the Trinity as the archetype
of truth and charity. He described holiness as the consequence of

---

4. For Keane's attitude toward formalism in devotions see *Pastoral Letter
(February 2nd, 1883)* (Richmond: Catholic Visitor Print, 1883) 18; "Inaugural Ser-
mon," *Catholic Mirror* 29 (August 31, 1878): 4–5; *Pastoral Letter, October 18,
1879*, reprinted in Zardetti, *Special Devotion to the Holy Ghost*, 179–83; *A Sodality
Manual for the Use of the Servants of the Holy Ghost* (Baltimore: John Murphy &
Company, 1880), 11.

5. *Pastoral Letter, February 2nd, 1883*, 15–22, with quotation from 17.

God's image and likeness in the person. Thus the foundation of his view was a theological anthropology which noted that people could be perfect only insofar as their minds, hearts, and wills expanded in the possession of truth and love. "Holiness of life," Keane wrote, "means turning to God and clinging to God, our First Beginning and Last End, with a pure conscience, a loving heart, and a prayerful soul."[6] This view correlated well with the bishop's republican political orientation which emphasized the universal aspiration for enlightenment, the capabilities of reason, and the rights of conscience. In his 1883 Lenten pastoral letter Keane equated holiness with "an intelligent Christian life," one marked by three requirements: the habitual recollection of the relation between God and our souls; a firm resolution to shape one's life by this recollection; the desire to draw "nearer and nearer to God as life goes on." Perfect union with God, he argued,

> is the work of divine grace. This is what God made us for; this is what our Divine Saviour redeemed us for; this is what the Holy Ghost lives and works in our souls for. This is what the Church exists for, what her Sacraments are dispensed for. Were we to fail in turning our people's hearts and lives to this, "then would our preaching be in vain, and your faith also in vain" (1 Cor. XV, 14).[7]

Precisely because of his focus on the perfection of the person, Keane was able to relate sanctity to the laity's exercise of responsibility, intelligence, and liberty in both Church and society.

Keane also followed Hecker in his understanding of the relationship between the Church and modern civilization. Both accepted a theology of history which presented a strong connection between creation and redemption. They believed that God had planted the

---

6. Ibid., 16. For the person made in the image and likeness of the Trinity see Keane, "Address to the Catholic Young Men's National Union," *Catholic Mirror* 30 (June 28, 1879): 1; "Catholic Societies," in *The Memorial Volume: A History of the Third Plenary Council of Baltimore* (Baltimore: The Baltimore Publishing Company, 1885), 190–208, with specific reference on 192–94.

7. *Pastoral Letter, February 2nd, 1883*, 20.

seeds of a primitive revelation in nature which came to complete frui-
tion in Christianity. This providential activity, Keane wrote, took
specific historical shape in the Roman Catholic Church. "In a
word," he argued, "she alone is the complete body of truth, possessing in entireness what the sects hold in scattered fragments, and
she alone has the vital organic force which is to render her life and
her evolution commensurate with the ages that will need the Redemption."[8] Such a view enabled Keane to take a more irenic position toward world religions while still insisting on the truth of
Catholicism. In a similar fashion he mixed amicably with Protestants
but guided his own people away from mixed marriages and toward
a strong parochial school system.

This providential interpretation of history which recognized
both the claims of Catholic truth and openness to new developments
surfaced clearly in Keane's understanding of the Church in the nineteenth century. In his 1878 essay on "The Providential Mission of
Pius IX," although he noted that the pope had moved away from his
early acceptance of representative government, Keane still argued
that the definition of infallibility merely made the Church more secure in its negotiations with liberal civilization. He believed that an
infallible teaching authority and a hierarchical organization provided
both the antidote to modern skepticism and socialism and the fulfillment of the age's legitimate aspirations for knowledge and liberty. He interpreted Vatican Council I's statements on rationalism to
mean the acceptance of "the sufficiency and reliableness of human
reason in its legitimate province, and the absolute certainty of its
knowledge of fundamental truth, but also its need of help from revelation in the investigation of Divine things." In the same way, while
accepting the Church's divine constitution, he pushed for a convergence between Catholicism and American civilization. Hecker had

---

8. John J. Keane, "The Conflict of Christianity with Heathenism," *American Catholic Quarterly Review* 5 (July 1880): 468–85, with quotation from 485. For
the Keane-Hecker interdependence see John J. Keane, "The Yorktown Centennial
Celebration," *Catholic World* 34 (Nov. 1881): 274–84, and Keane to Isaac T.
Hecker, October 22, 1881, PFA, where he acknowledges dependence on the Paulist;
also, I.T. Hecker, "The Mission of Leo XIII," *Catholic World* 48 (Oct. 1888): 1–
13.

taken the same basic approach in "The Future Triumph of the Church" and *Exposition.* In a very real sense, reconciliation between the Church and modernity was at the heart of both of their systems. As Keane put it, what was needed was "an element of unity, consisting of truth that all can believe, principles which all can admit, a rule which all can acknowledge their obligation to follow, an authority to which all can acknowledge their accountability in their dealings with their fellow men."[9] The real task before the pastor was to fashion that reconciliation.

Given Keane's view of sanctification, his emphasis on the person, and his vision of reconciliation, it was not surprising that his self-understanding took symbolic shape in devotion to the Holy Ghost. The Third Person of the Trinity was for him, as for the Paulist founder, the living principle of sanctification, personality, and synthesis. It was the Spirit who enabled Christians to "think in their heart" and led them to "interior and spiritual lives." It was the Spirit who was the providential guide of history. It was the Holy Spirit, "the soul of the Christian Church," who "finished and perfected" the work of creation and redemption. Devotion to the Spirit of Light and Love, Keane believed, would naturally be the dominant devotion of the future Church.[10] By focusing their lives around this practice, Christians could reconcile the Church and modern civilization, Catholicism and Protestantism, freedom and authority. When he became Bishop of Richmond, Keane looked for some way to give pastoral shape to his spiritual, religious, and political vision.

John Keane demonstrated a dedication to pastoral organization from his earliest days. He lived in a society that emphasized grouping together for a common purpose. In 1866 the National Labor Union formed; in 1869, the Noble Order of the Knights of Labor. Throughout the period, numerous fraternal organizations emerged in response to social and economic instability. In one way, Keane reacted strongly to the proliferation of these secret societies and to a theory

---

9. Keane, *The Providential Mission of Pius IX* (Baltimore: John Murphy, 1878), 20; "Address to the Catholic Young Men's National Union."

10. For the role of the Holy Ghost in Keane see *Pastoral Letter, February 2nd, 1883,* 20; Elliott, "Personal Reminiscences of Archbishop Keane," 642; Keane, *A Sodality Manual,* 5; "Catholic Societies," 198.

of government which viewed relationships between people as a balance of interests or a machinery of counterbalances. He believed that such an economic and political view had contributed to the Civil War. Yet, the bishop also knew that good organization could promote a social reconstruction which would be organic, enabling the people to relate in an ordered, free, and harmonious whole. He argued that Catholic unions and societies could best implement this reconstruction. They shunned secular "methods of organization," and in imitation of religious orders, retained local autonomy while still blending into one order regulated by a central authority. As a pastor, Keane recognized that Catholic associations were vital to the formation of community, the proper mingling of priests and laity, the integration of spiritual and charitable activity. His pastoral activity reflected these beliefs as he himself promoted numerous devotional and social welfare societies. Thus, it was natural for him to create a sodality which would embody his experience and understanding of the Holy Spirit.[11]

Bishop Keane promoted the Confraternity of the Servants of the Holy Ghost throughout his career in Richmond. In October 1879, fourteen months after his appointment, he issued a *Pastoral Letter* requesting that the confraternity be established in every mission of the diocese and that every Catholic who "has made his or her First Communion should be enrolled in this beautiful devotion." Although he definitely took the idea for the confraternity from Manning and Rawes, Keane clearly wished to implement in a practical way his own experience and vision of spirituality. He printed enrollment cards and in 1880 wrote *A Sodality Manual for the Use of the Servants of the Holy Ghost*. This small booklet interpreted the devotion for the people and recommended some specific practices. To further encourage the spread of the confraternity, Keane asked the priests in their annual reports to note explicitly the growth or decline in membership. The bishop also published a pastoral letter in 1883 empha-

---

11. For Keane's understanding of Catholic organizations confer "A Pastoral Letter," *Catholic Mirror* 30 (March 1, 1879): 4; "Address to the Catholic Young Men's National Union"; "Catholic Unions," *Catholic Mirror* (October 25, 1879): 2; *A Sodality Manual*, passim; "Catholic Societies."

sizing the importance of the confraternity, and in 1886 passed synodal legislation encouraging its development.[12]

Keane clearly saw membership in the Confraternity of the Servants of the Holy Ghost as the key expression of Catholic social and spiritual identity on both the personal and corporate levels. On the personal level, he argued that the devotion corresponded to the "providential tendency of the Church." With its emphasis on the interior and supernatural life, it provided a perfect response to the materialistic degrading of the person to the position of the beast. It was also not liable to the charge of mechanistic formalism. The only obligation was to be enrolled with "a sincere desire and resolution to love and honour the Holy Ghost, to think of Him more frequently and fervently, and to correspond to His grace more faithfully." Lastly, the confraternity furthered the requirement of an "intelligent Christian life," an habitual desire for union with God. To emphasize the devotion in the life of the individual, Keane issued an enrollment card titled "In Spiritu et Veritate." This means of identification enabled a person to move from one confraternity to another; it fit in the pocket, wallet, or prayer book. The bishop also advised people to recite every day some optional prayers in honor of the Holy Ghost: the "Glory Be" seven times; a prayer for the seven gifts; *Veni Sancte Spiritus; Veni Creator;* some portion of the "Little Office of the Holy Ghost." Lastly, and most significantly, Keane printed on the card a prayer "For the Conversion of All Erring Souls." For Catholics who mixed easily with Protestants and were a minority of the population, this prayer definitely reinforced their identity. Referring to the "poor separated brethren," it read:

> Thou knowest that our Divine Saviour shed His Precious
> Blood for them, and that they ought to be united with us
> in the security of the one fold, in the profession of the one

12. Keane, *Pastoral Letter, October 18, 1879,* reprinted in Zardetti, *Special Devotion to the Holy Ghost,* 182. The enrollment card was entitled "In Spiritu et Veritate," John J. Keane Papers, ACUA. For the synodal legislation see *Acta et Status Synodi Richmondensis Secundae* (Baltimore: Joannes Murphy, 1886), 50–51.

faith, and in the participation of Thy sanctifying sacraments. But, alas, the spirit of error keeps them wanderers
from the fold, deprived of the treasures of grace and truth.
O Spirit of Love, look on them in mercy, and bring them
back to the home of our souls, from which they so sadly
stray.[13]

Although the Confraternity of the Servants of the Holy Ghost
had no corporate existence and its members no social obligations,
Keane believed that the work of the Spirit, reflecting the Trinity,
would tend toward "as perfect union and organization as possible."
The *Sodality Manual* he wrote was therefore designed to coordinate
individual confraternities. The booklet encouraged each confraternity member to join in an association or sodality which would meet
monthly for spiritual instruction on the Holy Ghost, recitation of
prayers, the sharing of information and mutual aid, and the pooling
of financial resources. Members of the sodality were to receive communion in a body three Sundays a year in addition to the patronal
feast day, Pentecost. They were to increase their pursuit of individual
sanctification through frequent reception of communion, daily meditation, spiritual reading, visits to the Blessed Sacrament, recollection on the Holy Spirit "dwelling within us," the daily offering of
life to the Spirit, and the cultivation of a taste for "solidly good and
edifying reading." *A Manual* presented Keane's pastoral plan of renewal; it was designed to give substance to a Catholic spiritual and
social community identity around the Holy Spirit.[14]

The bishop organized the sodality in such a way as to try to reconcile a strong, republican, lay voice with the hierarchical constitution of the Church. The whole group was governed by a council of
one cleric and at least six lay members: a priest rector, prefect, two
assistants, secretary, treasurer (if there were funds), and consultors.
The prefect and two assistants were elected in private ballots by the
members at large. They, in turn, appointed the other lay members

---

13. "In Spiritu et Veritate," John J. Keane, ACUA. The prayer is reprinted
in *A Sodality Manual,* 67–68. For "an intelligent Christian life" see *Pastoral Letter,
February 2nd, 1883,* 18–20.
14. Confer *A Sodality Manual,* 3, 13, 19.

with the approval of the rector. If the sodality was composed of both male and female members, all officials except consultors were male. The rector directed all of the workings of the sodality. He saw to the observance of the rule, presided at the council's quarterly meetings, and gave the address at the monthly gatherings. Outside of these specific functions, the laity were encouraged to take the initiative. The prefect was the chief executive officer and led the members in the recitation of the office. The assistants replaced the prefect in case of absence and fulfilled the parts assigned to them in public prayers. The secretary kept the records of officers and members, and the treasurer handled the available funds. Heading bands of twelve members each, the consultors helped secure regular attendance at meetings, reported to the council, and gave example to all of strict fidelity to duties. To spiritually bind the group together Keane composed a "Little Office of the Holy Ghost" in which he encouraged communal singing and choral recitation of psalms. The bishop carefully assigned parts and specific places in the assembly to the lay leaders: "It should be a privilege if the Father Rector sometimes heads the parts assigned to the Prefect," he wrote. In this way the total structure encouraged the reconciling activity of the Holy Spirit; constitutionally and ritually it came as near as possible to coordinating the rights and duties of the laity with the authority of the clergy. Keane presented a similar vision of the Church thirty-five years later in his devotional meditation *Emmanuel*.[15]

Keane's vision also reflected the reconciling power of the Spirit in the way it connected devotion with social activity. *A Sodality Manual* urged its users to take an active part in every Catholic work of charity established in the locality, especially those designed to aid young men. They were to encourage Church literature by devoting funds to the support of Catholic periodicals and the distribution of publications. Keane described at length the mutual relations of charity which should exist among the members of the sodality: visiting the sick, attending funerals, and procuring employment for those who needed it. The bishop believed very strongly that devotion to

---

15. Ibid., 14–18, 22–26, 32–34, and 35–66 for the text of "Little Office of the Holy Ghost." Compare this structure with that in John Joseph Keane, *Emmanuel* (Philadelphia: John Joseph McVey, 1915), especially 115–121.

the Holy Spirit necessarily entailed active zeal and charity for others. Membership in the sodality could not be "spiritual" without at the same time being "social."[16]

John Keane's confraternity and its accompanying *Sodality Manual* embodied his vision of Catholic identity; it integrated personal experience, social involvement, and institutional structures in one common religious activity. The bishop drew on the ideas of Manning and the vision of Hecker, combining these with his own organizational abilities and pastoral sense. Still, the question remains: Was Keane's view popular? Was his pastoral plan instituted? Did the bishop's own experience and thought reflect the community's self-understanding? Available evidence does not provide a thorough answer to these questions. Fortunately, it is possible to compile a statistical table of membership in the confraternity/sodality for the first six years after Keane's *Pastoral,* and in this way make some tentative assessment of the community's acceptance of his vision. (Confer Table 1)

Although these pastoral reports were inconsistent, several conclusions can still be drawn: (1) from 1879 to 1885 devotion to the Holy Ghost was quite widespread in the Diocese of Richmond, at one time or another being practiced in almost every mission; (2) excluding the cathedral, six major missions showed a steady enrollment: Alexandria, Harrisonburg, Martinsburg, Portsmouth, Staunton, Winchester; (3) the confraternity, after an initial encouragement from Keane and the priests, never grew in the way the bishop hoped it would. The priests do not appear to have been as supportive as their leader. Devotion to the Holy Ghost never achieved the status of a truly popular devotion such as the Sacred Heart, Living Rosary, Forty Hours, all of which were practiced in the diocese during this same period. (4) By the time Keane moved from the diocese in 1888 trends indicated that the devotion would not continue on any large scale.[17]

---

16. *A Sodality Manual*, 21, 26–28.

17. The statistics are compiled from "Pastors' Annual Reports," 1880–1885, in Richmond Diocesan Archives. I could find no evidence of the people's reactions to the devotion in "Keane, Bishop John, 1878–1888," Box 4.

	1/1 1880	1/1 1881	1/1 1882	1/1 1883	1/1 1884	1/1 1885
1. Richmond: St. Peter's Cathedral						
St. Mary's	283	643				
St. Patrick's			36	46	50	174
2. Alexandria: St. Mary's	133	173		173	31	
3. Charlottesville: Church of the Paraclete					12	15
4. Fortress Monroe: St. Mary's, Star of the Sea		130	130			
5. Fredericksburg: St. Mary's		7				
6. Harper's Ferry: St. Peter's		–3*		75		
7. Lexington: St. Patrick's	84	100				
8. Harrisonburg: Church of the Transfiguration	36	36			24	25
9. Lynchly: Church of the Holy Cross	150	150				
10. Martinsburg: St. Joseph's		25	45	45		40
11. Norfolk: St. Mary's		175				
12. Petersburg: St. Joseph's	200	200				
13. Portsmouth: St. Paul's	225	300	90	240	240	250
14. Staunton: St. Francis of Assisi		128		80	80	
15. Warrenton: St. John's	133	133				
16. Winchester: Sacred Heart	90	90		87	87	87

*This indicates a decline in membership of three people.

In conclusion, the widespread initial enrollment in the confraternity/sodality and its steady continuation in some places coupled with its failure to grow numerically were significant. Keane hoped that devotion to the Holy Spirit would be the vehicle of a Catholic identity in the modern world. He promoted this with all the means at his disposal: pastoral letters, synodal legislation, personal visitation, questionnaires, and prayer books. Internally, the devotion to the Holy Ghost was designed to unite the community through bonds of mutual charity and religious ritual. Externally, the prayers reinforced the truth of Catholicism and the erring ways of Protestantism. Politically, by emphasizing the indwelling of the Spirit in the person and the active role of the laity in Church and society, the confraternity/sodality incorporated American republican ideals. Yet, in the light of the debates between the liberals and conservatives over education, ethnicity, ecumenical relations, and Catholic discipline in the 1890s, the lack of growth in the Bishop of Richmond's vision may have been prophetic. Perhaps Keane's presentation of devotion to the Holy Ghost, for all of its strengths and comprehensiveness, simply could not create community solidarity on a popular level. Its social definition was too weak to bind diverse nationalities together; its ecumenical posture too open to withstand the rise of nativism; its focus on individual initiative and an "intelligent Christian life" too educationally oriented to cope with a population which was still predominantly concerned about economic survival; its ecclesiological vision too republican to handle the need for disciplined boundaries, clear structures of authority, and precise role definition. To embody those values, devotion to the Holy Ghost would have to be approached from a different perspective, one closer to Henry Edward Manning's. Keane's contemporary in New York City, Thomas Scott Preston, attempted to do just that.

THOMAS SCOTT PRESTON:
DEVOTION IN NEW YORK CITY.

Thomas Scott Preston introduced devotion to the Holy Ghost into New York City on August 26, 1878, when he established the confraternity at St. Ann's Church. This group was aggregated to the archconfraternity in London in September. After holding meetings on the first Friday of each month in conjunction with exposition of the Blessed Sacrament, Preston took the occasion of his annual Advent sermons on Sunday evenings to explain the devotion to the congregation. Unfortunately, there are no records of the numbers of people who enrolled in the confraternity, and it is difficult to determine its popularity in comparison with the Sacred Heart devotion and Forty Hours. There is no mention of the devotion in the legislation of the fourth and fifth archdiocesan synods in 1882 and 1886. However, in addition to Preston's Advent discourses published as *The Divine Paraclete* (1879), there exist six other sermons which he preached on the Holy Ghost between 1864 and 1890. These homiletic materials indicate Preston's presuppositions about the society in which he lived, his continued efforts to shape a Catholic identity within it, and his focus on the Holy Ghost as one of the major symbols in its formation. They provide a counterpoint to the approach of John Keane, and reveal that the very real conflicts within the Catholic community in the United States extended even to the understanding of the religious practices of the people.[18]

Thomas Preston's career closely mirrored that of Henry Edward Manning. Born in 1824, Preston was educated at General Theological Seminary in New York. The Oxford movement, with its emphasis on tradition, ritual, and authority, strongly influenced him, and at one time he was refused ordination because of his High Church views. Preston eventually received orders as an Episcopalian priest in 1848 and worked as a curate under John Murray Forbes at St. Luke's Church, New York City. He converted to Roman Ca-

---

18. See Preston, *The Divine Paraclete, A Short Series of Sermons upon the Reason and Office of the Holy Ghost* (New York: The Catholic Publication Society, 1893 [1879]); *The Sacred Year: Sermons for the Principal Sundays and Holy Days, from the Feast of St. Andrew to the Nineteenth Sunday after Pentecost* (New York: Robert Coddington, 1880), 338–53; and five typescript sermons at the Sisters of the Divine Compassion, White Plains, New York. These last sermons were taken in shorthand by Mary Dannat Starr who together with Preston founded the Community of the Sisters of the Divine Compassion. Starr had the sermons typed and bound in 1901. For purposes of convenience they will be referred to by their dates: May 26, 1882; June 6, 1884; May 24, 1885; May 29, 1887; May 1890. All of them were given on or within the octave of Pentecost. I am very indebted to Sr. M. Teresa Brady, the present archivist, for her help in locating and copying the sermons.

tholicism in 1849, was ordained in 1850, and after working in Yonkers became pastor of St. Ann's in 1862. While at St. Ann's, he also served as secretary and vicar general to archbishops John McCloskey and Michael Corrigan. Preston died in 1891.

The New York priest's prolific writings indicated his deep similarities to Manning: unquestioning dedication to hierarchical authority; emphasis on the unity of Catholic dogma, discipline, and devotion; struggle against modern rationalism and laicism. Preston wrote in his 1873 commentary on devotion to the Sacred Heart that the purpose of the modern state in its battle with the Church was "to break down her spiritual power, to prevent obedience to her priests, to steal away her children, and pervert them, if possible, to the infidelity of the day."[19] Just as Manning fought with the liberal Catholics, Acton and Simpson, so Preston reacted strongly to Sylvester Malone, Richard Burtsell, and Edward McGlynn, a group of "Americanizing" clerics in New York. He stated his position very succinctly in a letter to Archbishop Domenico Jacobini: "We are devoted to the Holy See, we do not believe in the great folly and absurdity of Americanizing the catholic church. We propose to catholicize America."[20] "Catholicism" for Preston included a rigorously conservative stance on infallibility, parochial schooling,

19. Preston, *Lectures Upon the Devotion to the Sacred Heart of Jesus Christ*, 135. For general background on Preston see F.D. Colahan, "Preston, Thomas Scott," *New Catholic Encyclopedia* (New York: McGraw Hill Book Company, 1967), XI: 761–62. Preston's agreement with Manning can be followed in three of his most significant apologetic works: *Lectures on Christian Unity, delivered in St. Ann's Church, Eighth Street, during the Season of Advent, 1866* (New York: D. & J. Sadlier & Co., 1867); *Lectures on Reason and Revelation, delivered in St. Ann's Church, New York, during the Season of Advent, 1867* (New York: The Catholic Publication House, 1868); *Christ and the Church; Lectures delivered in St. Ann's Church, Eighth Street, during the Season of Advent, 1869* (New York: The Catholic Publication Society, 1870).

20. Preston to Jacobini, Jan. 2, 1890, as cited in Curran, *Michael Augustine Corrigan*, 309. Confer Preston's letters to Archbishop Corrigan, 1875–1880, in C-5, Archives of the Archdiocese of New York. Nelson J. Callahan, ed., *The Diary of Richard L. Burtsell, Priest of New York, the Early Years, 1865–1868* (New York: Arno Press, 1978), i–xxvii, has the latest assessment of the "Americanizing" clerics.

clerical discipline, Latin liturgy, the temporal power of the papacy, and the *Syllabus of Errors.*

Preston's pastoral situation differed markedly from John Keane's Diocese of Richmond. The archdiocese of New York contained the largest Catholic population in the United States; by 1880 there were 600,000 Catholics in the city and lower state counties. St. Patrick's Cathedral, dedicated in 1879, symbolized the emergence of a Catholic middle class, a social and political power within the city. In the 1860s, St. Ann's Parish containing the Peter Cooper Union, Academy of Music, and Union Square, was in the center of the metropolis. Preston built a French Gothic church on a new site in 1870. His parishioners represented the fashionable businessmen and politicians of the time as well as poor Irish laborers. Parish life was filled with activity: literary unions, annual fairs, a parochial school, May devotions, etc. On the one hand, Preston confronted a lukewarm faith preoccupied with status and acceptance in the social life of the city; on the other, an undignified and undisciplined group of poor Catholics longing for a spiritual home. The pastor's reaction, following the pattern of his own conversion and intellectual training, was to insist on the Church as an ordered, visible sign of triumph over the world, a corporate whole whose life shone with grandeur, holiness, majesty, and beauty.[21]

Thomas Preston's task of forming a Catholic community identity took firm shape in devotion to the Holy Ghost. His writings testified that he was preoccupied with the relationship between "Spirit" and "Body." "Spirit" was the agent through whom one shared in God's own life: invisible, peaceful, timeless, immutable, ordered by a Trinitarian unity. "Body" was something material and historical, possessing visibility, order, framework, shape, boundaries, form, substance, nature, humanity. Through the Holy Ghost,

---

21. For background see Henry J. Browne, *St. Ann's on East Twelfth Street, New York City, 1852–1952* (New York: The Roman Catholic Church of St. Ann, 1952), 10–28; Curran, *Michael Augustine Corrigan,* passim; John Talbot Smith, *The Catholic Church in New York,* I: 312–28. Preston paints a clear picture of a "triumphant Church" in his sermon on May 26, 1882, Archives of the Sisters of the Divine Compassion (ASDC).

the Son of God received a *body* in the womb of the Virgin Mary; the Spirit took possession of a visible *body,* the Church; Jesus was present in his eucharistic *body;* the individual believer's *body* was the subject of redemption and resurrection in the Spirit. In other words, "Spirit" and "Body" were the linguistic categories in which Preston expressed his pastoral task: to create, shape, form, mold in the middle of New York City a social structure which all could see, a divine and human organization called "Church." "We attribute to the Third Person of the Trinity," he wrote, "the special office in creation of establishing order, of harmonizing elements that might be in conflict, of causing life and beauty to bloom, where, without His celestial touch, all would be dead and shapeless."[22] Three major characteristic areas surfaced in Preston's presentation of the relationship between "Spirit" and "Body" in devotion to the Holy Ghost: an emphasis on the corporate whole; the importance of role differentiation within the body; the dignity of the person.

When Preston presented his theological understanding of devotion to the Holy Ghost he emphasized the Spirit as the creator of a corporate unity. The preacher's rhetorical technique was to lead the congregation through a schema of salvation history (Trinity/creation/sin/incarnation-redemption/recreation) which would move them to acknowledge their own salvation in the truth of what he said. At the beginning of his series of sermons he pictured to the listeners a home of bliss and peace, "lifted up above the storm of earth, far from its confusing strife." This home was the Trinity, a unity marked by order in procession and arrangement in which three were one in nature, essence, and existence.[23] The Holy Ghost, Preston argued, was the "life and power and might and love" of this unity. This reality was the foundation of all things, and when God created the world through

---

22. *The Divine Paraclete,* 45. The analysis of "Spirit" and "Body" is based on a reading of all the sermons. For particular examples confer *The Divine Paraclete,* 62–63, 89–93, 161–65; sermon on June 6, 1884, ASDC. Mary Douglas' reflections on the importance of the idea of "body" are particularly relevant here: *Purity and Danger, An Analysis of Concepts of Pollution and Taboo* (New York: Frederick A. Praeger, 1966); *Natural Symbols, Explorations in Cosmology* (Barrier & Rockliff: The Cresset Press, 1970).

23. *The Divine Paraclete,* 55. For the salvation history theme see the sermons for June 6, 1884, May 24, 1885, ASDC.

the Word, the Spirit brooded over the waters of chaos bringing unity of life and order. Unfortunately, humanity fell through sin, lapsed into disorder, its corporate life becoming invisible and passing into "the shadow of death away from God."[24] The second Adam had come to recreate the race and make visible on earth the unity and order of God. To do this, Christ laid the foundations of his Church, its constitution and organization, and then sent the Spirit to "quicken it and make it the dwelling of God."[25] Preston summarized his understanding of the relationship between "Spirit" and the "Body" of the Church as follows:

> Although He is an invisible Spirit, yet He came into the world with a visible triumph, and marvellous manifestation of His power. For He came to a visible Church, and to inaugurate an external dispensation, where the outward body is the sign or sacrament of the inward grace. He came not to the body of believers as individuals, but to the external organization in which He abides, and through which mercy flows to the members.[26]

This was a position modeled on that of Henry Edward Manning.

Similar to Manning, Preston insisted on a "rigid" physical and moral unity created by the Spirit in the visible Church. "Order," he wrote, "is the necessary mark of all the works of God. . . . Divine authority exacts order as its first essential."[27] Confronted with what he thought were the impieties and disobedience of both society and the Church's own priests, the vicar general stressed the integrity and purity of the Body of Christ. The Holy Spirit emancipated the Church from the law of decay, he argued. It gave the Church an indefectible supernatural life, an infallible teaching authority, and unsurpassed holiness. Speaking in his own French Gothic church, designed by one of the most prestigious architects of the day, Preston exhorted his people in the following words:

---

24. *The Divine Paraclete*, 62.
25. Ibid., 74.
26. Sermon, "The Temples of God," in *The Sacred Year*, 340.
27. *The Divine Paraclete*, 57, 66.

Behold the Church of God. Nineteen centuries have passed over her ministry. She has had her Gethsemani, she has had her Calvary; she has followed her Lord; she has suffered in every way; she has suffered from open enemies and from the treason of her friends, but she stands on God's holy mountain, till now unconquered and unconquerable. Waves have dashed against her in vain; she stands around the Vicar of the Lord, though a prisoner and vanquished to human eyes—of the God Man. In her loyalty and truth she is divine. No man can conquer her, no weapon hath ever been forged that can prevail against her. Even if she seem to die, she lives; even if she suffers, she only puts upon herself new strength. Behold miracle of miracles, the greatest, most wonderful work of God, the perpetuity of the holy Church, and in that Church, and only in that Church is that indwelling power of the divine Spirit.[28]

Here was the apocalyptic heavenly Jerusalem on earth, a society with clear boundaries and sharp definition anticipating the unity and integrity of the Triune God.

Preston's desire to give clear external definition to the Body of Christ corresponded to his sharp differentiation of the internal roles of the priests and bishops from those of the laity. For example, the Pastor of St. Ann's argued that on Pentecost, after "the whole flock of Christ had been given to Peter," the Spirit descended on the apostles to abide substantially and permanently in the Church. The apostles, in turn, preached the truths of revelation and through them the Spirit came to the other members.[29] In addition, Preston consistently used institutional and cultic categories: the Spirit created the divine authority and priesthood of the apostles, consecrated bishops as their successors, conferred grace through the sacraments, and enabled people to confess their sins. Because of this divine action the Church

28. Sermon on May 24, 1885, p. 1055, ASDC. Confer *The Divine Paraclete*, chapter 3.

29. Confer sermons for May 26, 1882 and May 24, 1885, ASDC; *The Divine Paraclete*, 66–77.

could have "no unmeaning rites" and "no formalism." At the center of the Church, he argued, was the eucharist, bread and wine transubstantiated by the "power of the Holy Ghost overshadowing the priest," making present to the people the Body of Christ. This interpretation of the action of the Holy Spirit was the devotional partner to synodal legislation enforcing the Roman collar, forbidding clerical attendance at opera houses and race tracks, and governing Forty Hours devotion.[30]

In a theological and pastoral system such as Preston's, devotion to the Holy Ghost had one other significant result. Received through the sacraments and mediated by the corporate Body, the Holy Ghost still granted great dignity and life to the individual believer. Preston's last Advent sermon argued that through the Spirit people were closely united to Christ, participated in his flesh, formed one body with him, partook of his divine nature. As a result, the body itself became the subject of redemption and resurrection; mortal sin was expelled; the person became upright and holy, a son and an heir of God.

Preston's writings were filled with statements about deification. He frequently cited from the Canticle of Canticles and painted a rich picture of supreme beatitude.[31] His May 1890 sermon to a charitable confraternity of lay women presented his most complete description of holiness. "Do we understand," he wrote, "how great is our dignity to have dwelling within us the everlasting Spirit of God, substantially, not only by power and by grace, but substantially?" This grand gift of the Spirit brought with it a great responsibility to avoid sin. It also enabled us to do anything we wanted to do in our spiritual life: to overcome our vanities, to act with a strengthened will, to grow in the grace of God by every single action. The pastor concluded with a short description of three degrees of the spiritual life

---

30. For examples of cultic language see *The Divine Paraclete,* 129–41; sermons for June 6, 1884 (on the eucharist) and May 29, 1887, ASDC. The comment on formalism is from "The Temples of God," *The Sacred Year,* 345. For synodal legislation see *Synodus Dioecesena Neo-Eboracensis Quarta* (Neo-Eboraci: Typis Societatis Pro Libris Catholicis Evulgandis, 1882).

31. *The Divine Paraclete,* chapter 4. Confer "The Temples of God," *The Sacred Year,* 346–50; sermon for June 6, 1884, ASDC.

and exhorted the confraternity members: "Let us make our life more and more the life of God, and the Holy Ghost will sanctify every moment of our existence. He is the tender Father, the gentle Mother; let us look up to Him and in His sight forget the things of the world. Continually, day and night, to aspire to Him. This is peace, this is happiness."[32] Through the words of Preston, the Holy Ghost, the "Father of the poor," promised to the people honor, dignity, treasure; the Spirit created the individual to be "a jewel of honor in the mansions of the just."[33]

In conclusion, the Confraternity of the Servants of the Holy Ghost symbolized in the early 1880s for John Keane and Thomas Preston two distinct pastoral approaches to the formation of the Catholic community. Through devotion to the Holy Ghost, with its many personal, communal, and educational dimensions, both men tried to communicate an experience and understanding of Catholic identity. The devotion as a specific expression of life in the Spirit carried anthropological, sociological, ecclesiological, and theological meaning. It stood at the intersection of the person, the Church, and the world. In retrospect, it does not appear that either pastor was highly successful in creating a devotion with popular appeal. However, it should be recalled that devotion to the Holy Ghost was for Keane, following Hecker, the very heart of his spiritual life; for Preston, following Manning, it was one expression among many in a single tapestry of Catholic truth. Ultimately what was at stake in their respective approaches was the spiritual shape and posture of the Catholic Church in the United States. In this conflict, subsequent events would give the nod to Preston.

---

32. Sermon, May 1890, pp. 478, 482, ASDC.
33. "The Temples of God," *The Sacred Year*, 353.

IV

THE TRANSFORMATION
OF THE DEVOTION

Between 1884 and 1899 the role of devotion to the Holy Ghost in the American Catholic community underwent a gradual transformation. What had represented in the 1870s and early 1880s two different experiences of Catholic identity gradually came to symbolize only one, the tradition of Henry Edward Manning. Three significant developments represented this transformation: the institutionalization of the devotion in seminaries and religious congregations; the synthesis offered by Otto Zardetti's *Special Devotion to the Holy Ghost;* and the authoritative interpretation of Leo XIII's two encyclicals *Divinum Illud* (1897) and *Testem Benevolentiae* (1899). Although this change did not occur without a struggle, by the early twentieth century the Confraternity of the Servants of the Holy Ghost became primarily directed to the fostering and promoting of clerical vocations, and, under the direction of the hierarchy, it was explicitly designed to strengthen the bonds of unity between the pastors and their people. What many had seen as a social and religious symbol of Catholic identity in the 1870s had now become an ecclesiastical prayer form. This chapter will attempt to describe this transformation.

INSTITUTIONAL MANIFESTATIONS.

Post-Civil War Catholicism experienced an increased emphasis on the importance of solidly established and well educated clergy in the formation of the Church. In 1868 the *Catholic Directory* listed fifty seminaries and 913 seminarians; by 1900; the number of institutions had more than doubled, and their occupants multiplied five times. Throughout the period, movements for priests' rights, the adoption of the Roman collar, the development of theological conferences, and the founding of periodicals specifically directed to the clergy reflected a growing professionalization. Numerous articles attempted to identify the role of the priest in society, the contours of his intellectual life, and the nature of his sacerdotal vocation. The Second Plenary Council of Baltimore (1866) passed extensive legislation on clerical deportment; less than twenty years later, the Third Plenary Council ruled on the rights of parish priests and their role in the selection of bishops. James Gibbons' *Ambassadors for Christ* (1896) became a best selling manual for pastoral activity and priestly spirituality. In the late 1890s John Talbot Smith's *The Training of A Priest* and John Hogan's *Clerical Studies* presented strong arguments for the reevaluation and strengthening of seminary education. In such an atmosphere it was only natural that many turned to devotion to the Holy Ghost as another means of defining clerical identity and mission in the world. Cardinal Manning summarized the connection very well when he wrote to Father Henry Augustus Rawes in 1879: "I rejoice all the more in this [the establishment of the confraternity], because I believe that Devotion to the Holy Ghost ought to be the special devotion of Priests. We are consecrated and anointed by Him, and our whole priestly work and pastoral office depends on Him."[1]

------

1. As quoted in Zardetti, *Special Devotion to the Holy Ghost,* 71–72. For general background on the development of clerical life see Robert Emmett Curran, "Prelude to 'Americanism': The New York Academia and Clerical Radicalism in the Late Nineteenth Century"; Eugene O'Callahan, *A Case for Due Process in the Church: Father Eugene O'Callahan, American Pioneer of Dissent* (New York: Alba, 1971); Donna Merwick, *Boston Priests, 1848–1910: A Study of Social and Intellectual Change* (Cambridge: Harvard University Press, 1973); Robert Trisco, "Bishops and Their Priests in the United States," in John Tracy Ellis, ed., *The Catholic Priest in the United States: Historical Investigations* (Collegeville: Saint John's University Press, 1971), 111–292; Michael O. Brown, "The Catholic Priest in Northern Ohio: Life-styles, 1860–1885," *Resonance* 7 (1972):53–93.

The Confraternity of the Servants of the Holy Ghost was first introduced into clerical life in the United States in June 1883. Otto Zardetti, rector and professor of dogmatic theology at the Seminary of St. Francis de Sales, Milwaukee, had been strongly influenced by Manning and decided that devotion to the Holy Ghost would greatly benefit the students. With the permission of Archbishop Michael Heiss he erected the confraternity and aggregated it to Bayswater, London. Any student of philosophy or theology could belong to the group, which became the spiritual branch of the Blessed Albertus Verein, a local society for the promotion and advancement of German culture. In 1886 it was decided that every new member would have to pay ten cents as an entry fee. After 1888, members attended a monthly votive Mass in honor of the Holy Spirit and a public novena before Pentecost and during the octave. On Pentecost Day itself, the confraternity gathered to listen to some dissertations on the Holy Spirit, declamations, poems, and an address by the priest moderator. Between 1883 and 1917 there were 1282 people enrolled for a yearly average of thirty-eight. English was allowed in the services for the first time in 1916, and the confraternity was formally dissolved on April 14, 1921, in order to suppress a German nationalistic spirit. This confraternity at St. Francis represented the longest-lived and most significant institutional manifestation of devotion to the Holy Ghost in the seminary.[2]

Clerical devotion to the Holy Ghost received its greatest legal support at Baltimore's plenary council in 1884. Addressing in a special way the education of priests, the council legislated the following:

> Finally, since it would be idle to hope that those who are raised up to the apostolic ministry will be worthy of their holy calling unless they have within themselves, live and are moved by, and work through the ecclesiastical spirit, which is a certain abounding or copious partaking of the

---

2. Cf. Zardetti, *Special Devotion to the Holy Ghost*, 170–71. A full history of the confraternity at the Salesianum can be found in Cyril A. Voltz, "Devotion to the Holy Ghost at St. Francis Seminary" (unpublished M.A. thesis, St. Francis Seminary, Milwaukee, 1936).

spirit of Christ, let devotion to the Holy Ghost be cultivated continually and fervently in the seminaries, so that
the Spirit of Christ the High Priest may enter into the clerics, abide in them, and operate in them. For this reason we
commend the propagation in the seminaries of the Confraternity of the Servants of the Holy Ghost, which confraternity has already been approved by the Holy See.[3]

For the most part the decree, inspired by John Keane, appears to have
remained inoperative. One direct outcome was the institution of the
confraternity as the central pious practice in Rome's North American
College. Denis O'Connell, the rector from 1885 to 1895, introduced
the devotion to the Holy Ghost in 1887 and received official approbation from the Holy See in May 1888. However, the "Rule of North
American College Under William H. O'Connell," written in 1897,
made no mention of the devotion. A survey of the oldest seminaries
in the country, conducted in the mid-1930s, found no evidence
"which would show that the Confraternity had been established at
any other seminary in this country at any time." Synodal legislation
which followed the plenary council in the dioceses of Baltimore,
New York, Brooklyn, Ogdenburg, Newark, Hartford, and Cincinnati did not mention the confraternity.[4]

---

3. *Acta et Decreta Concilii Plenarii Baltimorensis Terti, 1884* (Baltimore:
Joannis Murphy et Sociorum, 1886), Title V, ch. II, no. 165, pp. 84–85. The trans-
lation is taken from Joseph Clifford Fenton, "Devotion to the Holy Ghost and Its
American Advocates," *American Ecclesiastical Review* 71 (Dec. 1949):486–501,
486.

4. For the North American College and Denis O'Connell see Zardetti, *Special Devotion to the Holy Ghost*, 171 and especially 177–78 which reprints a letter
from Cardinal Manning to O'Connell, Whit Sunday, 1887; Robert F. McNamara,
The American College in Rome 1855–1955 (Rochester, NY: The Christopher Press,
1952), 309; "Rule of North American College Under William H. O'Connell,
1897," in Robert Francis McNamara Papers, 83–2, ACUA. For a survey of the
seminaries see Voltz, "Devotion to the Holy Ghost at St. Francis Seminary," 24,
which corrects the inaccuracies in Zardetti, Special Devotion to the Holy Ghost,
170–73. The synodal legislation is contained in the following: *Synodus Dioecesana
Baltimorensis Nona Quae Antecedentium Etiam Complectitur Constitutiones* (Baltimore: Foley Fratres, 1886); *Synodus Dioecesana Neo-Eboracensis Quinta, 17–18*

Other institutional embodiments complemented devotion to the Holy Ghost in the seminaries. Zardetti introduced the confraternity to the motherhouse of the Sisters of St. Agnes, Fond du Lac, Wisconsin, in 1885, and it was still practiced there in 1936.[5] From 1887 to 1901 the devotion existed at St. Vincent's Abbey, Latrobe, Pennsylvania, under the leadership of Abbot Augustus Schneider, O.S.B. This confraternity was explicitly directed toward priests and recommended the following pious exercises: daily recitation of the *Veni Creator* and *Veni Sancte Spiritus;* prayers to the Holy Spirit before Mass; offering the office of Terce in honor of the Spirit; invocation of the Paraclete before administering the sacraments and preaching; a Pentecost novena.[6] In addition to the Benedictines, the Holy Ghost Fathers, Divine Word Missionaries, and Carmelites were major orders promoting devotion to the Holy Ghost. A similar interest manifested itself in the Sister Servants of the Holy Ghost (San Antonio, Texas, 1888), Sisters of the Holy Ghost (Dubuque, 1890), and Mission Helpers of the Holy Ghost (Baltimore, 1890–95). Lastly, the Society of the Holy Spirit, a gathering of prominent laymen in New Orleans, was established in 1882 and numbered 500 by 1919. Its members received communion four times a year, attended periodic meetings, said a daily office, contributed to the Society, and distributed Catholic tracts, pamphlets, and books.[7] This organizational

---

Nov., 1886 (Neo-Eborace: Typis etc., 1886); *Constitutiones Diocesanae Brooklyniensis, quae in Synodo Diocesana Tertia, Dec. 27, 1894* (Neo-Eborace: Typis Missionis Virginis Immaculatae, 1895); *Statua Dioeceseos Ogdenaburgensis, 1886* (Troy, NY: T.J. Hurley, 1886); *Synodus Dioecesana Novarcensis Quinta, 1886* (Arlington, Neo-Coes: Typis Paedotraphii S.S. Cordis, 1887); *Constitutiones Synodi Hartfordiensis, IV* (Hartford, CT: The Case Lockwood et Brainard Company, 1886); *Concilium Cincinnatense Provincile, V, 19–20 May, 1889* (Cincinnati: Keating & Co., 1893).

5. Cf. Voltz, "Devotion to the Holy Ghost at St. Francis Seminary," 38.

6. Cf. *Confraternitas Servorum Spiritus Sancti,* an enrollment card of four pages used at St. Vincent's Abbey during the time of Augustine Schneider. I am indebted for this and other information to Brother Philip Hurley, O.S.B., assistant archivist, St. Vincent Archabbey, Latrobe, Pa.

7. For the Carmelites see *The Cenacle Retreat of Ten Days, Preparatory to the Coming of the Holy Spirit in His Gifts,* translated by the Carmelites of Boston (Boston: Carmelite Convent and Angel Guardian Press, 1905); the same press also published the Rev. Henry A. Barry, D.D., *God the Holy Ghost* (Boston: The Angel

growth paralleled the increased interest in the Holy Spirit in various editions of the *Raccolta,* or collection of indulgenced prayers.[8]

Running throughout all of these organizations was a general tendency to follow the approach of Manning and Preston by linking devotion to the Holy Ghost with the education of the clergy and the strengthening of ecclesiastical life. *Come, Holy Ghost,* a book published by Andrew A. Lambing in 1901, symbolized much of this development. Lambing, a diocesan priest, collected from European and American authors over 400 pages of excerpts on devotion to the Third Person of the Trinity. Although he included selections from Orestes Brownson and John Keane, his dominant interest was represented by Henry Edward Manning and Thomas Preston. Lambing dedicated the book to the members of the priests' Eucharistic League on the occasion of the thirty-first anniversary of his ordination. In a preface, Camillus Maes, Bishop of Covington, related the devotion to the priesthood. "The Church of Christ," he wrote, "is kept alive on earth by the indwelling of the Holy Ghost; the priest is begotten by His coming; and the ministrations of the priesthood impart His sanctifying grace to man." The Holy Ghost Provincial in the United States also argued for the importance of this approach in the contemporary world when he wrote:

> We Catholics of the United States have special obligations
> to foster this devotion, for the chief pastors in this country
> have been the instruments chosen by God to promote this
> devotion. When they were assembled in the Third Plenary
> Council of Baltimore, they recommended its practice to

Guardian Press, 1901). On the other congregations see the review of the Rev. William F. Stadelman, C.S.Sp., *Glories of the Holy Ghost. A Series of Studies, a Collection of Tributes, or Account of Certain Movements Bearing on the Third Person of the Blessed Trinity* (Techny, Ill.: Mission Press, 1919), 251–65, and passim.

8. Compare, for example, *The Raccolta; or, Collection of Prayers and Good Works, to Which the Sovereign Pontiffs Have Attached Holy Indulgences* (Maryland: Woodstock College, 1878), 32–34; *The Raccolta or Collection of Indulgenced Prayers and Good Works* (New York: Benziger Brothers, 1908), 27–34. This increase in indulgenced prayers was greatly encouraged by Leo XIII's encyclical *Divinum Illud,* 1897.

the students of our theological seminaries as to the future pastors of the flock of Christ.

Nor need we doubt that this devotion will be very fruitful not only to the clergy but also to the Church in general, and to the world at large. For the clergy, the Fathers of the Baltimore Council expect from it a large abundance of the ecclesiastical spirit; for the Church in general, the devotion to the Holy Spirit, the spirit of charity, zeal and union, will enkindle that charity and strengthen that union which perhaps we need more here, than anywhere else, in order to keep unbroken the bonds of Faith and Charity, since the Church makes us pray to the Divine Spirit: "Come, Holy Spirit . . . who through divers tongues didst bring all nations to the unity of faith"; for the world at large, it will bring into submission the false wisdom on which it prides itself, and lead the nation to the source of Truth, the Catholic Church, a hope that the present Sovereign Pontiff has already expressed.[9]

By 1907 a book on the *Glories and Triumphs of the Catholic Church* described the sole purpose of the confraternity as beseeching "the Holy Ghost to multiply the number of Priests, and enlighten them with the divine light."[10] Although the outline is sketchy, the fact that almost all the evidence for devotion to the Holy Ghost after 1884 was associated with seminary life and religious orders indicates that in the last twenty years of the century, the identity of the Catholic community was becoming firmly established along the ecclesiological lines elucidated earlier by Thomas Scott Preston. A major indicator of the change was the 1888 work of Otto Zardetti.

---

9. See the Rev. A.A. Lambing, *Come, Holy Ghost: or Edifying and Instructive Selections from Many Writers on Devotion to the Third Person of the Adorable Trinity* (St. Louis: B. Herder, 1901), ix, xvii, and xxii–xxiii for the statement from the Holy Ghost provincial.

10. *The Glories and Triumphs of the Catholic Church, Catholic Doctrine, Customs, and Ceremonies Explained* (New York: Benziger Brothers, 1907), 350–51.

OTTO ZARDETTI:

THE TRANSFORMATION OF DEVOTION TO THE HOLY GHOST.

Otto Zardetti was a pivotal figure in the development of devotion to the Holy Ghost in the United States. Born in Rorschach, Switzerland, in 1847, and educated at the University of Innsbruck, he spent several months in England and was personally acquainted with Henry Edward Manning and the future Archbishops of Milwaukee, John Martin Henni, and Sebastian Messmer. After an early career as professor of rhetoric in a Swiss seminary and librarian at St. Gall, Zardetti immigrated to the United States in 1881. He taught at St. Francis Seminary, Milwaukee, from 1881 to 1887, when he became Bishop Martin Marty's Vicar General in Yankton, South Dakota. Appointed Bishop of St. Cloud, Minnesota, in 1888, and consecrated in 1889, he served that diocese until he was appointed Archbishop of Bucharest in 1894. Zardetti died in 1902. A learned man, he read widely in the theology of his day, wrote extensively in German and English, and manifested a deep admiration for the thought of Manning. Zardetti pictured a dove on his episcopal coat of arms. In addition to starting the Confraternity of the Servants of the Holy Ghost at the Salesianum, he also published two works on the Holy Spirit: an edition of a seventeenth-century paraphrase of the *Veni Sancte Spiritus* and his own manual *Special Devotion to the Holy Ghost*. This last work, designed primarily for seminarians, attempted to synthesize previous interpretations of the Holy Spirit. Zardetti's synthesis was instead a testament to the transformation of the devotion.[11]

Special Devotion to the Holy Ghost was deceptively objective. Zardetti divided the manual into four parts: I, the relation of the de-

11. For biographical information on Zardetti see Benjamin J. Blied, "The Most Rev. Otto Zardetti, D.D., 1847–1902," *The Salesianum* 42 (Jan. 1947) 54–62; *The Diocese of St. Cloud. Official Record and Messenger* I (Dec. 1891), 1; II (Jan. 1892), 1; II (Feb. 1892), 1; Voltz, "Devotion to the Holy Ghost at St. Francis Seminary," passim; Sr. Mary Mark Donovan, O.S.B., "The Episcopate of the Most Reverend Otto Zardetti, First Bishop of St. Cloud, Minnesota, 1889–1894" (unpublished M.A. thesis, St. Louis University, 1954). On his relationship to Manning see Otto Zardetti to Cardinal Manning, October 14, 1889; February 14, 1892, Cardinal Manning, American Correspondence, ACUA.

votion to the age and country; II, the formalities of the confraternity; III, a theological explanation of the office of the Holy Ghost; IV, a compilation of prayers, hymns, and pious practices. Although the author relied heavily on Manning and Preston, it was his use of Hecker and Keane that revealed his basic slant. First, Zardetti quoted Hecker's 1875 *Exposition* extensively in arguing for a new reign of the Spirit after Vatican I. He agreed with the Paulist's observations on the importance of the devotion to counterbalance the materialism of the time and to produce the "men the age demands." But the vicar general also referred to Hecker's essay "Cardinal Gibbons and American Institutions." When the Paulist founder described Cardinal Gibbons as championing American institutions and liberty of action so as to make greater room for the action of the Spirit, Zardetti quoted the same passage to emphasize the support of authority. When Hecker attempted to present a nuanced understanding of the separation of Church and state, his interpreter quoted him as implying the need for the Church to guide the people. This was necessary, Zardetti argued, lest "the slavery of passion, only removable in the power and strength of the true religion and supernatural grace, will destroy in its very essence our noblest national privilege, freedom and independence, or that these prerogatives degenerate into licentiousness and lawlessness."

Second, Zardetti quoted Keane's 1879 *Pastoral* not in criticism of the plethora of pious practices in the Catholic community, as the bishop intended it, but in support of prayer to the Holy Ghost among the clergy. The difference was subtle but significant. It indicated that Zardetti was aware of the diverse interpretations of devotion to the Holy Ghost and his work collapsed the approach of Hecker and Keane into that of Manning and Preston. This was particularly evident in three major areas: Zardetti's presentation of the relationship between devotion to the Holy Ghost and the Sacred Heart; his clerical emphasis; his analysis of the "fruits of the Spirit."[12]

Given the tendency in the nineteenth century to join devotion to

---

12. For Zardetti's use of Hecker and Keane see *Special Devotion to the Holy Ghost,* 52, 54–56, 64, 99–100. The quotation "slavery of passion" is from 67. Hecker's essay "Cardinal Gibbons and American Institutions," first written in 1887, was reprinted in *The Church and the Age,* 100–114.

the Sacred Heart with a strong emphasis on hierarchical authority and reparation for the sins of the modern world, it was inevitable that some tensions would arise between proponents of the Sacred Heart and Hecker's and Keane's promotion of the Holy Spirit.[13] The use of the Sacred Heart as a symbol to encourage parochial schooling, a "visible Catholicism," and as an attack on Americanizing clergymen by the New York bishops and Thomas Preston in 1873 have already been noted. Perhaps the clearest statement of the issues at stake was the exchange of letters between Isaac Hecker and Henri Ramière, the founder of the Apostleship of Prayer and frequent contributor to the Jesuit journal, *Messenger of the Sacred Heart of Jesus*.

In late 1878 Ramière sent an article to Hecker for publication in the *Catholic World*. The Paulist responded by forwarding to the Frenchman a copy of his essay "The Catholic Church in the United States." Ramière, apparently angered by Hecker's refusal to print his article, wrote a stinging criticism in return. Hecker's contention that *"governments derive their just power from the consent of the governed"* simply could not "be said to be Catholic doctrine, as a universal principle." Ramière quoted Romans 13.1, a favorite text of the conservatives: "non est potestas nisi a Deo." The staunch monarchist also believed that the American's understanding of the effects of original sin was obscure. Reason, Ramière argued, had been greatly dimmed by ignorance and free will weakened by concupiscence. "Such being the case, one may doubt whether institutions which suppose all men (baptised and unbaptised) capable of judging rightly the interests of the State and of using dispassionately the political power, is in accordance with our belief of the corrupt state of human nature; and whether they do not rather imply the rationalistic hypothesis of the native righteousness of men."[14] Later in

---

13. For general background see Thomas A. Kselman, *Miracles and Prophecies in Nineteenth-Century France* (New Brunswick, N.J.: Rutgers University Press, 1983). On the Sacred Heart: Jacques Le Brun, "Politics and Spirituality: The Devotion to the Sacred Heart," *Concilium* 9 (1971):29–43; Michael J. Phayer, *Sexual Liberation and Religion in Nineteenth Century Europe* (London, 1977), ch. 7; "Politics and Popular Religion: The Cult of the Cross in France, 1815–1840," *Journal of Social History* 11 (Spring 1978):346–65.

14. H. Ramière to Isaac T. Hecker, Nov. 30, 1878; July 5, 1879, PFA.

the same year, representatives of the Apostleship of Prayer had an audience with Pope Leo XIII, who summarized the spiritual and political significance of devotion to the Sacred Heart in these words:

> It was a merciful design of the most beneficent Love, to put under the eyes of proud man, disdainful of all authority and of every restraint, immeasurably covetous of earthly things and of sensual delights, to put, we say, before his eyes a Divine Heart, animated by no other sentiments than by those of a most profound humility, an unalterable weakness, a perfect obedience, a poverty without example, and by a peerless purity and sanctity.[15]

In the light of this background, it was significant that in his address to the Third Plenary Council of Baltimore in 1884, John Keane noted his own support of the Sacred Heart devotion, by then vying with Forty Hours in popularity. Keane emphasized that it was the carrier of "a more intelligent, a more interior, a more truly spiritual piety." Keane's anthropology of "heart" differed sharply from that of Ramière or Leo XIII. The Bishop of Richmond also argued that devotion to the Spirit would be the devotion of the future Church.[16]

In July 1888, *The Messenger of the Sacred Heart* reviewed Hecker's *Church and the Age* under the title "Authority and Liberty—Father Hecker's New Book." The four-page article hardly made reference to the Paulist's writings. Instead, it presented a strong defense of the necessity of authority. The Church, it argued,

> is the Kingdom of Heaven on earth, wherein the union of her children is secured by their receiving the same faith from the same teachers, and having the same helps from common Sacraments, and uniting in the same line of action under the direction of common officers. And this authority of teaching, of administering the Sacraments, and of governing is made and preserved *one*—that is, *unity of action*

---

15. "Apostleship of Prayer," *Catholic Mirror* 30 (Dec. 13, 1879), 1.
16. John J. Keane, "Catholic Societies," 197–98.

> is secured in the Church—by all authority centering in one
> common Head, the Pope.

The reviewer criticized priests who resisted Church authority and defended a strong connection between religion and politics. Repeating a position which Manning had detailed, he noted that the promise of "an *assisting Spirit*" secured for the Church both "faith in her individual members and a proper exercise of authority in her officers."[17] The differences between this linking of authority, freedom and Spirit, and that of Hecker's presentation in *Church and the Age* could not have been more pronounced. In the 1880s those who supported the Sacred Heart devotion emphasized institutional structures, obedience to authority, the unity of the Church, and external practices which were identifiably Catholic. In contrast, Hecker's and Keane's approach had focused on the internal action of the Spirit in the minds and hearts of the believers, individual initiative, and openness to Protestants.[18]

In this context Zardetti's book defended devotion to the Holy Ghost while at the same time uniting it to the institutional values closely associated with the Sacred Heart. First, Zardetti argued that true devotion to the Holy Ghost implied allegiance to the Sacred Heart. He significantly used St. Paul—the patron of the Paulists and one of the patrons of the confraternity—as an example of someone who was filled with the Spirit and loved the heart of Jesus. Cardinal

---

17. "Authority and Liberty—Father Hecker's New Book," *The Messenger of the Sacred Heart of Jesus,* New Series III (July 1888):497–500, with quotations from 499.

18. For further information on devotion to the Sacred Heart in post-Civil War United States see "Prospectus of the Church in 1866," *Ave Maria* II (Feb. 17, 1866):109–10; (Feb. 24, 1866):125–26; "The Apostleship of Prayer," (May 13, 1865):20; (June 17, 1865):93–94; (Oct. 21, 1865):365–66; (Sept. 2, 1865):253–54; "The Era of the Heart of Jesus," ibid. I (Sept. 16, 1865):286; (Sept. 23, 1865):301–302; "The Sacred Heart the Salvation of Nations," *The Messenger of the Sacred Heart of Jesus* 8 (Jan. 1873):1–11. *The Messenger* presented its interpretation of the Holy Spirit in the following articles: "The Special Action of the Holy Spirit in the Work of Our Divinization," New Series 4 (Aug. 1877):323–34; "The Christian Spirit, the Seal of our Divinization," ibid. (Sept. 1877):369–76; "The Divinization of the Christian by the Heart of Jesus," ibid. (Dec. 1877):511–18.

Manning also defended the convergence between the two practices. Second, possibly refuting Keane's position in the 1884 speech before the plenary council, Zardetti noted that there could be no fear that devotion to the Holy Ghost would supersede the more "practical exercises" of the Sacred Heart. Third, any notion that the devotion to the Holy Ghost was too mystical or entailed another new practice was refuted by the few obligations attached to it and its purpose to awaken a consciousness of the Spirit in the other activities of life. Zardetti concluded the chapter by relating devotion to the Holy Ghost with pious practices associated with the Virgin and the saints. A later portion of the manual emphasized the connection between the Holy Ghost and the sacraments of Penance and Eucharist.[19]

Zardetti's effort to relate the devotion to the Holy Ghost to a more hierarchical understanding of the Church also emerged in his discussion of the Spirit in the life of the priest. Central to his clerical view was the interpretation of Pentecost. Although recognizing that the Holy Ghost came upon the "entire congregation" in the upper room in Jerusalem, Zardetti noted that the Paraclete came with a "special mission and plentitude to the Apostles." "The organic nature of this mystical structure, the Church," he argued, "requires that the Spirit especially, principally and preeminently dwells and works in the higher life-giving and life-preserving organs of the body—the Priests." In other statements, Zardetti claimed that the Holy Ghost came only on the apostles at Pentecost and only through them and their successors was the Spirit given to the people. As a rule, "man should be saved by man's instrumentality and the visible work of redemption performed by the Godman, should be continued by men divinely called, divinely ordained, divinely constituted, and therefore truly 'men of God.' " Bishops, pastors, and priests were the "first Fruits of the Holy Ghost." In scholastic fashion, he divided the Pentecostal effusion into three parts: the gift of God and the Spirit (*donum altissimi Dei*); ordinary gifts given to all in proportion to their merit or position; *charismata*, extraordinary gifts common in the apostolic age. Throughout his writings Zardetti emphasized the distinction between clergy and laity; following Manning

---

19. Zardetti, *Special Devotion to the Holy Ghost*, 89–103, 370, 385.

and Preston, he carefully noted the differences between the gift of
the Spirit in creation and its presence in the Church.[20]

Special Devotion to the Holy Ghost clearly reflected the growing preoccupation in the Catholic community with priestly identity
and training. Zardetti drew an analogy between the Son of God and
the mystical nature of the priest. Both constitutions were the work
of the Spirit: Just as the Spirit had come upon the holy men of the
Old Testament to prepare for the Incarnation, so it suffused priestly
calling, training, and education; just as the Spirit overshadowed
Mary, so it came over the elect of God and created "character" in
them; just as the Spirit rested on the Lord when he entered public
life, so it remained with the priest all the days of his life. The book
consistently called for a spiritual revival and public recognition of
the priesthood through study, theological treatises, the celebration of
ordination anniversaries, and the dedication of Pentecost as a special
feast honoring the clergy. It was certainly ironic that after quoting
Hecker and Keane in support of the revival of devotion to the Holy
Ghost, Zardetti argued for an equation between the Spirit and an ul-
tramontane ecclesiology.[21] The openness of the 1870s had given way
to more pressing institutional concerns in the late 1880s.

A third indication of this change in mood from the 1870s to the
1880s was reflected in Zardetti's treatment of the fruits of devotion
to the Holy Ghost. After describing the personal indwelling of the
Spirit and relating the devotion to an increase in charity, the theological virtues, habitual joy, and zeal for God's glory, the professor
of dogmatic theology spent several pages stressing the Spirit's call
to unity. Pentecost, he argued, destroyed both a nationalism which
clung to old world customs and a false nativism which excluded all
the resources from abroad. The Church like the country, Zardetti
noted, was *unum ex pluribus;* it was meant to gather all peoples into
one whole. Within the context of ethnic rivalries and increasing anti-
Catholicism, he balanced the expansive gifts of the Spirit with what
he called "characteristic *restraints* effected through the influence of

---

20. Ibid., 72, 73, 78, 83. See Zardetti's First Pastoral Letter as Bishop of St.
Cloud, printed in *The Diocese of St. Cloud. Official Record and Messenger* II
(Sept.–Dec., 1892); III (Jan.–May, 1893).

21. *Special Devotion to the Holy Ghost,* 74–75, 77, 85, 115–16, 256–83.

the Holy Ghost.'' Zardetti presented the three criteria which he believed were necessary to discern the true operation of the Spirit: *"a loving filial submission* to our Holy Mother the Church''; sincere appreciation for the Saints and theologians of the Church; wholesome suspicion and fear of all novelty and an honest mistrust of ourselves.

Special Devotion to the Holy Ghost criticized those who quibbled in any way at the teaching, dictation, and commands of ecclesiastical authority. Zardetti, following the exposition of Manning and Preston, presented his interpretation of the *spiritus ecclesiasticus* which the Third Plenary Council had urged upon the priests: loving appreciation of whatever the Church does or advises us to do; strict fidelity to ceremonies and liturgical functions; preference for ''words, forms and sentiments of prayers'' approved by the pope; unity of body, mind, and spirit between priests and people. Given Zardetti's explicit rejection of the ''spirit of independence, subjectivism and false liberty,'' the question could be posed: Is this how John Keane would have understood the Holy Spirit in the life of the Church?[22]

There is no direct evidence that Otto Zardetti purposefully designed *Special Devotion to the Holy Ghost* to refute the approach of Hecker and Keane. Still, his misinterpretation of them, his concentration on the relationship between the Sacred Heart and the Holy Spirit, the sharp differentiation of the clergy from the laity, and the definition of *spiritus ecclesiasticus* may be taken as a barometer of the ideological shift occurring in the Catholic community in the United States. An increased emphasis on the institution—represented by the codification of law at the Third Plenary Council, the growth of seminaries, the proliferation of religious orders; the concern to Americanize increasing numbers of newer immigrants and to avoid ethnic rivalries; and a defensive reaction to nativism would build on the impetus created by earlier disputes over public schooling to foster a strong consolidating party in the Church. Meanwhile, the political and social ground had shifted from beneath Hecker and

---

22. Ibid., 104–32. For the reflections on nationalism see 120–25; three criteria, 125–30; *spiritus ecclesiasticus,* 128. For a similar treatment in Manning see ''The Disciples of the Holy Ghost,'' in *Sermons on Ecclesiastical Subjects,* 309–41.

Keane. This story is well known. Here it need only be noted that if Zardetti truly set out "to gather into *one* volume as far as possible, all that could and should be said" of devotion to the Holy Ghost, he failed to incorporate one whole experience.[23] *Special Devotion to the Holy Ghost* thereby witnessed to the spiritual transformation taking place in the community. The only work on devotion to the Holy Ghost written after Zardetti and before 1900 which this researcher could find supported the position of Manning, Preston, and Zardetti.[24]

Pardoxically, the very success of this more institutional approach would at the same time lessen the importance of the devotion to the Holy Ghost. Once structures and boundaries were clearly defined and pious practices popularized, the need to emphasize an interior vivifying force which continually renewed and reformed Catholic identity in Church and society was no longer a pressing concern. In such an atmosphere, it was not surprising that devotion to the Holy Ghost as a major symbol of Catholic experience declined. Future generations would come to know this devotion primarily through its manifestations in the Portuguese immigrant community, celebrations marked by public processions, and community celebrations in which the clergy played a prominent role.[25] The condemnation of Americanism in 1899 enforced this development from the viewpoint of ecclesiastical authority.

POPE LEO XIII AND

DEVOTION TO THE HOLY GHOST.

Pope Leo XIII published an encyclical on the Holy Spirit, *Divinum Illud,* on the feast of Pentecost, 1897. The encyclical was intended to provide a spiritual foundation for the twin purposes of his

---

23. *Special Devotion to the Holy Ghost,* 7.

24. A Sister of Mercy, *Meditations on the Veni Sancte Spiritus, with Devotions for the Novena In Preparation for the Feast of Pentecost* (New York & Cincinnati: Fr. Pustet & Co., 1889).

25. Information taken from the reflections of Joao da Cunha Valim received through the kindness of the Rev. Vernon Petrich.

pontificate: "the restoration both in rulers and in people, of the principles of Christian life in civil and domestic life"; a reunion with the Catholic Church of those who had fallen away. Leo elaborated on the connection between the Holy Spirit, the Incarnation, and the Church. He concentrated on the Spirit's gift of doctrinal truth to "the mystic body of Christ," which he centered in the hierarchy: "By Him the bishops are constituted, and by their ministry are multiplied not only the children, but also the fathers—that is to say, the priests—to rule and feed the Church by that Blood wherewith Christ has redeemed her." Because of the fullness of this divine constitution, no "further and fuller 'manifestation and revelation of the Divine Spirit' " could be imagined or expected.

Leo then described the operations of the Holy Ghost in the soul of the just person. He carefully related the Spirit to the works of creation and the Old Testament but noted that a new "regeneration and revelation" was necessary. His reflections on human nature after the Fall provided the anthropological foundation for his view: "On account however, of original sin, our whole nature had fallen into such guilt and dishonor that we had become enemies of God. 'We are by nature the children of wrath.' There was no power which could raise us and deliver us from this ruin and eternal destruction." Through the mercy of God and His only begotten Son, the Holy Spirit received in Baptism and Confirmation expelled this unclean spirit and dwelt in the person as the source of inspiration and sanctification. *Divinum Illud* concluded by recommending devotion to the Third Person especially as the agent of forgiveness of sin and commanding that a novena to the Holy Ghost be made each year before Pentecost.[26]

Leo's encyclical on the Holy Ghost provided the mystical counterpart to his understanding of the state, the Church, the person, and the spiritual life. The pope approached the relationship between the spiritual and temporal powers from a structural point of view. In order to free the Church from the encroachments of the laicist state, he argued that both state and Church were perfect, hierarchical socie-

---

26. The English text of *Divinum Illud* is taken from John J. Wynne, S.J. (ed.), *The Great Encyclical Letters of Pope Leo XIII* (New York: Benziger Brothers, 1903), 422–40; longer quotations from 429–31.

ties, created as such by God. They differed in that one was founded by God as the author of nature, the other by God as the giver of grace. State and Church were also distinguished by object and end: the one temporal, the other spiritual; by way of knowing, reason, and faith; by the means of certitude, evidence, and divine authority. By sharply differentiating the state from the Church institutionally and juridically, Leo could then defend the integrity of the Body of Christ and its dealings with the modern world. In this view, the person sustained two types of relationship: a relationship with the natural order which embraced the essential constitution of the person as created, intelligent, and free, owing to God adoration, cult, and prayer, and having duties toward others; a relationship with the supernatural, comprising realities which God had freely added to human nature.[27]

Within Leo XIII's political and ecclesiastical framework, the person became very dependent on authority. Because concupiscence was also deeply rooted in the person, the Church, by virtue of its superior destiny, became the final arbiter of how Church and state were to be related, how the individual was to act as both citizen and churchperson. What Charles Curran says of Leo XIII's politics equally applied to his ecclesiology: "The citizens are called by Leo the untutored multitude who must be led and protected by the ruler. At best authority appears as paternalistic and the subjects are children who are to obey and respect their rulers with a type of piety."[28] Although the pope's nuanced position allowed for active participation by Catholics in the shaping of public legislation, it was still institutional authority, especially embodied in legislation, which took responsibility for the discernment of correct action; the person's duty was obedience. In a parallel fashion, *Divinum Illud* emphasized the

---

27. Cf. Patrick Granfield, "The Church as *Societas Perfecta* in the Schemata of Vatican I," *Church History* 48 (Dec. 1979):431–46; Ferd. J. Moulart, *L'Eglise et L'Etat ou Les Deux Puissances* (Louvain: Ch. Peeters, 1887), third edition, 2–3; John Courtney Murrary, S.J., "Leo XIII on Church and State: The General Structure of the Controversy," *Theological Studies* 14 (March 1953):1–30; "Leo XIII: Two Concepts of Government," ibid. (March 1954):1–33; James P. Scull, S.J., *The Relationship of Institutions of the Natural Law with the Supernatural Order* (Rome: Gregorian University Press, 1966).

28. "The Changing Anthropological Bases of Catholic Social Ethics," *The Thomist* 45 (April 1981):284–318, with quotation from p. 288.

mediation of the Holy Spirit to the person through the hierarchical Church. This orientation naturally encouraged a focus on external devotions, as it had with Manning, Preston, and Zardetti. In addition to this encyclical on the Holy Ghost, Leo also published ten letters on Mary, of which nine were on the rosary, and individual statements on the souls in purgatory, St. Joseph, the Holy Family, the Sacred Heart, and the Eucharist. Thus, *Divinum Illud* was part and parcel of Leo's overall vision of the Church and society.[29]

Leo XIII's teaching on the Holy Spirit came to bear directly on the Catholic community in the United States during the Americanist crisis. This story, as indicated in chapter one, has been told many times. Still, it should be recalled that the major European protagonists recognized that devotion to the Holy Ghost was a key component of the debate. In many respects, they simply repeated arguments which had been circulating in the United States since the early 1870s. Abbé Félix Klein, a professor at the Catholic Institute of Paris and a supporter of Hecker, presented a piety which he believed was more relevant to the modern world, one that emphasized individual initiative, personal responsibility, and the movements of God in the interior of the heart; in short, a piety focused on the Holy Spirit. In contrast, Père Delattre, S.J., discussed at length the new "American model of devotion": independent, republican, democratic. He argued that the Christian life was primarily characterized by docility and obedience. Delattre rejected Hecker's intimation that the age of martyrs, monks, and hermits was over, and quoted *Divinum Illud* to support attachment to the present structures of Church and state. Third, Charles Maignen addressed the issue of a lack of political vitality among Catholics, a criticism Brownson and Hecker had elaborated almost thirty years earlier. He also referred to *Divinum Illud*'s statement that there could be no "fuller manifestation of the Spirit." Maignen, significantly, raised the issue of Hecker's lack of devotion to Mary and the Sacred Heart. In large measure, Leo's response to Americanism was simply to pick up the argument outlined in *Di-*

---

29. For information on Leo's piety see Hubert Jedin and John Dolan, eds., *The Church in the Industrial Age,* vol. X of *History of the Church* (New York: Crossroad, 1981), translated by Margit Resch, 257–69; William Raymond Lawler, O.P., ed., *The Rosary of Mary* (Paterson, N.J.: St. Anthony Guild Press, 1944).

vinum Illud and the conservative French critics and apply it to the American scene.[30]

Testem Benevolentiae, Leo XIII's encyclical condemning Americanism in 1899, made three major points about devotion to the Holy Ghost. First, the encyclical censured the opinion that the Holy Ghost "pours greater and richer gifts into the hearts of the faithful now than in times past." Second, *Testem* acknowledged that the "Holy Ghost, by His secret incoming into the souls of the just, influences and arouses them by admonition and impulse," but it added this *caveat:* according to the common law, God had decreed that people for the most part would be saved by people. Given the encyclical's understanding of the person ("Who is there who is not disturbed by passions, sometimes of a violent nature, for the persevering conquest of which, just as for the observances of the whole natural law, man must needs have some divine help?"), it naturally avoided any understanding of the Spirit which would issue from an optimistic anthropology. Third, the papal statement explicitly strengthened the role of the spiritual director, presumably a priest, in the discernment of the Spirit. From the perspective of devotion to the Holy Ghost, it was significant that this encyclical was probably influenced by the Jesuit Cardinal Camillo Mazzella. At one time he had taught at Woodstock College in Maryland and was a friend of Thomas Scott Preston. In addition, he was a strong supporter of Michael Corrigan, Preston's archbishop. One of Corrigan's representatives in Rome had been Otto Zardetti.[31]

Within the context of the Catholic community in the United States, *Testem Benevolentiae* served to reinforce a pattern of devotional life which had been developing since 1830. Ann Taves in a study of Catholic devotionalism in mid-nineteenth-century America has argued that the growth of special devotions around the Blessed Sacrament, Jesus, Mary, and the saints helped shape a defensive

---

30. Félix Klein, "Catholicisme Americain"; A.-J.Delattre, S.J., *Un Catholicisme Américain,* vii, 26–33; Maignen, *Le Père Hecker: Est-Il Un Saint?,* ch. 5.

31. The English text of *Testem* may be found in John Tracy Ellis, ed., *Documents of American Catholic History* (Chicago: Henry Regnery Company, 1967), II:537–47. On Preston, Corrigan, Cardinal Mazzella, and Zardetti see Curran, *Michael Augustine Corrigan,* passim.

Catholic identity in the face of nativism; strengthened the community's psychological dependency needs for authority; represented the standardization and Romanization of piety; and nurtured a Church-centered spirituality divorced from the concerns of the public order. A juridical understanding of Church and state contributed to this development. Thus, Leo XIII's encyclical, while specifically addressing devotion to the Holy Ghost, corresponded to other sociological, theological, and devotional trends in the United States.[32] A final chapter will now examine two representatives of the transformation of devotion to the Holy Ghost and the significance of their work in the general development of American Catholic spiritual identity.

---

32. See Ann Taves, "Relocating the Sacred: Roman Catholic Devotions in Mid-Nineteenth-Century America" (Ph.D. diss., University of Chicago Divinity School, 1983); Joseph P. Chinnici, "Organization of the Spiritual Life: American Catholic Devotional Works, 1791–1866," *Theological Studies* 40 (June 1979):229–55; "American Catholics and Religious Pluralism, 1775–1820," *Journal of Ecumenical Studies* 16 (Fall 1979):727–46.

V

THE AFTERMATH OF AMERICANISM

Testem Benevolentiae gave the highest authoritative approval to one tradition of Catholic spirituality which had been developing in the United States since the Civil War. It would be incorrect to assume, however, that with the publication of the pope's encyclical, the struggle to fashion a Catholic spiritual identity around devotion to the Holy Ghost ceased. Immediate reaction to Leo's pronouncement would indicate that much of the succeeding history of the devotion in the community would continue to reflect the dual inheritance of the 1870s. This concluding chapter will examine two reflections on devotion to the Holy Ghost penned in the wake of the condemnation of Americanism, one by a Paulist who inherited the tradition of Isaac Hecker and another by a diocesan priest heavily influenced by Manning and Preston. In the course of this examination it should become clear what was the chief significance of the post-Civil War development of devotion to the Holy Ghost. It revealed the fundamental structures which shaped Catholic spiritual identity in the United States and the basic lines along which it would continue to develop.

THE UNEASY SYNTHESIS OF JOSEPH MCSORLEY.

In June 1900 the young Paulist Joseph McSorley (1874–1963) published an article on the Holy Spirit in the *Catholic World*. Coming just months after *Testem Benevolentiae*, McSorley's presentation addressed all the issues raised in the debates over Americanism and systematically supported the position of Isaac Hecker. The work was a carefully prepared statement. It cited scholastic theologians whose orthodox credentials could not be questioned: Aquinas, Camillo Mazzella, Johannes Franzelin, and Christian Pesch. McSorley also sprinkled throughout the article references to Leo XIII's *Libertas* (1887), *Divinum Illud, Annum Sacrum* (1899), and *Testem Benevolentiae*. The Paulist recounted the pope's efforts to encourage devotion to the Holy Ghost through novenas, sermons, conferences, and spiritual direction. He enumerated what he considered the most significant theological truths attached to the devotion, its practical implications, and its suitability for the present age. The article indicated the heart of the previous debates over devotion to the Holy Ghost and at the same time revealed the impact of history on the Paulist's position. Two key areas surfaced: the relationship between the devotion and the current age; McSorley's theological anthropology.[1]

Devotion to the Holy Ghost, McSorley argued, was particularly suited to the people of the United States, "earnest, intelligent, active, and liberty-loving." It turned their thoughts inward and encouraged a "vital spirituality": love of personal religion, loyalty to the inner promptings of grace, cultivation of the highest forms of prayer, and a sense of individual freedom and responsibility. The Paulist noted that by joining together devotion to the Holy Ghost and to the Sacred Heart of Jesus, the pope had given "a heaven sent indication of the spiritual ideals that will best avail for the perfecting of the existing social order." He then referred to Manning's statement that loss of devotion to the Holy Ghost had been one of the causes of the Reformation, but he elaborated on the cardinal's interpretation:

But the new religionists brought about a far worse state of affairs. Making no headway themselves, they still obstructed the path of others. For wild fanaticism such as they displayed was the one thing most likely to discourage

---

1. Joseph McSorley, "Devotion to the Holy Spirit," *Catholic World* 71 (June 1900):290–304.

authority from reposing confidence in the personal fidelity
of the subject. Catholics were forced to concentrate all resources on the defence of points attacked. External authority was of necessity emphasized most strongly and
became all dominant, while individual initiative in action
and individual freedom in methods were suspected to be,
and often developed into, the false and fanatical vagaries
of heresy.[2]

Fortunately, McSorley wrote, this siege was almost over, and devotion to the Holy Ghost could now be used to bind human liberty,
so capable of being exaggerated in the United States, to the chains
of divine love and to accomplish the "renewal of Christian life in
human society and the reconciliation to the faith of all those outside
the church."[3]

McSorley spent most of the article elaborating the fine points of
a theological anthropology which would have startled any conservative adherent of *Testem Benevolentiae*. First, he very carefully related the indwelling of the Spirit to the order of creation. The Creator
was present in the creature by ubiquity and omnipotence in addition
to the personal indwelling. Deification was effected "not by destroying human nature, not by nullifying its powers, but by elevating these
to a new and higher order wherein they become of greater and divine
worth." The Paulist argued that the Spirit came to all the people of
the Old Testament who "clung to God with firm and generous
hearts" and also to those within and without the church who had
been raised to the supernatural life of grace. In such a perspective
Pentecost completed what had already been started; it did not com-
mence an entirely new dispensation.

Second, in a very pointed fashion, McSorley noted that the personal indwelling was analogous to the presence of Christ in the Eucharist. In the life of the individual believer, it was even more
significant, since the Spirit's indwelling was permanent whereas the
time of sacramental communion was brief. Lastly, the article de-

---

2. Ibid., 302.
3. Ibid., 303.

scribed in some detail the life of a soul constantly recollected on the divine indwelling. McSorley forcefully emphasized fidelity to the personal inspiration of the Spirit and the importance of conscience. "The frequent advice of others," he wrote,

> may be perfectly indispensable to our success, and consequently is to be sought; but we should not neglect opportunities of useful work, merely because no one has suggested our embracing them. Nor can we always have a director within call, unless indeed it be the indwelling Spirit. And therefore the best direction is that which trains men in prompt and spontaneous fidelity to the guidance of God's Holy Spirit, as the normal spiritual life is that wherein the soul, instead of merely shaping itself on the minute details of a model provided by an adviser, uses its own intelligence to recognize, and its own will to execute God's particular designs in its regard. How simple in sublimity the rule of life which has for its supreme principle the conscience, instructed by authoritative teaching, and energized by the promptings of the Holy Spirit.[4]

The Paulist restated Hecker's position on the importance of obedience and the external authority of the Church, but he also noted that the perfection of the life of the Spirit often "conflicted with prevalent notions and cherished traditions." Significantly, he used Teresa of Avila and Ignatius Loyola, a founder and a reformer of important religious orders, as his ideals in the spiritual life.

McSorley's article contained inherent ambiguities. The Paulist recommended an external devotion symbolic of the triumphant Church, the Sacred Heart, while at the same time critiquing the "propaganda of minor devotions" and lauding the Holy Spirit who required no badge, medal, or affiliation, only a "lovingly attentive heart"; he stressed the republican values of freedom and initiative, yet referred to Leo XIII's program for the renewal of society; he argued for a "vital spirituality" focused on interiority and personal

---

4. Ibid., 292, 298–299.

responsibility, but carefully structured his arguments around appeals to authority; he quoted Manning on the historical significance of devotion to the Holy Ghost, but interpreted post-Reformation history in the same way as Brownson and Hecker; he emphasized the beauty of the Catholic position on indwelling, yet implied that God's presence was everywhere; he knew the centrality of the Eucharist but highlighted the Spirit's permanent presence in the individual. In short, McSorley seems to have been caught between his own personal views of the Holy Spirit and those publicly accepted by Church authority; between his understanding of the Spirit's support of individual liberty and responsibility, and how these values could be manifested in a Church which proclaimed itself the agent of society's regeneration.

This tension in McSorley's approach surfaced clearly in his private correspondence at the time. For example, in 1900 he privately acknowledged his studied use of Ignatius Loyola to defend his own position.[5] Two years later he wrote to his Paulist superior about a pamphlet on the function of authority in education written by the French Oratorian and modernist, Lucien Labrethonnière: "It is full of fine Americanism, i.e. defense of personal initiation etc. very thoroughly studied and defended. It is a bit à la Spalding." He recognized approvingly the Americanist sympathies of Henri Bremond.[6] With respect to devotion to the Holy Ghost, McSorley's synthesis betrayed an alliance in conflict.

McSorley's uneasy position can only be understood by examining the two general structures of experience and thought which shaped the development of devotion to the Holy Ghost after the Civil War: Church/state relationships and the understanding of the person. When Manning and Preston, Hecker and Keane, first reflected on devotion to the Holy Ghost it represented for them a practical and theoretical synthesis between the person, the Church, and the social order; it was an integrative symbol, albeit from different perspectives. Manning, for example, recognized the separation of Church and state but argued that the former, because of its superior end, was

---

5. Joseph McSorley to Alexander P. Doyle, July 13, 1900, PFA.
6. McSorley to Doyle, January 20, 1902; February 24, 1902; March 8, 1902, PFA.

the final arbiter of the relationship between the two. Presupposing a juridical framework, this view usually interrelated the Church and society through formal legal structures (civil and canon law, concordats) and through moral prescriptions interpreted by the teaching authority of the Church in pastoral letters, textbooks of theology, the sacrament of penance, and the interpretation of natural law.

Theologically, the juridical position on Church and state relationships presupposed either an anthropology of pure nature or a very pessimistic interpretation of the Fall. In either case, the structures of authority in the Church, symbolized in devotional life, exercised a dominant control over the individual's sphere of responsibility, reason, and freedom, while at the same time granting the person dignity in the "new dispensation." Preston presented the purest statement of this view in his numerous devotional works and his advocacy of the union of Church and state. Hecker and Keane, on the other hand, operated out of a Jacksonian commitment to democracy and a providential interpretation of modern history. For them, Church and state were separate and both were defined as communities, albeit structured ones, from the perspective of a sociopolitical anthropology rooted in the person's intelligence and freedom. The Church influenced the state primarily by persuading individuals to witness the truth. In the civil order, this meant concerted attempts to convert individual consciences to Catholicism through writing, publishing, giving missions, and lecturing; within the Church, it necessitated developing an ecumenical piety which encouraged cooperation and directed sacramental ministry, preaching, and spiritual direction toward the creation of socially responsible individuals.[7]

In the light of this history the significance of McSorley's article becomes clear. It should be noted that the Paulist did not refer to Hecker and Keane's vision of the Spirit as the regenerator of both Church and society. In fact, every time McSorley mentioned the perfection of the social order, he explicitly acknowledged Leo XIII's viewpoint. His overwhelming focus was on the consequences of de-

---

7. Preston's position on Church and state is presented in "American Catholicity," *American Catholic Quarterly Review* 16 (April 1891):396–408. Edward J. Langlois, C.S.P., "Isaac Hecker's Political Thought," in *Hecker Studies* is the best presentation of the Paulist's views.

votion to the Holy Spirit in the life of the individual. Although he could relate the Spirit to the development of freedom and responsibility, this "vital spirituality" remained unconnected with social action or ecclesiastical change. The reason was simple: When McSorley sat down to write, he simply could not ignore the fact that *Testem Benevolentiae* had given the juridical tradition of Manning and Preston an authoritative status; it had fixed the boundaries of the spiritual life within a particular framework of Church/state relationships. Yet he also could not deny his Paulist inheritance and his acceptance of the constitutional anthropology underlying Church/state separation in the United States. McSorley tried therefore to combine the two traditions by accepting the social question on Leo XIII's terms and affirming the anthropological issue on Hecker's terms. This meant that the only place left for the exercise of devotion to the Holy Ghost was in the mystical life of the person. Many of McSorley's early articles emphasized prayer and mysticism, and the development of an interior piety. He related the spiritual life to the social order through "the sacrament of duty." Other Paulists, Walter Elliott and John J. Burke, followed suit, giving devotion to the Holy Ghost a structured novena compatible with the juridical tradition of spirituality while emphasizing immediate indwelling in the person.[8] Inheritors of two traditions, they preserved the Spirit by limiting its social, political, and ecclesiological consequences. The transformation of devotion to the Holy Ghost which had been occurring since the Third Plenary Council was now manifesting its most significant consequences.

8. Cf. Joseph McSorley, "The Scale of Perfection," *Catholic World* 74 (Oct. 1901):33–46; "Saint Thérèse, A Child Contemplative," ibid. 75 (May 1902):198–214; "Saint Chantal: A Type of Christian Womanhood," ibid. 76 (Feb. 1903):571–84; "Soul Blindness," ibid. 76 (March 1903):782–93; *Progress in Prayer* (St. Louis: B. Herder, 1904); *The Sacrament of Duty and Other Essays* (New York: The Columbus Press, 1909); for Elliott see "The Paraclete and the Human Soul," *Catholic World* 73 (June 1901):278–86; *Novena to the Holy Ghost* (New York: Paulist Press, 1922); Burke's reflections can be found in *Novena to the Holy Spirit with Prayers from the Missal and Short Reflections* (New York: Paulist Press, 1925); *Daily Thoughts for Lent on the Holy Spirit* (1932, PFA).

THE FINAL WITNESS:
NOVENA OF SERMONS ON THE HOLY GHOST.

In 1901 "A Diocesan Priest" published anonymously a work entitled *Novena of Sermons on the Holy Ghost*. Michael Augustine Corrigan gave the book an *imprimatur* and James Cardinal Gibbons wrote the introduction. Current censorship records of the Archdiocese of New York indicate that the author was the Rev. Thomas F. Hopkins of St. Mary's Church, Charleston, South Carolina.[9] Hopkins, born in Philadelphia in 1841, was educated at the diocesan seminary there and ordained by Bishop Wood on July 28, 1864. He became rector at Glen Riddle preparatory seminary in 1868. After its closure in 1871, he served the diocese as pastor of the Chapel of the Sacred Heart of Jesus. Around 1875 Hopkins left the active ministry and became part of a company with property holdings in New York, San Francisco, and the state of Nevada. In July 1886 he wrote to his boyhood friend Cardinal Gibbons asking to be restored to the exercise of his ministry. Gibbons helped him locate under Bishop Marty in Yankton, South Dakota, where in 1889 he served as a business advisor and editor of the *Dakota Catholic*. The 1893 *Catholic Directory* listed Hopkins as a resident in Charleston, South Carolina. He was eventually incardinated into that diocese and appointed pastor and diocesan consultant at St. Mary's Church. Hopkins resigned in 1901 and died in Germany on August 22, 1904. In addition to editorial work, he published one apologetic pamphlet on *Papal Pretensions*. The diocesan priest preached his *Novena of Sermons* on the two Sundays before and the six Sundays after Pentecost, but the place and date are uncertain. The work was the last major representative of the post-Civil War history of devotion to the Holy Ghost.[10]

---

9. A Diocesan Priest, *Novena of Sermons on the Holy Ghost in His Relationship to the World* (New York: Cathedral Library Association, 1901). The imprimatur record was furnished by Sr. Marguerita Smith, archivist for the Archdiocese of New York.

10. Hopkins' biography has been compiled from the following sources: The Rev. William C. Burn, archivist of the Diocese of Charleston, provided information on Hopkins as pastor of St. Mary's, Charleston; Sister M. Felicitas Powers, R.S.M.,

Written after *Testem Benevolentiae,* the *Novena of Sermons on the Holy Ghost* reflected in much the same way as had McSorley's article the dual inheritance of the 1870s. This heritage affected content, method, and style. The book, consisting of three series of three sermons each, mixed various themes present in Manning, Zardetti, and Hecker.[11] It traced the relationship of the Holy Ghost to the Blessed Virgin Mary (1–3); to the Incarnate Word (4–6); to the written Word of God (7–9). While presenting a strong continuity between creation, incarnation, and the foundation of the Church, thereby implying a providential interpretation of history, it argued in an apocalyptic fashion against the "utterly reckless liberalism and shocking blasphemies of our times." The book linked devotion to the Holy Ghost with the Eucharist and the Sacred Heart, but also struggled to establish the Scriptures at the heart of Catholic spiritual life. In method, the citations from patristic authors were probably taken from Manning and Zardetti, but they were used to support an anthropology similar to that of Hecker and Keane. Sermons one to six and nine argued in a persuasive style; sermons seven and eight, obviously dependent on Manning's *Temporal Mission,* apologetically. Within the context of this dual inheritance, it should be noted that Gibbons's "Introduction" was especially bold. The cardinal emphasized the secret operations of the Holy Ghost in the soul, stressed personal enlightenment and action, and gave six criteria for the true discernment of the Spirit, only one of which was obedience to constituted authority.

The ninth chapter of *Novena of Sermons,* on the Holy Ghost as "our teacher and guide in the use of Scriptures," revealed the most

---

sent me copies of the following letters in the archives of the Archdiocese of Baltimore: Hopkins to Gibbons, July 29, 1886; August 27, 1886; Archbishop Feehan to Gibbons, September 28, 1886; Hopkins to Gibbons, June 21, 1887; April 26, 1888; August 19, 1889. Louis J. Delahoyde, chancellor of the Diocese of Sioux Falls, after a thorough search of the *Dakota Catholic,* assured me that there were no signed articles by Hopkins in that paper. For printed information confer the Catholic Directories for the period and Rev. George E. O'Donnell, *St. Charles Seminary, Philadelphia* (Philadelphia: American Catholic Historical Society, 1964), passim.

11. *Novena of Sermons,* 178. A few examples of literary dependence on Manning and Zardetti would be the following parallel passages: *Novena of Sermons,* 105–9, 126, 127, and Zardetti, *Special Devotion to the Holy Ghost,* 234–35, 252, 255; *Novena of Sermons,* 161ff. and Manning, *Temporal Mission,* 140ff.

important presuppositions which permeated the entire work and indicated Hopkin's own pastoral perceptions of the spiritual identity of the Catholic community. First, the preacher acknowledged that the people lived in a religiously pluralistic context whose hostility to Catholicism required both an ecclesiastically tight structure and a socially inoffensive posture. He knew that the constant cry which people heard was "The Bible, the Bible, and nothing but the Bible" and the accusation that the Catholic Church either discouraged its people from reading the Scriptures or substituted other devotions for the Word of God. Hopkins tried therefore to insist on the integrity of the Catholic faith and yet create a common field of discourse. He exhorted the people to use only the true Scripture approved by the Church and follow its "notes and comments." He also urged the people to read and treasure the Word of God and noted the centrality of Scripture in the Mass, vespers, official prayers, breviary, and devotional books of Catholics.

With respect to devotions, the diocesan priest affirmed the priority of a specifically Catholic symbol, the presence of Jesus in the Eucharist, and also compared Scripture to a sacrament. He argued that meditation on the Word should be the second most important object of people's devotional lives. Again, *Novena of Sermons* indicated the need for both discourse and defense by recommending four ways that people could witness to the Gospel: avoidance of wrangling and heated discussions; learning "the truths and doctrines really taught by the Church"; prayer; individual example. When Hopkins referred to the presence of the Church in society he did so, on the one hand, in apocalyptic terms which insisted on a firm loyalty to the Church, and, on the other hand, in irenic language which relegated the Church to the background. For example, in contrast to Manning and Preston who emphasized the Church's public role, or Hecker and Keane who argued for the fulfillment of American culture in Catholicism, Hopkins presented fruits of the Spirit which were socially acceptable: "full and perfect union with our Lord" and "bringing man, and the whole world to a true—a living faith in God's Incarnate Word." Although Hopkins rooted his whole approach in devotion to the Holy Ghost, banished from the argument was the Holy Ghost as a symbol and agent of social renewal. Like McSorley, this preacher at the beginning of the twentieth century was the inheritor of two traditions, one of which had received authoritative status. He also fought with the American Protective Association and insisted on the tight divorce between Catholic belief and public policy.[12] The spirituality of Hopkins's community had lost its social sting.

Second, Hopkins's ecclesiological reflections indicated that he lived within the boundaries defined by Manning, Zardetti, and Leo XIII, yet sympathized with the approach of Hecker and Keane. In an indicative passage in the last sermon, the diocesan priest paralleled the work of the laity with the priestly ministry of preaching. "And what is thus true of the ministers of God," he wrote,

> is in some sense, true of each one of you also. For you also are to engage in the work of the Lord. It is your duty to be able "to give reason for the faith that is in you," and to defend it against the many onslaughts daily made. Above all, it is your duty "to let your light shine before men," and to show forth in your daily lives the fruit and effects of the truths God gives you in the Holy Scriptures. For St. Peter assures you: "You are a chosen generation, a kingly priesthood."

Presupposing the Church's divine organization, as he had done in his earlier pamphlet on *Papal Pretensions,* Hopkins insisted throughout his sermons on defining the Church as the "mystic body of Christ," "a people gathered into one body from all nations."[13] He used passages from Ephesians, Romans, and I Corinthians to emphasize the unity of everyone in the Spirit. His interpretation of Pentecost mentioned the presence of Mary, the apostles, the women, and brethren. Perhaps because he had been for a time a layman himself, Hopkins broadened out the recommendation of the Third Plenary Council of Baltimore to include the laity.

Finally, it should be noted that *Novena of Sermons* began with three discourses on the relationship of the Holy Ghost to the Blessed

---

12. For the struggle with the American Protective Association see Rev. T. F. Hopkins, *Papal Pretensions* (Charleston: Edward Perry & Co., 1894). The "apocalypticism" and "fruits of the Holy Ghost" can be found in sermon six.

13. For the ecclesiology see especially sermons three and six.

Virgin Mary. Hopkins argued that she was the model of Christian perfection, the mother of Jesus, and the mother of the faithful "in the daily life of the Church." As Hecker had done before him, he related the activities of the mystic body of Christ to the anthropological goal of "full and perfect union with our head." As a pastor, Hopkins followed in the tradition of Keane. He exhorted the people, encouraged them, reminded them of their baptismal dignity, castigated them for their indifference, and called them to repentance. His goal was the renewal of community. But what did community mean? Nowhere in his sermons did Hopkins present a practical vision for the Church. The fact that the unity he strove for was "mystic" only indicated again that devotion to the Holy Ghost had undergone a transformation; as a pastoral symbol of renewal it had become ecclesiologically spiritualized. This was particularly evident in the Christological passages.[14] From the perspective of Hecker and Keane, "Spirit" had been divorced from "Body."

With the publication of McSorley's article and Hopkins' *Novena of Sermons on the Holy Ghost,* one history of devotion to the Holy Ghost ended and another began. Living within both the juridical inheritance of Manning, Preston, Zardetti, and Leo XIII, and also the anthropological tradition of Hecker and Keane, future generations of people promoting devotion to the Holy Ghost would reflect the fundamental problem at the heart of the spiritual identity and experience of the Catholic community in the United States. They could either ignore the Holy Spirit as an integrative force symbolizing social, political, and ecclesiological renewal and concentrate

---

14. The Christological theme which emerged in the second series of *Novena of Sermons on the Holy Ghost* had been interconnected with devotion to the Holy Ghost throughout the period under consideration. It surfaced clearly in the controversy over the Sacred Heart, and in the reflections of Hecker and Keane on the humanity of Christ. For purposes of length, I have omitted a detailed discussion of this somewhat subsidiary issue in the development of devotion to the Holy Ghost. It requires a separate and full treatment. Suffice it to note that in early commentaries devotion to the Holy Ghost as a symbol of renewal in Church and society was accompanied by reflections on the suffering of Christ. This element has significantly lost its bite in Hopkins. For example, compare *Novena of Sermons* with Preston, *Lectures Upon the Devotion to the Sacred Heart of Jesus Christ;* or Keane, *Emmanuel.*

on its purely interior significance as an animator of "Catholic Action"; or they could struggle to refashion a new synthesis within the respective positions outlined by Manning and Preston, Hecker and Keane. The former alternative would empty spirituality of any specific social content or application; the latter would entail far-reaching reforms affecting the structures of both Church and state. A survey of articles on the Holy Spirit in Catholic periodicals from 1900 to 1960 indicates that the discussion would begin anew in the 1930s and 1940s.[15] This struggle would culminate in the decisive events of the 1960s and 1970s. Throughout the whole time, from 1870 to 1980, the Holy Spirit would serve as a central symbol for the American Catholic experience, the community's spiritual identity, and some of its most significant choices.

---

15. I am indebted to a graduate student, Carol Mathis, for her thorough survey of major periodicals. See her unpublished manuscript, "Streams into a River: Devotion to the Holy Spirit in the Twentieth Century" (Graduate Theological Union, Berkeley, 1984).

Texts

JOHN JOSEPH KEANE

A SODALITY MANUAL FOR THE USE OF THE SERVANTS OF THE HOLY GHOST

The following excerpt, ''The Little Office of the Holy Ghost,'' is taken from *A Sodality Manual,* pages 35–66, 73–78. ''The Little Office'' was composed by Keane. Each hour is carefully structured around one of the seven gifts of the Spirit according to the following formula:

Opening Prayer
Antiphon
Hymn
Psalm (composed of seven selected verses)
Scripture quotations
Final Prayer (composed of petitions for a gift of the Spirit; for strength to avoid a dominant passion; for the joy of eternal beatitude)

''The Little Office,'' to be recited in public or private, is a noteworthy example of American Catholic devotionalism in its personal tone, its free use of Scriptures, and its underlying ecclesiology. For further comment see chapter three of the commentary.

Air to which all the Hymns may be sung.

O   Ho - ly   Ghost, we   Thee   a - dore, Thou Breath and

Bliss   and   Life— of   God; Thou glo - rious Bond of   Love   in

Whom The   Fa - ther and   the   Son— are one.   A - men.

Another Air for the Hymns.

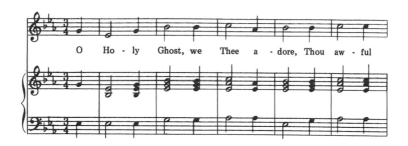

O Ho - ly Ghost, we Thee a - dore, Thou awful

Ho - li - ness of God, Whose Ma - jes - ty with trem - bling

song Ce - les - tial choirs a - dor - ing praise. A - men.

THE LITTLE OFFICE OF THE HOLY GHOST.

The Opening Prayer. (Read by the Prefect, all kneeling.)

Open, O Lord, our mouths to bless Thy holy name; cleanse our hearts from all vain, bad, and distracting thoughts; enlighten our understanding, inflame our will, that we may worthily, attentively and devoutly recite this holy Office, and may deserve to be heard in the presence of Thy Divine Majesty. Through Christ Our Lord. Amen.

O Lord, in union with that divine intention with which Thou, whilst on earth, didst render homage to God, we offer these prayers to Thee.

Our Father. Hail Mary.

(*First Assistant.*) The Spirit of the Lord shall rest upon Him; the Spirit of Wisdom and of Understanding, the Spirit of Counsel and of Fortitude, the Spirit of Knowledge and of Piety, and He shall be filled with the Spirit of the Fear of the Lord. (*Isaias* xi, 2, 3.)

(*Here and in all passages from Scripture, the reference is given, but not to be read aloud.*)

MATINS AND LAUDS.

The Gift of Wisdom.

(*Wisdom is the Gift of the Holy Ghost by which we know and bear in mind the end for which God created us, and use all things as means for its attainment.*)

Ant. (*Pref. all standing.*) Come, O Holy Ghost, fill the hearts of Thy faithful;

(*All.*) And kindle in them the fire of Thy love.

V. (*Pref.*) Send forth Thy Spirit, and they shall be created;

R. (*All.*) And Thou wilt renew the face of the earth.

(*All.*) Glory be to the Father, &c.

Hymn.

> O Holy Ghost, we Thee adore,
> Thou Breath and Bliss and Life of God,
> Thou glorious Bond of Love, in Whom
> The Father and the Son are one.
>
> Thou brooded'st o'er creation's dawn,
> Awaiting Thy abode in man;
> That, made for Love, his soul should seek
> No other end save Love Divine.
>
> O grant us Wisdom for our guide
> That our life-journey may not err,
> That nought of earth may lead astray,
> But all things help us up to God. Amen.

(All sit down.)

Psalm VIII.

(First Asst.) O Lord, our Lord * *(First side)* how admirable is Thy name in the whole earth!

2. For Thy magnificence is elevated: above the heavens.

3. For I will behold Thy heavens, the works of Thy fingers: the moon and the stars which Thou hast set.

4. What is man that Thou art mindful of him? or the son of man that Thou visitest him?

5. Thou hast made him a little less than the Angels, Thou hast crowned him with glory and honor: and hast set him over the works of Thy hands.

6. Thou hast put all things under his feet: all sheep and oxen, yea, and all the beasts of the field.

7. O Lord, our Lord: how admirable is Thy name in all the earth!

(All.) Glory be to the Father, and to the Son and to the Holy Ghost.

As it was in the beginning, is now, and ever shall be, world without end. Amen.

Psalm CXVI.

(*First Asst.*) O praise the Lord, all ye nations * (*First side*) praise Him, all ye people.

For His mercy is confirmed upon us: and the truth of the Lord endureth for ever.

(*All.*) Glory be to the Father, &c.

(*First Asst. standing alone.*)

The Voice of the Holy Ghost Concerning the Gift of Wisdom.

The Lord hath made all things for Himself. (*Prov.* xvi, 4.)

Wisdom reacheth from end to end mightily, and ordereth all things sweetly. (*Wis.* viii, 1.)

Wisdom is an infinite treasure to men, which they that use become the friends of God, being commended for the gifts of discipline. (*Wis.* vii, 14.)

If any one want Wisdom, let him ask of God, who giveth to all abundantly, and upbraideth not, and it shall be given him. (*James* i, 5.)

Hath not God made void the wisdom of this world? . . . For we preach Christ crucified: unto the Jews indeed a stumbling block, and unto the gentiles foolishness; but unto them that are called, Christ the Power of God and the Wisdom of God. (*I Cor.* i, 20–24.)

(*At the end of the reading, he says*)

V. And do Thou, O Lord, have mercy on us.

(*All.*) R. Thanks be to God.

(*All rise.*)

V. (*Pref.*) Blessed are the peace makers;

R. (*All.*) For they shall be called the children of God.

(*Pref.*) Let Us Pray.

O Holy Ghost, adorable Spirit of Wisdom, we beseech Thee, make us truly wise. Make us ever bear in mind that God alone is our First Beginning and our Last End, and that all things must be used as means to bring us to Him. Save us from the concupiscence that would lead us astray after earthly ends; and grant that we may at last reach safely the bosom of our Eternal Father. Through Christ Our Lord. (*All.*) Amen.

PRIME.

The Gift of Understanding.

(*Understanding is the Gift of the Holy Ghost by which the mind is enlightened to perceive and accept the truths of Faith.*)

Come, O Holy Ghost, &c, *as at Matins and Lauds.*

Hymn.

> O Holy Ghost, we Thee adore,
> Thou key to all God's mysteries,
> Thou Sea of Light, in whose calm depths
> God's Self and all His works are seen.
>
> The Prophets found their light in Thee,
> And all who e'er have taught of God;
> And Revelation's heights and depths
> To "little ones" Thou makest plain.
>
> O grant us Understanding's ray,
> That, in this age of darksome doubt,
> By Faith our straining eyes may see
> God's radiance shining through the veil.

Amen.

Psalm XV.

1. Preserve me, O Lord,* for in Thee have I put my trust: I have said to the Lord, Thou art my God, for Thou hast no need of my goods.
2. The Lord is the portion of my inheritance and of my cup: Thou art He that will restore my inheritance unto me.

3. The lines are fallen unto me in goodly places: for my inheritance is goodly unto me.

4. I will bless the Lord, who hath given me understanding: moreover my reins also have corrected me even till night.

5. I set the Lord always in my sight: for He is at my right hand that I be not moved.

6. Therefore my heart hath been glad, and my tongue hath rejoiced: moreover my flesh also shall rest in hope.

7. Thou hast made known unto me the ways of life: Thou shalt fill me with joy with Thy countenance; at Thy right hand are delights for evermore.

Glory be to the Father, &c.

The Voice of the Holy Ghost Concerning the Gift of Understanding.

I am the Light of the world, saith Jesus. He that followeth me walketh not in darkness, but shall have the light of life. (*John* viii, 12.)

I confess to Thee, O Father, Lord of heaven and earth, because Thou hast hid these things from the wise and prudent, and hast revealed them to little ones. (*Mat.* xi, 25.)

The sensual man perceiveth not the things that are of the Spirit of God, for it is foolishness to him, and he cannot understand; because it is spiritually examined. (*I Cor.* ii, 14.)

Eye hath not seen, nor ear heard, nor hath it entered into the heart of man, what things God hath prepared for them that love Him. But to us God hath revealed them by His Spirit: for the Spirit searcheth all things, yea the deep things of God. (*I Cor.* ii, 9, 10.)

We see now through a glass, in a dark manner; but then we shall see face to face. (*I Cor.* xiii, 12.)

V. And do Thou, O Lord have mercy on us.

R. Thanks be to God.

(*Pref.*) *V.* Blessed are the clean of heart;

R. For they shall see God.

Let Us Pray.

O Holy Ghost, adorable Spirit of Understanding, we beseech
Thee, enlighten our minds for the better appreciation of our holy
Faith. Enable us to see more and more clearly the truth, the beauty,
and the necessity of the Divine Revelation which Thou hast given
us, and which is taught us by Thy holy Catholic Church. Save us
from the darkness spread over so many minds by pride and sensual-
ity. Be a light to our steps till in Thy light we shall see God face to
face. Through Christ our Lord. Amen.

TIERCE.

The Gift of Counsel.

(*Counsel is the Gift of the Holy Ghost which guides the conscience, for the shunning of evil and the accomplishing of the holy
will of God.*)

Come, O Holy Ghost, &c., *as at Matins.*

Hymn.

O Holy Ghost, we Thee adore,
Thou Rule of all that's rightly done;
Inspiring all the works of God,
And guiding ours in paths divine.

Thou wast Our Lady's Counsellor,
When Gabriel for her *fiat* sued;
The prudent Handmaid of the Lord
Thou makest Mother of the Word.

O grant us Counsel, that our lives,
From self and earthly motives free,
May ever know but one blest aim—God's glory and our
    neighbor's weal.

                                                        Amen.

Psalm XXII.

1. The Lord ruleth me * and I shall want nothing: he hath set me in a place of pasture.

2. He hath led me on the paths of justice: for His own name's sake.

3. For though I should walk in the midst of the shadow of death, I fear no evils: for Thou art with me.

4. Thy rod and Thy staff: they have comforted me.

5. Thou hast prepared a table before me: against them that afflict me.

6. And Thy mercy will follow me: all the days of my life.

7. And that I may dwell in the house of the Lord: unto length of days.

Glory be to the Father, &c.

The Voice of the Holy Ghost Concerning the Gift of Counsel.

The just man liveth by faith. (*Rom.* i, 17.)

Enter ye in at the narrow gate; for wide is the gate and broad is the way that leadeth to destruction, and many there are who go in thereat. How narrow is the gate and strait is the way that leadeth to life, and few there are that find it. (*Mat.* vii, 13, 14.)

Seek the things that are above, where Christ is sitting at the right hand of God; mind the things that are above; not the things that are upon the earth. (*Coll.* iii, 1, 2.)

We are debtors, not to the flesh, to live according to the flesh. For if you live according to the flesh, you shall die: but if by the Spirit you mortify the deeds of the flesh, you shall live. For whosoever are led by the Spirit of God, they are the sons of God. (*Rom.* viii, 12–14.)

V. And do Thou, O Lord, have mercy on us.

R. Thanks be to God.

V. Blessed are the merciful;

R. For they shall obtain mercy.

Let Us Pray.

O Holy Ghost, adorable Spirit of Counsel, we beseech Thee, direct our daily and hourly lives in the ways of righteousness. Make our every decision, our every thought, word, and act, worthy of disciples of Jesus Christ. Save us from having our judgment warped or our will perverted by the allurements of avarice and self-love. Enable us ever so to live as we would wish to be found when called by our Divine Master to give an account of our stewardship. Through the same Christ our Lord. Amen.

SEXT.

The Gift of Fortitude.

(Fortitude is the Gift of the Holy Ghost which strengthens the will to do and to bear all things for God.)

Come, O Holy Ghost, &c., *as at Matins.*

Hymn.

O Holy Ghost, we Thee adore,
Thou Will of the Almighty God,
Thou Fire of Love, which nought can quench,
Thou Strength of God in feeble man.

Thou camest like a rushing Wind,
To fill th' Apostles' souls with strength.
That Faith and Love 'gainst every shock
Of earth and hell might stand unmoved.

O grant us Fortitude, to bear
The cross for love of our sweet Lord,
To run the race, to win the fight,
And gain the victor's crown at last. Amen.

Psalm XXVI.

1. The Lord is my light and my salvation * whom shall I fear?
2. The Lord is the protector of my life: of whom shall I be afraid?
3. If armies in camp should stand together against me: my heart shall not fear?
4. If battle should rise up against me: in this will I be confident.
5. For He hath hidden me in His tabernacle: in the day of evils, He hath protected me in the secret place of His tabernacle.
6. Be Thou my helper, forsake me not: neither despise me, O God my Saviour.
7. Wait on the Lord, do manfully, and let thy heart take courage: and wait thou on the Lord.

Glory be to the Father, &c.

The Voice of the Holy Ghost Concerning the Gift of Fortitude.

The Lord saith: My grace is sufficient for thee; for power is made perfect in infirmity. Gladly therefore will I glory in my infirmities, that the power of Christ may dwell in me. (*II Cor.* xii, 9.)

I can do all things in Him who strengtheneth me. (*Phil.* iv, 13.)

In the world you shall have distress, saith the Lord; but have confidence, I have overcome the world. (*John* xvi, 33.)

To him that shall overcome, I will give to sit with me in my throne, as I also have overcome, and have sat down with my Father in His Throne. (*Apoc.* iii, 21.)

Blessed is the man that endureth temptation; for when he hath been proved, he shall receive the crown of life, which God hath promised to them that love him (*James* i, 12.)

V. And do Thou, O Lord, have mercy on us.
R. Thanks be to God.

V. Blessed are they that hunger and thirst after justice;
R. For they shall have their fill.

Let Us Pray.

O Holy Ghost, adorable Spirit of Fortitude, we beseech Thee, strengthen our feeble wills with the power of Thy divine grace, that we may be able to do all things and suffer all things for God and our salvation. Thou seest, alas! how vacillating are our resolutions, how innumerable our failures. Save us from enervating self-indulgence and sloth. Enable us, by true nobleness of soul, to deserve a crown at the hands of the Just Judge. Through the same Christ our Lord. Amen.

NONES.

The Gift of Knowledge.

(Knowledge is the Gift of the Holy Ghost which stores up in the memory the truths of Faith which are received through the Gift of Understanding.)

Come, O Holy Ghost, &c., *as at Matins.*

Hymn.

O Holy Ghost, we thee adore,
Whom Jesus "Spirit of Truth" hath named,
Receiving from th' Eternal Word
Faith's treasures for the souls of men.

In Tongues of Fire Thy radiance beamed
Above the rapt Apostles' heads.
That, cleansed with Fire, their tongues might pour
Thy truth forever o'er the world.

With heavenly Knowledge fill our mind,
That, deaf to error's syren tongue,
From toils of darkness and deceit
Thy truth may ever keep us free. Amen.

Psalm XVIII.

1. The heavens show forth the glory of God * and the firmament declareth the works of His hands.

2. Day unto day uttereth speech: and night unto night showeth knowledge.

3. There are neither speeches nor languages: where their voices are not heard.

4. Their sound hath gone forth into all the earth: and their words unto the ends of the world.

5. The law of the Lord is without spot, converting souls; the testimony of the Lord is faithful, giving wisdom to little ones.

6. The precepts of the Lord are right, rejoicing hearts: the commandment of the Lord is lightsome, enlightening the eyes.

7. For Thy servant keepeth them: and in keeping them there is great reward.

Glory be to the Father, &c.

The Voice of the Holy Ghost Concerning the Gift of Knowledge.

If you continue in my word, saith the Lord, you shall be my disciples indeed, and you shall know the truth, and the truth shall make you free. (*John* viii, 31, 32.)

I will ask the Father, and He shall give you another Paraclete, that He may abide with you forever, the Spirit of Truth, whom the world cannot receive, because it seeth Him not, nor knoweth Him: but you shall know Him, because He shall abide with you, and shall be in you. He will teach you all things, and bring all things to your mind, whatsoever I shall have said to you. (*John* xiv, 16, 17, 26.)

The things that are of God no one knoweth but the Spirit of God. Now we have received not the spirit of this world, but the Spirit that is of God, that we may know the things that are given us from God. (*I Cor.* ii, 11, 12.)

V. And do Thou, O Lord, have mercy on us.
R. Thanks be to God.

V. Blessed are they that mourn:
R. For they shall be comforted.

Let Us Pray.

O Holy Ghost, adorable Spirit of Knowledge, we beseech Thee preserve in our minds the treasures of Divine Truth. Above all other knowledge, help us to advance in the knowledge of God, in the science of the Saints. Deliver us from the darkness of ignorance; save us from the illusions of error; bring back them that have strayed from the truth. Grant that, ever following the voice of the Good Shepherd, we may enjoy here the sweetness of His pastures, and hereafter the abundance of Our Father's house. Through the same Christ our Lord. Amen.

VESPERS.

The Gift of Piety.

(*Piety is the Gift of the Holy Ghost which warms the heart with filial love towards God.*)

Come, O Holy Ghost, &c., *as at Matins.*

Hymn.

O Holy Ghost, we Thee adore,
Thou Fount of Love in Jesus' Heart,
Poured forth in ours, that we, made sons,
May with Him, "Abba, Father," cry.

When Jesus the baptismal flood
For our regeneration blessed,
Thou, Spirit Dove, wast there to teach
Our souls to wing their way to God.

O grant that Piety may melt
The ice from round our frozen hearts;
That, winged with love, our souls may soar,
In Jesus' Heart to find their rests. Amen.

Psalm XLI.

1. As the hart panteth after the water-springs * so panteth my soul after Thee, O God.

2. My soul hath thirsted after the strong living God; when shall I come, and appear before the face of God?

3. My tears have been my bread day and night; whilst it is said to me daily, Where is thy God?

4. These things I remembered, and I poured out my soul in me: for I shall go over into the place of the wonderful tabernacle, even unto the house of God.

5. With the voice of joy and praise: the noise of one feasting.

6. Why art thou sad, O my soul? and why dost thou disquiet me?

7. Hope thou in God, for I will yet praise Him: *He is* the salvation of my countenance, and my God.

Glory be to the Father, &c.

The Voice of the Holy Ghost Concerning the Gift of Piety.

God sent His Son . . . that we might receive the adoption of sons. And because we are sons, God hath sent the Spirit of His Son into our hearts, crying: Abba, Father. (*Gal.* iv, 4–6.)

We have known and have believed the charity which God hath to us. God is charity; and he that abideth in charity abideth in God, and God in him. Let us therefore love God, because God first hath loved us. (*I John* iv, 16, 19.)

I am come to cast fire on the earth, saith the Lord, and what will I but that it be enkindled. (*Luke* xii, 49.)

He that hath my commandments and keepeth them, he it is that loveth me. If any one love me, he will keep my word, and my Father will love him, and we will come to him, and will make our abode with him. (*John* xiv, 21, 23.)

To them that love God, all things work together unto good. (*Rom.* viii, 28.)

V. And do Thou, O Lord, have mercy on us.

R. Thanks be to God.

V. Blessed are the meek;

R. For they shall possess the land.

Let Us Pray.

O Holy Ghost, adorable Spirit of Piety, we beseech Thee, inflame our hearts with that blessed Fire which Jesus came to cast on the earth, and which He so ardently desires to see enkindled. Thou seest, alas! how our souls are chilled by this cold world in which we have to live. Save us from not loving God, and save us from serving Him with lukewarmness. And since we are made the children of God, through Thee, the Spirit of His Son, O grant that our hearts may ever share in that filial love with which the Heart of Jesus burns for His Father and our Father. Through the same Christ our Lord. Amen.

COMPLINE.

The Gift of the Fear of the Lord.

(*The Fear of the Lord is the Gift of the Holy Ghost which restrains us from evil by a salutary dread of our own weakness, the heinousness of sin, and the judgments of God.*)

Come, O Holy Ghost, &c., *as at Matins.*

Hymn.

O Holy Ghost, we thee adore,
Thou awful Holiness of God,
Whose Majesty, with trembling song,
Celestial choirs adoring praise,

On Thabor, in the shining Cloud
That veiled our radiant Saviour's brow,
Thou show'st how dread th' Omnipotence
That deigns our puny love to crave.

O may Thy Fear surround our lives
With ramparts 'gainst the wiles of sin,
And spur our lagging steps to where
We'll praise Thy name for evermore.

Amen.

Psalm XXXIII.

1. I will bless the Lord at all times,* His praise shall be always in my mouth.

2. My soul shall glory in the Lord: let the meek hear and rejoice.

3. I sought the Lord, and He heard me: and He delivered me from all my troubles.

4. The angel of the Lord shall encamp round about them that fear Him: and shall deliver them.

5. O taste, and see that the Lord is sweet: blessed is the man that hopeth in Him.

6. Fear the Lord, all ye His saints: for there is no want to them that fear Him.

7. The Lord is nigh unto them that are of a contrite heart: and He will save the humble of spirit.

Glory be to the Father, &c.

The Voice of the Holy Ghost Concerning the Gift of the Fear of the Lord.

The Fear of the Lord is the beginning of Wisdom. (*Eccl.* i, 16.)

Be not afraid of them who kill the body, and after that have no more that they can do. But I will show you whom ye shall fear: fear ye Him, who after He hath killed, hath power to cast into hell; yea, I say to you, fear Him. (*Luke* xii, 4, 5.)

His mercy is from generation unto generations, to them that fear Him. (*Luke* i, 50.)

With fear and trembling work out your salvation. (*Phil.* ii, 12.)

He that thinketh himself to stand, let him take heed lest he fall. (*I Cor.* x, 12.)

Grieve not the Holy Spirit of God, whereby you are sealed unto the day of redemption. (*Eph.* iv, 30.)

The fear of the Lord is honor, and glory, and gladness, and a crown of joy. With him that feareth the Lord it shall go well in the latter end, and in the day of his death he shall be blessed. (*Eccli.* i, 11, 13.)

V. And do Thou, O Lord, have mercy on us.

R. Thanks be to God.

V. Blessed are the poor in spirit:

R. For theirs is the kingdom of heaven.

Let Us Pray.

O Holy Ghost, adorable Spirit of the Fear of the Lord, we beseech Thee, keep ever Thy salutary restraint on our wayward inclinations. Make us fear sin above all evils, and the loss of God above all calamities. Save us from the folly of presumption, the snares of self-deceit, and the blindness of false security. Guide us through the safe paths of Thy holy Fear to that blessed end of our journey, where all fear will be cast out by perfect love, and Thy Seven Gifts will be transformed into the plenitude of eternal bliss. Through Christ our Lord. Amen.

HYMNS.

The "Veni Creator Spiritus."

In the Name of the Father, and of the Son, and of the Holy Ghost. Amen.

Come, Holy Ghost, Creator, come;
Dwell in us as Thy chosen home;
Thy servants' minds with truth inspire,
Their hearts inflame with heavenly fire.

O Paraclete, to Thee we cry,
Thou priceless gift of God most high:
Thy living unction from above
Is fire of grace and light of love.

Thou bindest with a sevenfold band,
O finger of the Father's hand:
O promised Spirit, Thou dost teach,
Enriching all our mouths with speech.

Thy blessed light to us impart,
And pour Thy love on every heart;
The weakness of our flesh supply
With ceaseless succor from on high.

Far from us drive the deadly foe;
Thy peace and joy on all bestow;
In every path be Thou our Guide,
And with us evermore abide.

O may Thy grace on us bestow,
The Father and the Son to know;
Coequal Spirit, we adore
Thy majesty for evermore.

All glory to the Father be;
All glory, only Son, to Thee;
All glory to the Spirit blest
The bond of Their eternal rest. Amen.

V. Send forth Thy Spirit, and they shall be created:
R. And Thou shalt renew the face of the earth.

Let Us Pray.

O God, who hast taught the hearts of the faithful by the light of Thy Holy Spirit; grant that we by the same Spirit may love what is right, and always rejoice in his consolation.

May Thy grace, we beseech Thee, O Lord, so go before our actions and follow them, that all our prayers and all our works may begin from Thee, and in Thee be ended; through our Lord Jesus Christ Thy Son, who liveth and reigneth with Thee in the unity of the Holy Ghost, God, for ever and ever. Amen.

The "Veni, Sancte Spiritus."

In the Name of the Father, and of the Son, and of the Holy Ghost. Amen.

> Come, Holy Ghost, Thou Lord of love,
> Pour on us from Thy throne above
>   Thy unction and Thy light:
> O come, Thou Father of the poor;
> O come, with gifts, both large and sure,
>   And make our spirits bright.

> Thou of consolers art the best;
> Thou art our soul's most treasured guest,
>   And drivest from us fears:
> In labor Thou art rest most sweet,
> Refreshing coolness in the heat,
>   A solace amid tears.

> O Light most blessed, brightly shine
> Within our souls and make them Thine;
>   O make them all Thy own;
> Without Thy Godhead is no rest,
> And work is worthless at the best,
>   If Thou be all unknown.

> O wash away all sinful stains,
> And water all that dry remains,
>   And heal the wounded soul:
> Bend, bend the stubborn mind and heart;
> To frozen souls Thy warmth impart;
>   Our wandering feet control.

To all Thy servants trusting Thee,
Faithful wherever they may be,
　　Give sevenfold gifts of grace:
O give them gladness when they die,
That they may dwell with Thee on high,
　　And ever see Thy face. Amen.

V. May the grace of the Holy Spirit
R. Enlighten our minds and hearts.
V. O Lord, hear Thou our prayer:
R. And let our cry come to Thee.

Let Us Pray.

O God, to whom every heart is open and every desire speaketh, and from whom no secret is hidden; cleanse the thoughts of our hearts by the inspirations of Thy Holy Spirit, that we may merit to love Thee perfectly and praise Thee worthily; through Jesus Christ our Lord. Amen.

Grant, we beseech Thee, O merciful God, that Thy Church, being gathered together in Thy Holy Spirit, may not be disturbed by the powers of evil; through our Lord Jesus Christ, who with Thee and the Holy Ghost liveth and reigneth, one God, world without end. Amen.

V. O Lord, hear our prayer:
R. And let our cry come to Thee.
V. May the souls of the faithful departed through the mercy of God rest in peace.
R. Amen.

(For the Hymn, "Veni, Creator Spiritus;" and the sequence, "Veni, Sancte Spiritus;" there are the following Indulgences:

1. A Plenary Indulgence once a month, if said with the intention of praying for peace among Christian princes, &c.

2. Three hundred days on Whit Sunday and during its Octave.

3. One hundred days, any other day, once a day.

For gaining the plenary indulgence, confession and communion are required.)

A DIOCESAN PRIEST [THOMAS F. HOPKINS]

NOVENA OF SERMONS ON THE HOLY GHOST IN HIS RELATIONSHIP TO THE WORLD IN THREE SERIES OF THREE SERMONS EACH

Sermons are one of the most important sources for understanding the formation and development of American Catholic spirituality. Hopkins' Novena of Sermons *is the finest single representative in this genre of the post-Civil War tradition of devotion to the Holy Ghost. The work draws freely on the writings of Cardinal Manning and Otto Zardetti while reflecting in many places the vision of Isaac Hecker and John J. Keane. The "Introduction," written by Cardinal Gibbons after* Testem Benevolentiae, *is an important witness to the continuing appeal of an "Americanist" spirituality. For further comment see chapter five of the commentary.*

INTRODUCTION.

There are three teachers in the spiritual life. First, Christ teaches us, through His Gospels; secondly, the Church teaches us, through her ordained ministers, and, thirdly, the Holy Ghost teaches us, through His secret inspirations.

We cannot always have access to the words of the Gospel nor of earthly teachers. But the Holy Spirit, is ever at our call, ready to impart His life and grace to us. He speaks to us at home and abroad, in solitude and in company, by night and by day. The Paraclete is at all times and places attentive to our entreaties.

115

The instructions imparted to us by human agents are more or less colored and tinged by the earthly channel through which they flow, but the waters of grace flowing into our hearts directly from the Holy Ghost come to us from their heavenly source without any human mediation.

If we approach the Divine Paraclete in the spirit of Samuel when he said "Speak, Lord, Thy servant heareth," we shall receive abundant blessings. God's chosen servants have acknowledged that they obtained more light from Heaven, and more consolation by secret communings with the Holy Spirit, than by labored study and intercourse with men. I was once called by a pious convert—a lady—to the bedside of her sick husband, who was an avowed unbeliever. I used every argument which the occasion suggested to win him to belief in Christ. But he frankly told me, that while grateful for my services, I made no impression on him; that there was a chasm between him and me, which could not be bridged over. I finally asked him to promise me, that he would have recourse to the Spirit of God and implore Him to give him light to see the truth and the grace to follow it. He promised to comply with my request. In a few days I was again sent for and entering his room, I immediately saw that a change was wrought in him. It was the right hand of the Most High. He launched forth into an eloquent and impassioned vindication of the truths of Christianity, and begged for the grace of baptism. In order to give emphasis to his conversion, he desired that his non-Catholic friends should assist at the ceremony. He died a few days after in the full profession of Catholic faith.

You would like to have some sign or criterion by which you can judge whether or not you possess the Spirit of God. "Believe not every spirit, but try the spirits if they be of God." (1 John, 4. 1). Just as we judge of a tree by its fruits, so do we judge of the Spirit by His operations within us.

And the Spirit of God is not an idle Principle but an active power, constantly working within us.

The Spirit of God is a Spirit of Light. "God is Light and in Him there is no darkness." (1 John 1.5).

The Spirit of God is a Spirit of Prayer. "We know not what we should pray for as we ought, but the Spirit Himself asks them for us with unspeakable groanings." (Rom. 8. 26). If you have the Spirit of God you will be devoted to prayer; you will instinctively turn to the Divine Paraclete for comfort and light, and on every occasion of temptation.

The Spirit of God is a Spirit of Obedience, while the Devil is a spirit of revolt. They who are swayed by the Holy Ghost, have a reverential obedience for the Divine Law and respect for all constituted authority.

The Holy Ghost is a Spirit of Truth. He is expressly so called in the Gospel, while the Devil is called the "father of lies." "When the Spirit of Truth will come He will teach you all truth." He is "the Spirit of Truth who proceeds from the Father"; "the Spirit of Truth whom the world cannot receive." It is a good sign that you are animated and prompted by the Holy Ghost if you are always truthful, open, candid, sincere and ingenuous in your speech and conduct; and if you abhor lying, deceit, and all kinds of duplicity.

The Holy Ghost is a Spirit of Temperance in eating and drinking: "Be not drunk with wine wherein is luxury, but be ye filled with the Holy Ghost, speaking to yourselves in psalms, and hymns, and spiritual canticles, singing and making melody in your heart to the Lord." (Eph. 5. 18, 19).

The Holy Ghost is a Spirit of Mortification and Self-denial. "If you live according to the flesh you shall die, but if by the Spirit you mortify the deeds of the flesh you shall live." (Rom. 8. 13).

The Holy Ghost is a Spirit of Love. "The fruit of the Spirit is Charity. Let us love one another for love is of God. God is love." (1 John, 4. 7, 8).

It is my earnest prayer that all who shall read this work may be inspired with a greater devotion to the Holy Ghost, and may live under the sweet influence of the Divine Comforter.

James, Cardinal Gibbons.

FIRST SERIES.

THE RELATIONSHIP OF THE HOLY GHOST
TO THE BLESSED VIRGIN MARY.

I.

In Her Immaculate Conception. She is the "Spouse of the Holy Ghost."

"I came out of the Mouth of the Most High, the first-born of all creatures" (Eccl. 24, 5.)

My Brethren, the Church is even now looking forward to and preparing for the annual celebration of one of the greatest, most solemn, and most fruitful festivals of the Christian year. The revolving circle of her calendar will soon bring us to the great Feast of Pentecost, the festival of God, the Holy Ghost, Third Person of the Adorable Trinity, distinct in personality, yet, in all that constitutes the Godhead, co-equal with the Father and the Son.

Though the mystery of the Holy Ghost in the Divine Trinity is unfathomable to our human minds, and unspeakable by our human lips, yet it contains so much of importance to your spiritual interests and mine that I venture to make it the subject of your pious consideration in a series of instructions to which I invite your attention during this season preceding and following the great festival itself. Not that I can hope to discourse worthily on this subject so exalted, so divine, even though my lips and heart were cleansed as were those of Isaiah with a coal of fire from Heaven. But we may hope, from the mercy and love of God poured out upon us through His Holy Spirit, that as we thus reverently seek to know Him better and to learn to love Him more deeply, He Himself, the "Spirit of Truth," will enlighten the darkness of our minds, will dispel the clouds and errors of our intellects, will banish the coldness and hardness of our hearts;—and, taking us by the hand as we grope in the banishment of our sin-laden condition, will, of His own great love, lead us into the "ineffable light" of His knowledge and His sanctifying grace.

For he alone can be our Guide in these our searchings after His truth. In her beautiful prayer to the Holy Ghost, the Church proclaims to the Almighty her firm faith and confidence: Send forth Thy Spirit and they (our hearts) shall be created (made entirely new) and Thou wilt renew the face of the earth,"—this earth of ours now lying in the chaos and confusion of sin, will be renewed into perfect spiritual order and beauty, upon which the Spirit of God will move as of old it did upon the waters, and from which, if we remain faithful, the sunlight of His presence and grace will never more be banished. We, sharing this confidence of our Mother, the Church, will re-echo from our inmost hearts her earnest prayer: "Come, Oh Holy Ghost, fill the hearts of Thy faithful, and kindle in them the fire of Thy love."

The great scene of Pentecost, the visible descent of the Holy Ghost upon the Apostles and the infant Church of Christ, is told us in the Acts of the Apostles in tones truly divine, because inspired. It is so glorious a fact, one so unique, so singular, so constantly though not visibly renewed, so perpetual a fact in the Church of God, that, if we look upon it with the reverent eyes of devout minds, our lips cannot remain sealed, but must spontaneously burst forth into glad thanksgiving, and influenced by the Spirit of God, we, like the converts of that first Pentecost Sunday, joyously "speak in our own tongues the wonderful works of God." (Acts 2. 11.) In external splendor and impressiveness, no historic fact in our redemption seems so glorious, so public and so productive of immediate, palpable effect, as this solemn effusion of the Holy Spirit, this His visible descent upon the Apostles. The birth of our dear Lord was accomplished in the secret watches of the night, while the heavens glittered with stars that sang to one another in gladness, and found their radiance dimmed by the brightness of angel's eyes who looked on the mystery that was concealed from men. The triumphant Resurrection of Christ from the dead was effected in the dim dawning of that first Easter morn, while enemies slept in indifference, while guards lay stricken senseless with fear, and while the faithful ones, unconscious of the triumph of that very hour, wept because, believing He had come to redeem Israel, they thought He had failed in the effort. But the Holy Ghost descended "when the day of Pentecost was fully come," in the perfect brilliancy of the morning sun, heralded by a sound from Heaven as of a mighty, rushing wind, visible to the eyes of all men—coming in the form of tongues of fire—fulfilling the sayings of the Prophets—redeeming the promises of Christ—moving the heavens by the might of His coming—loosening the tongues of the hitherto fear-stricken Apostles, striking off the chains of their weakness and cowardice—leading them, a band of unconquerable heroes, into the very hosts of the enemy, changing the whole face of the earth—and from that triumphant moment forevermore remaining in the midst of the nations by means of the Church of Christ, an everlasting miracle! I say, an everlasting miracle; for He Who on that fiftieth day after the Resurrection of Christ was thus solemnly given to the disciples has never since left the Church to which He then united Himself. The coming glad day of Pentecost whose rosy dawn is almost upon us, will not record merely a past event, but a living,

perpetual fact. Even as on that first Pentecost, so to-day does the
Holy Spirit dwell in the mystic body of Christ, the Church. And even
as the human soul lives and acts in our visible body, so does the Holy
Spirit daily live and act in the Church, giving life and energy, binding together all the faithful and making them all members of the one
great, living body, whose head is Christ Jesus, Our Lord!

If all this be true, can we doubt the importance of the Holy
Ghost to each of us individual members of the Church—our constant
and complete dependence on Him for our very spiritual life—and the
vital importance of placing ourselves and remaining in intimate
union with Him, without Whom we are spiritually dead! The Church
teaches us that the sanctification of human souls is in a special manner the work of the Holy Ghost.

I pause here for a moment to remind you of a fact important in
all our meditations on the Holy Ghost—that God is one and inseparable. By the mystery of the Holy Trinity we know that in this unity
of the God-head there are three distinct persons in one God. All divine worship is rendered to these three in one, all divine perfections
are common to these three in one, and belong equally to them all.
And all the divine operations in creation and in created objects are
equally to be attributed to, because they are equally effected by the
three in one. And yet in the outward work of the God-head, outside
of Himself, and relating to us, (*"ad extra"* or external, as the Church
terms it,) the several persons of the Holy Trinity have a relationship
and an attributed province peculiar to each of them. Thus God the
Son, has a special relation to God's creatures as the Incarnate Word,
Who by the hypostatic union united our human nature to Himself and
became our Redeemer. So the Holy Ghost is specially related to us
in the office of Sanctifier. The grace of the Triune God is poured out
upon us by the action of the Holy Ghost in a special manner. This
work in us is indeed one that is common to the three persons of the
God-head, for neither of them is excluded from the work of our sanctification, just as they all operated in the work of our redemption.
But the operations of charity and grace by which we are sanctified,
are by "appropriation," as theologians term it, specially the work of
the Holy Ghost. In thus adoring, honoring, venerating and invoking
the Holy Ghost we never, and by no means exclude the Father or the
Son. In the triple invocation with which the Church directs us to begin the "Litanies," we adore and invoke, "God the Father Al-

mighty, God the Son, Redeemer of the world, and God the Holy Ghost." But the climax of the invocation, comprising all the others, is: "Holy Trinity, One God, have mercy on us." In a special manner the Scriptures teach us that "the Charity of God is poured out into our hearts by the Holy Spirit who is given to us," and as this charity is the link that binds us to God, and is the special action of the Holy Ghost, it is through Him in a special and peculiar manner that our souls are sanctified.

Therefore, resuming the thread of my discourse, I desire to impress upon your minds the importance to us of the Holy Ghost, and our entire dependence on Him. He it is Who "filled the Apostles" (Acts 2, 4.) The disciples "were filled with the Holy Ghost" (Acts 13. 52.). Through Him we "are built together into an habitation of God in the Spirit." (Eph. 2. 22.). He it is "who is given to us." (Rom. 5. 5.). He, "the Spirit, helpeth our infirmity. For we know not what we should pray for as we ought, but the Spirit Himself asketh for us with unspeakable groanings." (Rom. 8. 26.). His anointing "teaches us all things and is the truth." (1 John 2. 27.). Nay, without Him we are utterly incapable of any good, even of speaking that name in which alone is our salvation, for St. Paul assures the Corinthians "that no man can say the Lord Jesus, but by the Holy Ghost." (1 Cor. 12. 3.). With these evidences do you still doubt the importance and the necessity of the Holy Ghost in the work of our salvation? We cannot do so.

Then have our past lives in their veneration and love and devotion to the Holy Ghost shown us to be persuaded of this great truth? Have we not to admit that we have been singularly cold and indifferent to Him, that He has been a mere abstract idea to us even while we perhaps thought we were working zealously for our salvation? We honor and adore the Father, and He becomes a living reality to us as our Creator and Sovereign Lord. We love and worship the Son, and, in the infinite, loving humility of His Incarnation, we realize Him as of our human nature and our Brother, even though our Redeemer and Judge. But how few of us have sought to cultivate a warm, personal, living, active devotion to the Holy Ghost, Whom, indeed, we always name with the Father and the Son, but to Whom our hearts have been so sadly indifferent and cold, and yet through Whom alone the benefits and the love of the creating Father and the redeeming Son can be poured out upon us!

To awaken us from this apathy, this sad indifference that threatens our eternal ruin, the Church each year invites us to celebrate the great festival of the Holy Ghost. As we specially worship the Incarnate Son at Christmas, so do we specially adore the Holy Ghost at Pentecost, which St. Augustine calls the *"Dies natalis Spiritus Sancti,"* the Nativity of the Holy Ghost. But the great festival of Pentecost will pass without fruit for us, unless we learn this lesson of increased love and tenderness and devotion to the Holy Ghost. In this deep conviction and in the desire that our past indifference may give way to fervor, and that our hearts; hitherto cold and thoughtlessly indifferent and negligent towards the Third Person of the Holy Trinity, may grow warm with the fire of His love, I propose to speak to you, during this sacred season, of His claims on our love by the various relationships existing between the Holy Ghost, and our eternal interests. For if we desire His influence in our souls, if we hunger for His sweet and consoling presence in our hearts, if we long for the light by which He alone can illuminate us in divine truth, our cry to Him must be the voice of earnest longing and tender devotion. We must implore Him with intense love to enter our hearts. We must join in the grand supplication of the Church "Come, Oh Holy Spirit, and send from high Heaven the ray of Thy light. Without Thy divine aid, there is nothing in man, nothing that is innocent." Believe me, a cold and indifferent invitation will not bring Him into our hearts, yet we cannot earnestly desire that of which we ourselves are ignorant. If, therefore, my feeble words to you may serve to make Him better known to you and more desired by your hearts, then will you also the more anxiously seek for Him, and He will come to you, and, fulfilling the sweet promise of Our Lord, will make His dwelling place with you.

In calling your devout attention to the various claims of the Holy Ghost on our love and the various manners and methods in which He has shown His relationship to us, I am happy to remember that, however feeble my voice, I speak His praise and seek to make Him better known to you, in this beautiful month of May, dedicated by the Church to the special honor of Mary, the Mother of Jesus, Our Lord. You remember how the Scriptures testify that she formed a central figure in the group upon which the Holy Ghost visibly descended on that first day of Pentecost. If His special province is the sanctification of human souls, what grander work of His sanctifying hand can we contemplate than this spouse of the Holy Spirit, upon whom He poured out the very fulness of grace! And what time more appropriate to reflect on the work of the Holy Ghost in the human soul than this month in which the Church proposes to our daily contemplation this one creature of whom she declares, "Thou art all fair, Oh Mary, and there is no spot in thee!" The month of May, with its reflections and its reminders of the holiness of Mary, seems a specially appropriate time for considering the operations of God the Holy Ghost, through Whom she became the perfect vessel of election that the Church holds up for our imitation and our love.

Our first reflections, therefore, on the Holy Ghost shall be on His relationship to that Queen of God's people. And while His grace, I pray, may purify my lips, I shall endeavor to lead your minds to the very beginning of His work in Mary, and to remind you of the action of the Holy Ghost in her Immaculate Conception, thus explaining and justifying for you that mysterious and tender title which the Church solemnly and constantly gives to Mary, when she hails her as the "Spouse of the Holy Ghost."

Remembering the active part of the Holy Ghost in the work of creation, we understand why the Church names Him *"Digitus Paternae Dexterae,"* "The Finger of God's right hand." Through Him the link is formed between the Creator and His creation. In the great six days of the creation, this Spirit of God was borne upon the face of the deep and brooded over each new development of the creative power of God. In the opening words of the Sacred Text describing the great scenes of the creation, we are told, "The Spirit of God moved over the waters." (Gen. 1. 2.). The wonderful evolution by which all things were made from nothing, and by which the primitive chaos dissolved itself into the material beauties that are ever new, was the work of the Holy Ghost. Then came the crowning work of creation, when, on the sixth day, man was made and fashioned to the image and likeness of God. The body was formed of the dust, and in itself, perhaps was not superior to other works of the creative hand that had gone before. But when God's image was to be stamped upon that material clay—when the soul was to enter, bringing with it all the dignity of manhood, it is God's Spirit that effects this work. God breathed into his face the breath of life, and man became a living soul, because of this indwelling of God's own Spirit. And now remember that, in his first creation, man stood forth holy and sinless.

The Spirit of God breathed not only into the face of Adam, but into the face of his soul, thus sanctifying him, endowing him with a newly-created sanctity which was a participation of His own un-created holiness. The original innocence of the first created soul was the direct and glorious work of God's Holy Spirit, Who thus, in the crowning work of the first creation already shows Himself to us as the Sanctifier.

That work of God, man constituted in original innocence and holiness, was ruthlessly destroyed by sin. "Confusion worse con-founded" would have been the continued result of man's sin, had not the mercy of God planned a remedy even at the first appearance of the evil. A new creation of justice restored and holiness regained was even then promised by an all-merciful God, while the outrage of the first sin was yet in fresh enormity. To the serpent, as the in-carnation of sin and evil, God declared: "I will put enmities between thee and the woman, and thy seed and her seed. She shall crush thy head." (Gen. 3. 15.). And at once in this vista of the future the mercy of God shows the coming work of the Holy Ghost, the Sanctifier. As Adam was created in original innocence, so, faith teaches us, she through whom the remedy of Adam's sin came to us, was held free from all sin from the first moment of existence in her mother's womb, by an anticipation of the merits of her Divine Son. Now, if, as we have seen, the innocence of the first man was the direct work of the Holy Ghost, do we not readily understand that the preservation from all stain of sin for this new Eve, this mother of the new spiritual creation of justice and holiness renewed, was equally and worthily a work eagerly assumed by this Divine Sanctifier of souls?

Here begins that special and mysterious relationship between the Holy Ghost and the Blessed Virgin which continued so clearly throughout her life. Its first workings are shown in her Immaculate Conception, by which the Holy Ghost, her Sanctifier, preserved her from the first shadow of sin. The article of faith which teaches us that Mary was free from sin in the first moment of her existence, also and necessarily presents her to us as the special handiwork upon whom the Holy Ghost exerted His Divine influence and power. Faith and reason teach us the intimate manner in which, because of her Immaculate Conception, she was related to the Holy Ghost from the very beginning. We can have no doubt of this direct influence of the Holy Ghost upon all her life—of this intimate connection between her sanctified soul and Him Who sanctified her. It is the theme, the keynote of the salutation and message first brought to her by the angel from on high: "Hail, full of grace." (Luke 1. 28.) "The Holy Ghost shall come upon thee and the power of the Most High shall overshadow thee. And therefore, also, the Holy which shall be born of thee shall be called the Son of God." (Luke 1. 35.). She is declared to be already "full of grace," due entirely to the action of the Holy Ghost. But all her future life is to be shaped—all the further designs of God now disclosed to her by the Angel, are to be carried out under the influence and by the action of this same Holy Spirit, and not otherwise. The Fathers of the Church in every age seem fully to realize this and constantly term Mary "The Spouse," "The Sanctuary," "The Dwelling Place" of the Holy Ghost. And we must remember that the praises with which the Church honors her Saints, and her Queen of all Saints, are not idle words nor empty titles, but have a real significance, and are founded in the very truth of God.

In the Nicene Creed, the symbol of Catholic faith throughout the world, we profess, with the Church, that Jesus Christ, "became incarnate by the Holy Ghost of the Virgin Mary and was made man." Not only does the Liturgy of the Church everywhere teem with this idea—the intimate relationship between the Holy Ghost and the Blessed Virgin, but it is shown to us most markedly when, in the votive Mass of the Blessed Virgin, the Church directs that the second prayer shall always be that of the Holy Ghost. This being the sense and mind of the Church, we, reverently inquiring when this mysterious connection began, know that it dated from the very beginning of her life which was all sinless, and we are inevitably borne back in thought to that first moment of her existence, in which, as she came from her Creator's hand pure and sinless, the Holy Ghost first embraced this spotless spouse whom He had sanctified.

To make this favorite title, "Spouse of the Holy Ghost," more intelligible to you, let me remind you that spiritual writers approved by the Church, speaking of the justification or sanctification of the soul, and the union thus established with Almighty God, very frequently, and by preference, compare it with that union of heart and mind and sympathy and love that exists between two spouses. The Church assures us that not only do the gifts and beauties of the Godhead shine forth in holy souls, but that such souls become true, concentrated, spiritual temples of the Holy Ghost, Who dwells in them by personal presence. He is in substantial union with the just. St. Gregory of Nazienza says, speaking of just souls: "The Holy Ghost is no longer present with them only in operation," (for in this sense He is present even in sinful hearts, moving them by the inspirations of His grace,) "but He is with us and converses with us substantially, so to speak; for it was fitting that as the Son had dwelt among us bodily, so the Holy Ghost should be manifested bodily, Christ returning to Himself, and the Holy Ghost descending to us." (Forty-first Sermon on Pentecost.)

Now remember the beauty of holiness that Mary enjoyed from the moment of her Immaculate Conception. If so close a union exists at all times between the Holy Ghost and each sanctified soul, who shall worthily speak of the most intimate and sacred union that sprang up by the very action of the Holy Ghost in the creation of her sinless soul, and which was never throughout her life interrupted by one moment's estrangement of sin! Yes, in perfect holiness her beautiful soul was in its very creation wedded to this Divine Spouse, and Divine Love linked her as a spouse to the Holy Spirit of God in the moment of her Immaculate Conception. She, created by the Father, was prepared for the Son by her espousal to the Holy Ghost, and in the new creation of mercy and restored justice, she is the first fruits of the action of the Holy Ghost, the first embodiment of unstained holiness in a creature. Therefore the Church puts into her mouth the words of my text: "I came out of the mouth of the Most High, the first born before all creatures." (Eccl. 24. 5.). In this new creation of holiness, she is the first work of the finger of God's right hand! No merit of hers, indeed, entitled her to this first unspeakable honor and distinction. It was God's pure mercy and love that thus singled her out among all creatures; but, having so chosen her, the holiness of God allied itself to her so closely that she herself, wondering, exclaims: "He hath showed might in His arm." "He that is mighty hath done great things to me." (Luke 1. 49, 51.) The work of the Holy Ghost was perfectly done in her Immaculate Conception. He made the first human soul holy in its creation, and the same Holy Spirit so invested her with grace, that, by the future merits of her Son, she also was made holy in her very creation. In her case alone was raised the ban that rested upon every created soul by original sin, and this singular sanctification in Mary could be accomplished, and was accomplished only as the work of the Holy Ghost, the Sanctifier.

God's Spirit was breathed upon her also. He, the Spirit of God, through Whom all the work of the first creation had been disposed, and ordered and perfected, lovingly occupied Himself also in this new creation of a perfectly just soul, in the forming of the soul of her who was to become the very ark of the Living God. And thus with all the glory of His Infinite Holiness beaming upon her, she comes into existence pure, spotless, holy, and in the first dawn of her blessed existence her soul utters the glad chant which Isaiah had sung in prophecy ages before, and with which the Church in our age begins each celebration of the Mass of the Immaculate Conception. "Rejoicing, I will greatly rejoice in the Lord, and my soul shall be joyful in my God, for He hath clothed me with the garments of salvation, and with the robe of justice, He hath covered me, as a bridegroom decked with a crown, and as a bride adorned with her jewels." (Is. 61. 10.). This Bridegroom comes decked with the crown of Divine Majesty and glory. She, His spouse, newly created, is adorned by Him with the jewels of perfect innocence and holiness. The Holy Spirit, Whose graces and operations are manifold, seems to have exhausted all the resources of His divinity in fashioning this His spouse, for His grace made her perfect! In that moment of her creation, which, because of her holiness, was also the happy moment of her espousals with the Holy Ghost, He poured out upon her such an abundance of His gifts and treasures that even He, wondering, and admiring this His perfect work, and in the very rapture of His divine love, might well exclaim, "Thou art all fair, oh Mary, my beloved, and there is no spot in thee."

Here let me close while the eyes of your soul are fixed in wrapt contemplation upon the glorious picture of Mary the spotless spouse of the Holy Ghost. He Who sanctified her as His spouse, gave us in her, for all future time, a most glorious specimen of His work and power in her original sanctification. Remembering her wealth of holiness and her wondrous, close relation to the God-head, St. Bernard's words are clear to us when, in his second discourse on Pentecost, he says: "Justly are the eyes of all creatures raised to thee, dear Mother, because in thee, by thee, through thee the benignant hand of the Almighty hath re-created all that He had formerly made."

As on that first Pentecost Sunday the Holy Ghost visibly descended upon the infant Church, so in her Immaculate Conception

He had previously descended upon this virgin whom holiness allied to Him as His sacred spouse. He was united to her in that first moment of her existence, and from that moment forth His real, personal presence never left that chosen tabernacle and sanctuary. So that what is true of every pure soul, is true of Mary in a much more sublime sense—she is "the temple of God and of the Holy Spirit dwelling there."

And as we reverently look upon this great picture, can our hearts remain cold and indifferent to the influence of that Holy Spirit Who wrought so stupendous a work in this human soul! What can He not do in and for our hearts, if we but open them to His influence?

And these thoughts must awaken new love, new confidence towards her, whom we see so closely allied to the Holy Spirit of God. Did we ever before fully realize how closely Mary, in the very dawn of her existence, stands to that Holy Spirit through Whom alone our souls can be made holy, and can be saved? Then, let us enter into the devotional spirit of the Church at this season, and seek to develop increased devotion to the Holy Ghost, and increased confidence and love towards her, His sacred spouse. She will intercede in our behalf with her Spouse, and even as "He that is mighty" did great things for her in preserving her innocent and sinless, so, through her prayer, will He work miracles of grace in our hearts.

The path of unstained innocence has been lost by us through our many sins. But through the paths of penance and reparation for sin, He will lead us into "His admirable light," and, sanctified by the benediction of His grace, we shall again know the happiness of His restored love.

FIRST SERIES.

THE RELATIONSHIP OF THE HOLY GHOST
TO THE BLESSED VIRGIN MARY.

II.

In the Divine Incarnation. She is the Mother of Jesus.

"Behold, a Virgin shall conceive, and bear a Son, and His name shall be called Emmanuel." (Is. 7, 14.).

My Brethren, the great day of Pentecost, the glorious festival of the Holy Ghost is drawing nearer and nearer. The Pentecost sun will rise upon a world whose Christian elements will celebrate the yearly, solemn commemoration of the public, visible pouring out of God's Holy Spirit upon the Church founded and established by Christ Jesus. It will be a day of joy and gladness to all those who enter into its spirit, and seek to realize the greatness of the divine gift thus given to men. You have been blessed with the gift of faith. To you, the Feast of the Holy Ghost should be most solemn and beneficial. Your spiritual vocation has called you, not to the "ministrations of the flesh" as in the old law, but of the Spirit in the new law of love. "To you it has been given to know the mysteries of the Kingdom of God" by the priceless boon of your faith. Upon you in your Baptism and in the various Sacraments has been given the overshadowing of the Spirit with power from on high. And each one of you is bound not only to use these great gifts to your best advantage, but also, by the profession of your faith and by the example of your lives, to herald the message of divine mercy and truth even to the uttermost parts of the earth. It may be that you have failed to remember Him through Whom, as your Sanctifier, the graces of the Sacraments have been given to you—Him to Whom you owe the very gift and virtue of faith. Let us then seek to arise from this sad indifference to the Holy Ghost through Whom "every good and every perfect gift" has been given to us—let our minds in holiest reverence resume our considerations of His Mercy to us, and our dependence upon Him. For, aided by His light in our souls, these thoughts will open the eyes of our minds to see the "things that are of the Spirit," and seeing them we will burn with an ardent desire for the coming of Him Whose festival the Church is about to celebrate. There can be for us no worthier preparation for the great solemnity of Pentecost than our devout reflection on the work and relationship of the Holy Ghost to us.

We have already considered one manifestation of this stupendous work of the Holy Ghost in our human nature by reflecting on that which He did for our Blessed Mother Mary in her Immaculate Conception. To-day it is my desire to speak to you of a mystery far greater and more sublime, and one of which not the tongue of an angel could hope to speak worthily. If we justly are astounded at the power and virtue of the Holy Ghost as shown in His preserving Mary from all taint of sin, what shall we say of, or how can we properly conceive the divine relationship in which He stands to her in the Incarnation of the Eternal Son of God, to Whom she by the operation of the Holy Ghost was really and truly MOTHER!

In some limited sense we may judge of the greatness of Mary's work in the mystery of the Incarnation by reflecting on the greatness of preparation by which her Divine Spouse prepared her for this work. We have given some thought to this, in remembering the manner and circumstances of her Immaculate Conception. We know that the Holy Spirit operates with the very power of God, and from His Divine hand we are prepared to witness marvelous results. But He whom the inspired book of Wisdom describes to us as "Spirit of understanding, holy, one, manifold, subtile, eloquent, active, undefiled, sure, sweet, loving that which is good, beneficient," (Wisdom 7.22), even he seems in His work in Mary to have given us the evidence of His best and most perfect work possible towards a creature. God is light, and "He upon whom the angels long to look," "dwelleth in inaccessible light."

But this His sacred spouse He called into "His marvelous light" (1 Pet. 2.9), shed upon her the brilliancy of His own holiness, and made her so far to outshine all the other works of His hand, that the virginal Apostle in the Apocalypse (12.1) wonderingly exclaims: "A great sign appeared in Heaven: A woman clothed with the sun, and the moon under her feet, and on her head a crown of twelve stars." God the Holy Spirit is the distributor of all divine gifts and treasures. But while His benedictions and graces are always given to the elect with a divine liberality, yet in measured degrees, they were all poured out without limit upon His spouse upon whom He "heaped up joy and the exultation" of holiness.

If I thus dwell upon the work accomplished by the Holy Ghost in Mary, it is that from her wondrous preparation we may form some idea of her wondrous mission, and also, realizing how closely she is related to the source of all grace and holiness, may find our confidence in her increased by the conviction of her power with our Sanctifier. If my words seem to you an exaggeration of her excellence, remember how the great Doctors of the Church have spoken of the work and effects of the Holy Ghost in her. Read the astounding words of St. Thomas, the angelic Doctor, who says: "As the plenitude of grace was perfected in Christ, so a certain beginning of that fullness had preceded in Mary'' (S. Thom. III p. Ques. 28 Art. 3). The cherubim and seraphim sing her eternal praises in Heaven, venerating her as the perfect work of the Holy Spirit. But the echo of their song is caught up on earth by St. Bonaventure, when he declares: ''All the rivers center in the ocean, and all the gifts of the saints and the graces of all angels center in Mary. The rivers empty into the sea without causing it to overflow. Why wonder then that all grace centers in her through whom grace is given so abundantly to all other creatures!'' Mystic writers have claimed that the beauty of Mary's spotless soul was reflected and expressed even in her bodily form. We all know how the sentiments of the heart and the qualities of the soul are often shown in the very countenances of men, which tell us, now the sad story of sin, and again the indication of a pure and upright soul. And in this sentiment these writers maintain that the graces and beauty of soul given by the Holy Ghost to His spouse were so abundant that they shone forth in the material beauty of her exterior form. So the Blessed Albert the Great declares that ''Mary was necessarily endowed with exquisite form and incomparable beauty, and more justly so than either Esther the wife, or Judith the widow, or Rachel and Rebecca the virgins; for all these were but types and figures of herself. She possessed all the perfection of beauty that could possibly exist in a mortal body. As our Lord Jesus Christ was 'beautiful in appearance beyond all the sons of men,' so was the most Blessed Virgin the most beautiful and lovely among the daughters of men'' (Alb. Mag. Chap. 13 p. 92).

Now all this was the exclusive work of the Holy Spirit in Mary. Why were His gifts and graces thus poured out upon her with divine lavishness, but that she might be prepared for the great work for which she had been chosen? She was to be the actual dwelling-place of the Incarnate, Eternal Son of God, and for this reason was she clothed with the splendor of His Divine beauty. The fitness of her exalted sanctity is apparent to us when we remember that she was holy because of the office to which God had elected her; and, on the other hand, this office demanded perfect holiness for its worthy accomplishment.

The fitness of her perfect holiness is plain to us when we remember that it was only proportionate to the dignity of the divine maternity that was to crown her life. And her sanctification by the

Holy Ghost becomes reasonable and intelligible even to our frail minds, when we remember that only a Divine Hand could properly prepare her for her coming dignity as Mother of God.

Thus by the action and influence of the Holy Ghost and by His alliance with His spouse, the dwelling place had been prepared for the Eternal Son in the body and soul of Mary. The tabernacle now awaited the coming of the Most Holy One, the temple awaited the Eternal World to be enshrined there. As the special influence of the Holy Ghost had been required in the preparation of this virginal "temple not made by hands," so a new operation of the Holy Ghost was now demanded, by which the Eternal Word might enter this sanctuary and the Redeemer of the world might put on the garments of our humanity. Who but God's Holy Spirit dare assume this stupendous work. The Prophet had declared ages before: "This gate shall be shut; it shall not be opened and no man shall pass through it; because the Lord, the God of Israel, hath entered in by it, and it shall be shut for the prince, the prince himself shall sit in it" (Ezech. 44.2). Of old, Ozam was struck dead by Jehovah because he irreverently touched the ark of the Old Testament. Could human hand then dare to lay its violating touch on this living ark of the New Testament, which was to contain not the mere tables of the law and the emblems of mercy, but the very Author of all law, the very God of all mercy and holiness! None could dare approach her, save her Divine Spouse, "he that hath the key of David, he that openeth and no man shutteth, and shutteth and no man openeth" (Apoc. 3.7). Aye, and this most solemn assurance and guarantee is given her from the very Heaven of Heavens. The islands of the sea heard it and the people of the earth recognized it, when the angel-messenger reassured the Virgin who trembling asked "How shall this be, seeing I know not man," "The Holy Ghost shall come upon thee and the power of the Most High shall overshadow thee" (Luke 1. 35). As though He said to her: The jewel of thy virginity shall remain untouched, and yet shalt thou have all the honor and the joy of maternity, for He Who in the moment of thy creation espoused thee, will now unite Himself to thee by a new and most mysterious bond, and by virtue of His operation "thou shalt conceive and bring forth a son and shalt call His name Jesus." "The holy one that shall be born of thee shall be called (because He shall really be) the Son of God," and the Spouse by Whose operation this shall be effected is none other than He Who sanctified thee, espoused thee and prepared thee for this work, the Holy Ghost Himself.

And thus, in a new manner, her Divine Spouse Who from her Immaculate Conception had truly dwelt with her, now again came to her, and by a new operation of His Divine power she whom He had made and preserved a spotless virgin, now became the most spotless Mother of God, the Eternal Son made man. Can I dare to speak of this new relationship thus established between her and the Holy Ghost? Dare I attempt more than to recall to your devout and grateful hearts the fact that the Holy Ghost allied Himself to her by a new title and in a far more than ever sacred union, in thus effecting the Incarnation of the Eternal Son of God? Why in a certain sense, this union with the Holy Ghost and His operation in her chaste womb, created a new Heaven, since it opened up a new dwelling place for the Adorable Trinity. For, bearing in mind what the theology of the Church teaches us as to the indivisibility of the Triune God, and what is termed the "circuminsession" of the three Divine Persons of the God-head, we cannot doubt that Heaven was there, for God was there; and from the moment of Christ's Sacred Incarnation there dwelt in her in a new and special manner with the Incarnate Son, the Father and the Holy Ghost also!

This is indeed an incomprehensible mystery taught us by faith, but the same Holy Spirit Who effected it had long before by Isaiah's prophetic lips foretold the divine truth. "Therefore the Lord Himself shall give you a sign: Behold a virgin shall conceive and bear a son, and His name shall be called Emmanuel." (Is. 7.14).

Now remembering the ineffable, divine character of all this work, think how close is the relationship established between Mary and the Holy Ghost in the Incarnation of Christ. In her sacred body the Humanity of Jesus the Eternal God was effected, and His body with all its perfections, His soul with all its gifts and powers was there produced by the Holy Ghost. In every Mass, the priest, bowing low in reverence, recalls this great fact and, in the name of the Church, avows that it was done *"ex voluntate Patris, co-operante Spiritu Sancto,"* "by the will of the Father with the co-operation of the Holy Ghost." In her sanctified soul and sacred body God the Son assumed our human nature.

The Father and the Holy Ghost assisted Him as He invested Himself with the habiliments of our nature and with princely raiment prepared Himself for the sacrifice in which He was both the priest and the victim! But while it was Mary's unspeakable privilege to aid in all this divine work, it was accomplished by the agency and the operation of the Holy Ghost! Surely our human hearts, bright with the hopes of eternity, tremble with joy as we realize how closely, through Mary, the Holy Ghost has allied Himself to us creatures. In her He wrought this mystery, and the relationship which He formed with His spouse in the Incarnation of her Divine Son, is a new claim He makes on our devotion and love. For is she not a creature, even as we?

Rupert, a devout writer, states that the overshadowing of the Holy Ghost was necessary even to sustain the Blessed Virgin in the great part she bore in the Divine Incarnation. She was but a fragile virgin, weak not only because of her age and sex, but weak as a mortal for this participation in God's work. And yet she conceived and bore the "strong Word of God," the truth, substantial God Whom the angels tremble to behold. It needed, therefore, nothing less than "the power of the Most High to come upon" her, that power alone capable of the miracle by which human substance could be united to the Eternal Word.

Thus her conception of the Eternal Word was the operation of the Holy Ghost. He dwelt with His spouse really and truly before the Incarnation; for her sinless soul was wedded to Him in the moment of her first existence. But who will deny that a new and far more intimate and sacred relationship sprang up between Mary and her Divine Spouse when the "fullness of time" arrived, and "the Word was made flesh"?

The angels veil their faces before the holiness of God. She, a creature, stood face to face with her Creator. His human flesh and bone was formed of hers, she held Him in her arms, she hushed His infant cries, she ministered to His daily wants, and exercised a mother's care and authority over Him, she daily looked into His divine eyes, she pressed her lips upon His, she shielded Him from want and care with all the solicitude of a mother's love. She saw Him go forth on His great mission to the world; she witnessed His sorrows and humiliations; she saw Him scourged and spit upon and rejected by men. She stood beneath His cross while all nature was convulsed and, in darkness, trembled to its rock-bound centers. Ah, do we not realize in these thoughts that, mere creature as she was, she needed the constant presence and overshadowing of the Holy Ghost in all the scenes of the Incarnation and human life of her Divine Son? What lesser power could have fitted her for her sacred duties, what lesser strength could have sustained her in her anguish, when even His agonizing cry rang out over the darkened world, "My God, My God, why hast Thou forsaken me." She did discharge with superhuman fidelity every function and duty of her motherhood, and in the dread hours of His agony and death she stood beneath the cross, not quailing, not shrinking even from that fearful sacrifice; but as the Scripture says, she "stood beneath His cross," heroically participating in His great sacrifice. What sustained her in all this? What enabled her to rise above every weakness of her humanity? What, but the constant presence of her Divine Spouse Who supported her with divine strength, and Who was ever-present with her? The angel had promised that the power of the Most High would overshadow her, not for a moment, nor for a given time only; but she justly relied on that divine support in the discharge of every sacred duty to which God called her in selecting her as the Mother of the Eternal Son, and until she had fully and completely done her part in all the work connected with and flowing from the Incarnation of Jesus, God and man.

Do we not readily understand, then, that she who was dear to the Holy Ghost as His spotless spouse from the beginning of her existence, was infinitely more dear to Him as the Mother of the Eternal Word Who was incarnate through His operation? If even in our own poor, miserable, human lives, the child forms a new link and new bond binding together yet more closely the two human hearts from which that child drew its material being, can we not readily understand that the All-Holy Son of God, Who by the operation of the Holy Ghost was also really and truly the Son of Mary, formed a new and divinely-holy bond between this Mother and her Divine Spouse the Holy Ghost? Yes, she who in her Immaculate Conception became the spouse of the Holy Ghost, was bound to Him in yet more intimate, sacred and inseparable relationship when, by His operation, she united in herself the honor of unstained virginity and the dignity of Mother of God.

Few of us are so cold and indifferent that our hearts are not moved with love and gratitude as we remember the great gift God gave us in His Son, and the infinite humility and love of that Son in assuming our poor human nature. But how few of us have ever be-

fore reflected how we owe this very mystery of God's love, the Incarnation of His Son, to the Holy Ghost, by Whose operation it was
effected? If we love the Son for His mercy in coming to us, do we
not also owe a similar debt of gratitude for all eternity to that Holy
Spirit through Whom he came to us?

And yet we have been so wanting in living, practical love and
devotion to the Holy Ghost. Even while we have perhaps reflected
on Mary's honor and glory and power and influence as the Mother
who bore our Redeemer, we have almost forgotten Him by Whose
power the Redeemer came to us. Oh, let our coldness end now! Let
these thoughts show us how the Holy Ghost has loved us, how He
has bound Himself closely to us, how many are His titles and claims
to our love and deep devotion. And during these remaining few days
let us seek to prepare for the worthy celebration of His festival. And
let us open our hearts to Him with so warm a welcome that when the
annual recurrence of the festival of His love will gladden the Christian world, He may indeed fill our hearts with His grace, and remain
with us forever more.

> "Veni Creator Spiritus, Mentes tuorum visita.
> "Imple superna gratia, quae Tu creasti pectora!"
> "Come, O Creator, Spirit blest!
> "And in our souls take up Thy rest.
> "Come with Thy grace and heavenly aid,
> "To fill the hearts which Thou hast made."

FIRST SERIES.

THE RELATIONSHIP OF THE HOLY GHOST
TO THE BLESSED VIRGIN MARY.

III.

In the Daily Life of the Church. She is the Mother of the
Faithful.

*"And all these were persevering with one mind in prayer with
the women, and Mary the Mother of Jesus, and with his brethren"
(Acts 1. 14.).*

"It is truly meet and just, right and available to salvation that we at all times, and in all places render thanks to Thee, O Holy Lord, Father Almighty, Eternal God, through Jesus Christ, Thy Son, Who ascending beyond the highest Heavens and sitting down at Thy right hand, sent, on this day, to the children of His adoption, that Holy Spirit whom He had promised. And therefore with exultant gladness the whole world rejoices" to-day. This is the song of our Holy Church in the Preface of to-day's Mass. This is the motive and spirit of to-day's solemnity—joy, gladness, thanksgiving, because the Holy Spirit of God Who proceedeth from the Father and the Son, and Who with the Father and the Son is adored and glorified, was to-day sent to the Church of Jesus Christ.

At the coming of the Holy Ghost the mission of our Divine Lord on earth had been accomplished. His Church had been founded, her ministers had been instructed and had received their divine commission to preach the Gospel to every creature. He Who with divine love loved the Church He had consecrated with His precious blood had ascended, and stood as her Advocate with the Father; for we know, with the Apostle, that "we have an Advocate with the Father even Jesus Christ the Just." Then why did not the work go on? Where were the ministers whom He had chosen to carry to every creature the glad tidings of salvation? Fifty precious days had gone by since His triumphant resurrection stamped the seal of divinity on His work, and where were the fruits that Heaven might have expected from the work and the life of the Saviour? Why did the old pall of darkness and sin and death still hang over the world newly redeemed by the blood of Jesus?

We nowhere hear resounding the message of God's love and mercy. Nay, when we look for them, we find the very Apostles whom Christ had sent even as the Father sent Him, hidden away in an upper chamber in Jerusalem for fear of the Jews, while the world pursued its old course of crime and rebellion in ignorance of God. Plainly, something was wrong; something was yet needed to give life and energy; the touch of a divine hand was yet needed to set into motion the body which Christ had founded, the Church He had established. This listless, ineffective, trembling, fear-stricken organization was certainly not the Church which Christ had desired to be His "glorious spouse having no spot or wrinkle."

Yes, something was yet wanting. There were certain promises given by the Divine Founder which were yet to be redeemed for His Church. "I will ask the Father, and He will give you another Paraclete" (another Advocate, for this is the meaning of the word Paraclete), "that He may abide with you forever. The Spirit of truth whom the world cannot receive because it seeth Him not, nor knoweth Him" (John 14. 16–17). "I will not leave you orphans; I will come to you" (John 14. 18). "The Paraclete, the Holy Ghost whom the Father will send in my name, He will teach you all things, and bring all things to your mind whatsoever I shall have said to you" (John 14. 26). His last words to them on earth even while they stood wonder-stricken, speechless witnesses of the miracle of His Ascension, even while their hearts sank into the sorrow of His leaving them—His last greetings were a renewal of the same promises, and from His Divine lips as the clouds concealed His ascending form, cause His last Testament to them, "You shall receive the power of the Holy Ghost coming upon you, and you shall be witnesses unto me in Jerusalem and in all Judea and Samaria, and even to the uttermost part of the earth." (Acts 1. 8.)

And the glorious day of Pentecost witnesses the fulfillment of all these promises. The Church is a new creation of God's love and mercy. But as in the first creation all things were ordered and perfected into form and harmony only when "the Spirit of God moved upon the waters," so now in the divine decrees was it necessary that God's Spirit should move over this new spiritual creation and bring it into the harmony and effectiveness of God's designs. He came upon them in tongues of living fire; and, oh, the great, the divine change effected by His coming! They who before had trembled at each unwonted sound, now lift their eyes and hearts in glad welcome to the "sound from Heaven as of a mighty wind coming." (Acts 2.2.)

At once they are transformed; they are "all filled with the Holy Ghost." They stand forth before the multitude, who, aghast at their holy courage and boldness, mockingly declare that they who dare to speak thus are "filled with wine." Do they shrink from the jeers and scorn of the people whom their bold preaching of the despised and crucified One has startled? Ah, the day of shrinking is past. Listen to Peter, their divinely appointed head, "These are not drunk, as you suppose." You are witnessing the actual fulfillment of "that which was spoken of by the Prophet Joel . . . I will pour out of my Spirit upon all flesh" (Acts 2. 15–16–17). Jesus Whom you despised and crucified, "being exalted therefore by the right hand of God and having received of the Father the promise of the Holy Ghost, He hath poured forth this which you see and hear." (Acts 2. 33.) It is His Spirit by Whom these things are said and done, and in spite of your prejudices and your deep attachment to sin, you must accept this one great truth, that "there is no other name by which you can be saved," but that of the "same Jesus, whom you have crucified." (Acts 2. 36). Yes, the Holy Ghost descends, and the active mission of the Church has begun, never to end until she shall lay the last-created soul of the human race into the arms of its Creator. The Spirit of God has been breathed upon the body of the Church and it has become a living power to work for the salvation of souls. The great organism founded by Christ shall never more lie dormant as during the days preceding Pentecost, for He, the Holy Ghost, Who awakened the Church to life, and Who spoke by the mouth of Peter and the others on that day, shall never more desert her, but until the very end of time shall make her the fruitful mother of many children of God. This Feast of Pentecost may be said truly to be the birthday of the Church, for her life and activity began with His visible coming to her on this great festival. You see then how appropriate are the joy and gladness with which the day is celebrated by the Church and by her faithful children. You now understand why, in her ritual and liturgy, she makes it like unto the glorious festival of Christ's Resurrection, and why her paeans of joy and her resounding alleluias of to-day are second to those of no festival in all the Christian year.

The glorious celebration of Pentecost, in this year of grace, comes to us soon after the close of Mary's May-days. And from our contemplation of the perfections and holiness of the Mother of Christ, we go on most appropriately to consider on this, His festival, the wondrous work the Holy Spirit accomplished in His spouse. The two thoughts are most suitably linked together—the power and virtue and glory and love of the Holy Ghost as shown in His coming on Pentecost, and the proof of effectiveness of all these, in the Mother whom He consecrated as His spouse.

And therefore I deem it suitable, amid the abundance of spiritual food for thought that this festival supplies, to confine your pious attention to the new relationship established between the Holy Ghost and Mary on this birth-day of the Church, and which is shown by Mary's influence and position in the daily life of that Church which to-day was born of the Holy Ghost.

We have already considered how this chosen virgin was sanctified by the Holy Ghost in the dawn of her existence, and how she was allied to Him yet more closely in the great mystery of Our Lord's Incarnation. A new and most solemn link was, on this sacred day of Pentecost, formed between her and her Divine Spouse, by which she became the Queen and Mother of all those upon whom, on this day, the Holy Spirit breathed the breath of a new, spiritual life. To the mind of faith there is nothing remarkable in the fact that the inspired writer describing the work of the Holy Ghost in the birth of the Church, on this day, in a special and solemn manner states that the Apostles were, in the words of my text, "assembled with Mary the Mother of Jesus!" He would specially impress us with the truth that she, the spouse of the Holy Ghost, was present, in that great scene, and received a new overshadowing of her Divine Spouse, Who thus connected her most intimately with the new-born Church of Christ. The wording of the text is not a mere coincidence. Her full name and glorious title are given, "Mary the Mother of Jesus," so that the sacred emphasis on the statement may be impressed upon every heart. When "the fullness of time had come" what more central and conspicuous creature figures in the scene of Christ's coming than she from whom the Saviour of the world was born! In that other "fullness of time" when His work was done, and the dying lips of the Redeemer declared to all the world, "It is finished," she again is, after her Son, the central figure of that scene upon Golgotha, as she "stands beneath His cross," and in union with His great sacrifice fulfills the prediction of Simon, "And thy own soul a sword shall pierce, that out of many hearts thoughts may be revealed." (Luke 2. 35). The same inspired pen that recorded her presence in those great events now again distinctly testifies to her presence in this third "fullness of time" when the Church of her Son began its great work under the influence of the Holy Spirit, her Spouse. Her presence was not a mere matter of chance. We are told in the Acts that the Apostles, assembled in Jerusalem and awaiting the coming of the Holy Ghost "were persevering with one mind in prayer with . . . Mary the mother of Jesus." (Acts 1. 14.) There were others also present. Who they were is not specified beyond the general statement "the women" and "His brethren." But, as though it were an important item in the history of this divine event, her presence is specially mentioned and her identification is made complete.

A little reflection will show us the beautiful harmony and appropriateness of all this—why this, her third espousal with the Holy Ghost, consecrated that union with Him that was begun in her Immaculate Conception and was strengthened and increased in the Incarnation of God's Eternal Word. She, the mystic spouse of the Holy Ghost, was truly the mother of God made man, and throughout eternity will she continue to be the mother of Him spoken of by Isaiah the prophet: "And there shall come forth a rod out of the root of Jesus and a flower shall rise up out of his root. And the Spirit of the Lord shall rest upon him, the spirit of wisdom, and of understanding, the spirit of counsel and of fortitude, the spirit of knowledge and of godliness. And he shall be filled with the spirit of the fear of the Lord" (Is. 11. 1. 2. 3).

Was it not fitting and proper that upon Mary, "the rod out of the root of Jesse" as the Church terms her, when He had ascended to the glory of the Father, her Divine Son should shed the unction and radiance of His Holy Spirit first and before all others, and through that Spirit should enrich His mother with the superabundance of merits gained by His precious blood? In the work of our redemption by the second Adam, Mary was and will forever remain the mystic Eve, who, reversing the order of the first creation gave bone of her bone and flesh of her flesh to the God man from Whose sacred, spear-opened side was formed the Holy Church of God. She was of the stock of David, the plant from whose roots sprang forth that flower of Jesse by Whom we are redeemed. Was it not fitting then that that "rod" should be the centre of that divine planting, the Church of God, which first, small as the grain of mustard seed, when once enlivened by the Holy Spirit was destined to grow "and becometh a tree, so that the birds of the air come and dwell in the branches thereof." (Matt. 13. 32.) By her consent to the work God proposed to her by the angel's message. Mary became the mother of the Redeemer, and therefore the spiritual mother of the faithful souls whom He redeemed. She offered herself to the Most Holy One as the instrument for carrying out His designs of mercy hidden with Him from eternity, when Gabriel bore back to the Throne of the Holy Trinity the cry of her humility, "Behold the handmaid of the Lord;

be it done to me according to Thy word.'' (Luke 1. 38.) Then was it not fitting that she, the link between God and man, whose Son, dying on the cross, committed her as mother to John, the representative of the Church there present, should in a special, primary and most solemn manner share in the consecration of that Church when the Holy Spirit came to enliven it and make it fruitful?

In this thought lies, my brethren, the reason for that mutual, intimate relationship existing between Mary the ''spouse of the Holy Ghost'' and the Church, which by the action of the Holy Spirit became the spotless ''Bride of Christ.'' St. Augustine says to us: ''The Church has begotten you; but Mary, Virgin and Mother, begot your head, who is the head of the Church.'' Cornelius à. Lapide makes this strong assertion: ''Christ desired His mother to survive, to outlive Him on earth, that she might become the support of the Church, the teacher of the Apostles, and the comfortress of the faithful.'' (1st Treatise on Acts.) The Divine Spirit descended into His chosen sanctuary of her heart, and this virginal mother was filled with a new warmth, a new splendor of the Power from on High. And thus she who in her Immaculate Conception had been consecrated by the Holy Ghost—she who in the Incarnation of Jesus Christ had been overshadowed by the Holy Ghost—now, in the fullest sense and by her union with this same Holy Spirit, became the fruitful mother of immortal life. On this most joyous day of Pentecost her Spouse descended specially upon this mother of Christ; the power of His love and fruitfulness rested as a tongue of fire upon her virginal brow, and by His Divine consecration she then and there became the Queen of the Apostles, the Guide of the Evangelists and the splendid model as well as the august patroness of the priesthood of this new dispensation. The unction of God's Spirit descended upon this first born of the new creation, that she alone of women might speak in the midst of the faithful, might teach the Apostles, might instruct the Evangelists, might direct and guide the priesthood, might preside over the work of the daily life of the Church! The Blessed Rupert, in his commentary on the book of Canticles, exclaims: ''Thy voice, Oh Mary, was to the Apostles as the voice of the Holy Ghost, and from thy consecrated lips did they receive whatever fuller instruction or evidence they needed for strengthening them in the gifts they had received from the Holy Ghost.'' The great Bishop of Milan, St. Ambrose, says: ''It is not to be wondered at that St. John spoke more fully of the divine mysteries than the other Evangelists, for he had with him as his constant companion the Virgin who was the treasury of heavenly gifts.''

This is a most fruitful subject from which I select this one thought. The functions of Mary in the early days of the Church are hers to-day also, for to-day as then, the Holy Spirit, her Spouse, lives in and gives life and fruitfulness to the Church. The daily life of the Church, begun on the great day of Pentecost, has never been interrupted, will never cease until the trumpet of the great angel shall announce that "time shall be no more." And therefore Mary continues in the Church's work of to-day the mission to which she was consecrated when the tongue of living fire on Pentecost rested upon her as she sat in the midst of the Apostles and disciples. And as her Spouse then made her the central figure in the work of the new-born Church of Christ, so does He to-day continue the same relationship with her and make her the effective means of grace in the daily life of the Church.

Consecrated to Him in her Immaculate Conception, united to Him by unspeakable ties in the Incarnation of Christ, and made by Him the Mother of the Faithful in the Church of Christ, we understand at length how true and eloquent and deep-meaning is her title "Spouse of the Holy Ghost."

Now what shall be the practical fruit of these thoughts for us? The same Holy Spirit Who is so closely bound to her has come into our hearts also. In Baptism He entered there, and through the days of our innocence until sin drove Him from us He dwelt with us also. By the grace of the various Sacraments He has again and again come back to us, only to be again driven out by our renewed sins. Even to-day, on His glorious festival, He longingly, lovingly seeks an entrance into our hearts, desires to give to each one of us the benefits and fruits of His coming. Shall our hearts remain closed to Him? Shall our old indifference towards Him continue? Shall the great Feast of Pentecost pass and bring to us no benefit of increased love and devotion to Him Who is the Source and Author of all grace? We are indeed bowed down by the weight of sin, and with the royal penitent of old each of us must cry aloud: "Behold I was conceived in iniquities and in sins did my mother conceive me" (Ps. 50. 7). But the way of penance is open to us. In that Holy Sacrament does the Spirit of God act upon us, regenerating us, cleansing us from sin, so that it may be said of us also, as St. Paul said to the Ephesians, "You were heretofore darkness, but now light in the Lord." (Eph. 5. 8.) By true penance and contrition for sin we who were enemies of God may become His beloved friends, and the Holy Ghost will become the Spouse of our repentant hearts as He is of all just souls, by His grace dwelling there. Repentant, weighted with the burden of sin, let us bend deeply and striking our breast, as does the priest at the foot of the altar, confess our sin committed by our triple and multiplied fault. Then will the Comforter come to our hearts. Then may we gladly raise our eyes and look upon the gift of the altar, Christ's most sacred Body and Blood. For, "by the co-operation of the Holy Ghost," the Heavens have been opened and have rained down the Just One upon our altars for the food and nourishment of our souls to enable us to enjoy the living, bodily presence of Christ within us, and, by that same privilege, to become the living temples of the Holy Ghost.

May this great day of Pentecost accomplish this divine work in us! May we realize how the Holy Ghost is the Sanctifier of our souls, through Whom alone the love and service of God can be perfected in us. The Mass, the divine office, the hymns, the prayers of the Church to-day all are burdened with one great and ever-repeated cry, "Come, O Holy Ghost, fill the hearts of Thy faithful!" Our lips and hearts will not refuse to echo with love and faith, the words the Church puts into our mouths. With her priest at the beginning of Mass we will cry: "Send forth Thy light and Thy truth; they have conducted me, and brought me unto Thy holy hill and into Thy tabernacles" (Ps. 42. 3), to that Holy Sacrament, which, as St. Ambrose says, "God has placed in the power of the Holy Ghost." Our own unaided efforts are fruitless—my earnest words to you are valueless without the aid and mercy and unction of the Holy Ghost: "The sensual man perceiveth not these things that are of the Spirit of God, for it is foolishness to him" (1 Cor. 2. 14). "Neither he that planteth is anything, nor he that watereth; but God, that giveth the increase" (1 Cor. 3. 7)—that God Who works in our hearts by the influence and operations of the Holy Ghost. It is useless for me to preach to you, if your hearts remain indifferent, if they be wanting in living, active, practical faith and love towards the Holy Ghost, which are the fruits of your invitation to Him to come to you. All else is mere idle sound, "for no man cometh to the Son unless the

Father draw him,'' and He draws us to Himself only by the spiritual, sweet and strong power of the Holy Ghost.

So while my words die in your ears, may they live in your hearts, may the prayer of the Church, and of Mary, the spouse of the Holy Ghost, ascend in our behalf, and bring down upon each one of us, as on the early disciples who were assembled with Mary the Mother of Jesus, the living fire of God's love Who will make us wise and strong and holy.

Thus will the day of Pentecost be a happy and a beneficial one for us. The face of the earth, the spirit and earnestness of our hearts, will be renewed; He will abide with us, He will teach us all truth, He will inflame our hearts with His love, and the promise of the beloved Apostle will be fulfilled in us: "As for you, let the unction which you have received from Him abide in you. And you have no need that any man teach you: but as His unction teacheth you of all things and is truth, and is no lie. And as it hath taught you, abide in Him." (1 John 2. 27.)

> "Come Holy Spirit, Thou in toil art comfort sweet;
> Pleasant coolness in the heat;
> Solace in the midst of woe!
>
> Heal our wounds—our strength renew—
> On our dryness pour Thy dew;
> Wash our stains of guilt away.
>
> Give us comfort when we die.
> Give us life with Thee on high.
> Give us joys that never end!
>
> Amen. Alleluia."

SECOND SERIES.

THE RELATIONSHIP OF THE HOLY GHOST
TO THE INCARNATE WORD.

I.

In Preparing the World for the Mystery of the Incarnation.

"I believe in the Holy Ghost . . . who spoke by the Prophets." (*Nicene Creed*).

In the discharge of my pastoral duties towards you who have been committed to my spiritual care, I am deeply and reverently impressed with the conviction that I shall be most faithful and effective, if happily I lead you to increased love and devotion towards God the Holy Ghost, the Sanctifier of our souls. If my feeble words and exhortations convince you of the importance, nay the absolute necessity of this devotion, and arouse in you a holy desire that He come into your hearts and dwell with you, it will show itself in the increased fervor and piety of your lives, and will insure your eternal salvation if you persevere to the end. It is an important work for both of us. Important to you, that you take seriously to heart these urgent words I address to you; important to me, that the greatness of this subject lose none of its impressiveness by my negligence or weakness. In the hymn to the Holy Ghost which the Church so repeatedly sings, and especially during this octave of Pentecost closing to-day, she speaks of Him as *"Sermone ditans guttura,"* enriching our tongue with the gift of speaking His honor and His praise. I feel my insufficiency to treat this great subject worthily. I beg that He to Whom I would lead you may supply what is so needed in me, and may endow me with such wealth of speech that your hearts may be aroused from an indifference so sadly prevalent towards the Holy Ghost, may burn with His love and be adorned with His gifts and graces. It is no mere choice of mine that thus leads me to urge upon you the devotion to the Holy Ghost. It is His will. Knowing that He, the Spirit of Holiness, desires to dwell in our hearts and make them holy, I reverently dare to say to you, as did the first preachers of the Gospel to their hearers, "It hath seemed well to the Holy Ghost" and to us to hold up to your minds as the one perennial fountain of all grace, this devotion to the Holy Ghost Who once spoke by the Prophets, and now speaks to you by my unworthy lips. For to His Apostles and to all their successors in their holy functions did our Lord declare: "It is not you that speak, but the Spirit of your Father that speaketh in you." (Matt. 10. 20.)

And so I resume with you the consideration of this great subject, the claims of the Holy Ghost on our love and tender devotion. And if, as the Church declares in the "Preface of Pentecost," the whole world rejoices with exultant gladness on the Feast of the Holy Ghost, surely I also in speaking and you in considering this great subject, will find our hearts filled with the joy of the Holy Spirit. The holy thoughts here opened to us will sink like good and very good seed into our hearts, and nourished, developed, by the warmth of the Holy Spirit's love, will in good time bring forth the hundred-fold fruit of our improved lives. So shall my poor utterances prove even as were the words of Him in Whose name I speak to you, ''Spirit and Life'' (John 6. 64) to your souls.

In opening to-day the second series of our meditations on the Holy Ghost, which is to embrace the wonderful relationship He bears to Our Lord in the mystery of the Incarnation, I recall the words of the Fathers who under the guidance of the Holy Ghost assembled in the Third National Council of Baltimore. Urging this devotion to the Holy Ghost, and advising that everywhere be established the con-fraternities of the ''Servants of the Holy Ghost,'' warmly approved by the Holy See, and whose special object is the spreading of this devotion, this Sacred Council speaks of the Holy Ghost as ''the Spirit of Christ, the great High Priest,'' by Whom and through Whom alone are developed in our hearts the qualities suited to our sacred vocation. It was then the sense and teaching of this venerable Council that there is a special relationship between the Holy Spirit and Jesus Christ Who in His Divine Incarnation became the High Priest offering ''acceptable sacrifice'' to the Eternal God. We have already reflected in detail on the intimate union existing between Mary the Mother of Jesus and the Holy Ghost, her Divine Spouse—in her triple espousal with Him, His triple descent upon her, and her triple relationship to Him. The ascending step is a natural one—from the Mother to her Divine Son, Jesus Christ Our Lord, Who ''was conceived by the Holy Ghost, was born of the Virgin Mary, and was made man.''

Full well I know that I attempt to speak of a divine mystery, and that any mere human words on so stupendous a subject are but as a tinkling cymbal. But I remember also that, during her month, praises and prayers of untold thousands have daily risen to Mary the Mother of Jesus, and that her clemency will be poured out upon us to make fruitful our reflections on her Divine Son and her Almighty Spouse. I gladly remember that on this octave day of Pentecost, closing the formal celebration of that great festival, the Spirit of God fills His Church. While ''the sound of a mighty wind from Heaven'' that heralded His coming still is ringing in the ears of our souls, and He fills the whole world, we may reverently hope that the ''Spirit Who speaketh mysteries'' will enlighten our minds to understand His ways and His truth. And as we reverently touch the veil of mysteries ''hidden from the foundation of the world,'' we shall not profane those things that surpass our finite understanding by touching with irreverent hand, but, under His guidance, shall become as those who ''beholding the glory of the Lord with open face, are transformed into the same image from glory to glory, as by the Spirit of the Lord.'' (2 Cor. 3. 18).

''When the fullness of the time was come God sent His Son, made of a woman, made under the law.'' (Gal. 4. 4.) The general consent of theologians and spiritual writers interprets, in the strict sense, this ''fullness of time'' as relating to all that sacred period from the moment when the Eternal Son of God assumed our humanity in the womb of the Blessed Virgin, to the hour of His glorified ascension into Heaven—that moment, when as Leo the Great says, our ''human nature rose high above all celestial creatures, took precedence of all the orders of Angels, and upon the throne of His Glory was associated with Him Whose Divine nature was united to it in the Eternal Son.'' St. Paul says; ''Evidently great is the mystery of Godliness which was manifested in the flesh, was justified in the Spirit, appeared unto Angels, hath been preached unto the Gentiles, is believed in the world, is taken up in glory'' (1st Tim. 3. 16.). But, in a larger sense, ''the fullness of time'' may be understood as ''the dispensation of the mystery which hath been hidden from eternity in God, who created all things . . . according to the eternal purpose which He made in Christ Jesus Our Lord'' (Eph. 3. 9–11.) It includes the periods both preceding and following the Incarnation of the Eternal Word; and the operations of the Holy Ghost are special and well defined in each of these divisions of time.

The first essential and fundamental mystery of all Christianity is that of the Eternal Trinity, Father, Son, and Holy Ghost. Next to it, stands the great mystery of the Incarnation, surpassing all other mysteries in its dignity and immeasurable depth. It is God's mightiest, grandest external work. (*ad extra.*) It is the intimate alliance of the divine nature with the creature, a mercy and condescension to be forever adored and praised.

But when we speak of this union between God's Eternal, coequal Son and our human nature, does not our mind instinctively turn to the Holy Spirit by Whom faith tells us this union was effected, and sinking upon our knees we take up the daily song of the Church resounding throughout the world, re-echoed by all the choirs of angels, "He was incarnate by the Holy Ghost of the Virgin Mary, and was made man"? (Nicene Creed.) The Holy Ghost was the effective agent and factor by Whom Christ assumed human nature, and therefore we can understand how reasonably He was also the great Preparer for this entire work of the Incarnation.

He was borne upon the waters of creation, and, where all was empty and waste, He brought out beauty and harmony and order. He was breathed into the soul of the first man, and man stood forth in original innocence. Can we suppose that He abandoned the work of His hand when the misery of sin had again made creation waste and desolate, and the human family lay trembling under the weight of God's anger? No; God's decree of great mercy went forth even in the midst of that ruined paradise. Upon the unhappy wreck of a once happy creation, He, the Spirit of God's love, was again borne. His vital presence and influence began the work of that second and more sublime creation in which we were destined to "rejoice and our joy should be full." (1 John 1.4.) Of this new creation by the Holy Ghost does the beloved disciple speak, when he says: "That which was from the beginning, which we have heard, which we have seen with our eyes, which we have looked upon, and our hands have handled, of the word of life. For the life was manifested; and we have seen, and do bear witness, and declare unto you the life eternal, which was with the Father and hath appeared to us." (1 John 1.1–2.)

And so for 4000 years the Holy Spirit breathed upon, was borne upon the turbid, storm-tossed waters of the history of the Jewish people. It is a frequent declaration of Scriptural writers that, just as, by His daily ministrations in the Church, the Holy Ghost perpetuates the mystery of the Incarnation, so in a peculiar manner did He inaugurate and prepare the world for this mystery—in the synagogue of the Old Law. This His continued influence in the Old as well as in the New law, is indeed a profound truth, yet it commends itself to our reason, and, since all holiness even in the Old Law was in Him and through Him, we recognize Him without difficulty as preparing the world for the coming Incarnation of Christ, by all the religion and sanctity of which the Old Law was the source and inspiration. The whole economy of that Old Law led up to this mystery, however unconscious of the fact men may have been, for, "who hath known the mind of the Lord, or who hath been His counsellor"? (Rom. 11. 34.) "Oh the depth of the riches of the wisdom and of the knowledge of God! How incomprehensible are His judgments and how unsearchable His ways!" (Rom. 11. 33.), exclaims St. Paul, as His glance into the past rests upon the first ray of the coming light of the world, this first sign of the coming new divine dispensation. It was the operation of God's Holy Spirit that prepared the Heavens in which, in God's fullness of time, the Sun of Eternal Justice would appear; His work to precede the rising of that Sun by the aurora of all the types and figures of the Old Law. For, as the Book of Wisdom declares, he is "the worker of all things, the Spirit of understanding, holy, one, manifold, subtle, eloquent, active . . . having all power, overseeing all things." (Wisdom 7. 21–23.)

Of old he went before God's chosen people, as a bright cloud by day and a column of fire by night, and guided their feet dry-shod through the depths of the sea. It was the type and promise of that more glorious day when He, "as a bright cloud overshadowed" (Mat. 17.5) the Eternal Son from Whom and the Father He Himself proceeded. Once upon the cloud-capped mountain, amid pealing thunders and flashing lightenings, the Almighty announced the law of fear. But even then was the Holy Spirit preparing unto Himself a more chosen people, in whose hearts He would write the new law of love, preparing a new Sion vivified by Himself and, under His inspiration, preaching God's law in fiery eloquence to all the world, while He dwells there forevermore as her Guide and Teacher. The Holy Spirit Who once made man "a living soul," also lifted him up from the subsequent degradation of sin, "raising up the needy from the earth, and lifting up the poor out of the dung-hill." (Ps. 112. 7) Thus enlightened, the holy ones of the Old Law looked forward to the fulfillment of the divine promises, and spoke of Heaven's coming gifts. "the holy men of God spoke, inspired by the Holy Ghost." (2 Pet. 1. 21.) These were the types and precursors of the One God, made man. The Holy Ghost "spoke by the Prophets," "searching what or what manner of time the Spirit of Christ in them did signify, when it foretold those sufferings that are in Christ and the glories that should follow." (1 Pet. 1.11) At length the day of God's mercy dawns, and the Holy Spirit, in her very creation, sanctified the future mother of the uncreated Son, making her "fair as the moon" because most fair in grace, and sending her forth as a morning star to herald the near rising of the Sun of eternal justice. The Holy Ghost announces to Zachary in the temple, the coming of the Lord of the Temple. Already the sweet zephyrs of His mystic coming are breathed into the desert of human life as the angel promises to this aged Prophet a son who "shall be filled with the Holy Ghost even from his mother's womb . . . and he shall go before Him (the promised Saviour) in the Spirit and power of Elias." (Luke 1. 15 and 17.)

And at length, while the whole great court of Heaven bends low in wondering adoration, the Holy Spirit descends to the chosen virgin, and overshadowing her with the power of the Most High God, produces the substance of Christ's most sacred humanity, and effects the union of our poor human nature with the Second Person of the Most Holy Trinity.

To you has it been given, by your faith, "to know the mystery of the kingdom of God," (Mark 4.11) and therefore I need do no more than again remind you here, that the Holy Ghost alone is not to be considered or thought the Author of the Divine Incarnation. For He is one and indivisible with the Father and the Son. But, as St. Thomas declares, it is entirely proper, on account of His mysterious "appropriation" of that office in the Holy Trinity, to attribute the forming of the most sacred body of Christ, the Eternal Son, to the operation of the Holy Ghost. As mysterious and obscure as this may seem to worldly minds, it is quite clear to the mind considering these things by the light of the Holy Ghost. As Durandus writes, "The entire Trinity was active in the work of the Incarnation, but the entire Trinity did not become Incarnate." The Incarnation of Christ is certainly God's greatest and most sublime work *"ad extra,"* outside of Himself, and, like all other external works of God, is to be attributed to the Three in One. While the Eternal Father and the Holy Ghost cooperated, the uncreated Word of God arrayed Himself in the vestments of our salvation; yet must we not close our eyes to the special operation of the Holy Spirit in this divine mystery. The Incarnation of Christ was the loving decree of the Eternal Father the Creator and Beginning of all things. "For God so loved the world as to give His only begotten Son." (John 3.16) The "emptying of Himself" in becoming man, and the infinite humility of the Divine Incarnation, were in a special and unique manner the functions of God the Son, into Whose mouth St. Paul puts the words of the thirty-ninth Psalm: "Then said I, Behold I come! In the head of the book it is written of me that I should do Thy will, O God." (Heb. 10.7)

And the Holy Ghost became the operator, the complete means by which were carried out the decree of the Eternal Father and the ready acquiescence and self-sacrifice of the Divine Son.

"The Holy Ghost shall come upon thee, and the power of the Most High shall overshadow thee," (Luke 1.35) is the angel's promise to Mary, and throughout the world, prostrate in grateful adoration, the Holy Church sings the fulfillment of that promise, "He was incarnate by the Holy Ghost of the Virgin Mary, and was made man." And to the last hour preceding the coming of the Eternal Son, the work of the Holy Spirit continued to prepare the way for Him. "Elizabeth was filled with the Holy Ghost, and she cried out with a loud voice and said: Blessed art thou amongst women and blessed is the fruit of thy womb. And whence is this to me that the mother of my Lord should come to me." (Luke 1.41.43) That first act of adoration, offered to the yet unborn Saviour of the World, is recorded for us as the special inspiration of the Holy Ghost, Who prepared the way before Him.

These thoughts must convince us of the close relationship between the Holy Spirit and the Incarnate Word and of the great work done by the Holy Ghost in preparing the world for the mystery of Christ's Incarnation. They bring home to our hearts also a new title by which the Holy Spirit of God claims our devotion and love. He loved us from all eternity, and from eternity, while the Incarnate God was yet unknown, to our humanity. He labored for us and prepared humanity for the coming of the Redeemer. If, in the infinite mercy of His Incarnation, our dear Lord claims our tender love and gratitude, shall we refuse these to that Holy Spirit Who so urged His coming and so earnestly sought to make men ready for His coming? Every good thought and holy word and saintly deed in the Old Law, every uttered cry and whispered prayer for the coming of the Saviour of the world, the sighs and tears and pleadings of the Prophets, the hopes and longings of all just ones from Adam and Eve to Joseph and Mary—all were the inspirations and work of the Holy Ghost— all pleased to Heaven for the promised One of Israel; and who shall say by how many long ages the mercy of God may have been hastened by these workings of the Holy Ghost in the hearts of men?

Then let us resolve no longer to ignore or remain indifferent to the mightly claims of this Holy Spirit to our love. In the hearts of each one of us who has once fallen into sin, He has done this same work of divine preparation. He is doing it in every sin-darkened soul to-day. The Saviour of our souls cannot come to us save by the work of His Holy Spirit in us, awakening us from the sleep of death, and working in us the mystery of His grace. In how many ways does He thus seek to prepare in us the way of the Lord! He enlightens our intellect to show us the worthlessness of all things but God alone, Whom we have lost by sin. He arouses us by the stings and chidings of conscience. He gives us the desire to rise and go to our Father by repentance. It is in our unhappy power to stifle His voice and undo His merciful work in us. But if we will only obey Him, and be led by Him, He will prepare our hearts for the coming of Our Lord by a renewal of our longing for lost innocence, and from the deepest darkness of sin He will lead us into the light of divine pardon and love. Our only hope is in Him; our repentence and salvation can come only through Him. Let us realize this truth. It is vital to our spiritual life and interests. And recognizing how He alone can prepare our sinful hearts for their return to God, let our repentant souls cry to Him, in the words of our Holy Church

> "Bend the stubborn heart and will,
> Melt the frozen; warm the chill;
> Guide our steps that go astray!"

SECOND SERIES.

THE RELATIONSHIP OF THE HOLY GHOST
TO THE INCARNATE WORD.

II.

In the Life and Mission of Christ on Earth.

"He upon Whom thou shalt see the Spirit descending and remaining upon Him, He it is that baptizeth with the Holy Ghost." (*John 1.33*).

This glad Sunday finds us midway between two great and most solemn festivals. The week just passed brought with it the celebrations of "Corpus Christi," the glorious festival of the Blessed Sacrament of our altars. The week opening to-day will witness the Church's celebration of the solemn festival of the Sacred Heart of Jesus. Both are days in which divine love for our souls is the crowning thought of the Church. We recognize the Blessed Sacrament as the climax and concentration of all the love of Jesus towards us, for it is the means devised by the divine mind for perpetuating all His work of love, and binding us to Him in a union so sacred, so close, that all the angels look on in rapturous wonder and adoration whenever a soul receives Holy Communion. The Feast of the Sacred Heart is celebrated by the Church with the wish that we realize the great truth, that as the heart is the seat and centre and source of all affections, so that Sacred Heart of Jesus is to us the embodiment and concentrated expression of the wondrous, infinite love with which Our Lord loves us. And there seems a special appropriateness in celebrating the Feast of the Sacred Heart in close connection with that of the Blessed Sacrament. It seems to crystallize all the beauties and glories of the Blessed Sacrament, in some sense to remove the mystic veils that conceal Jesus in the Tabernacle, and present Him to us a living, palpable, realizable embodiment of divine love.

"Corpus Christi" recalls to us the mysterious, divine evidence of infinite love. The Sacred Heart of Jesus is held up to us as the very source and fountain of all that love—living, breathing, palpitating for us in the Blessed Sacrament. Therefore, I say that the great theme of both these festivals is divine love, inviting our poor love in return. It is our happiness and our duty to reciprocate the infinite love of Our Lord's Sacred Heart dwelling with us in the Sacrament of the altar. How have we fulfilled this duty? The memories of our past lives recall so many faults and sins that prove us not only to have forgotten our duty of loving God in return, but even to have turned away from Him in gross outrages to His Majesty and love. Why have we been so unhappy, so thankless? Has it not been because, by our indifference, we have driven from our hearts that Holy Spirit by Whom alone the love of God can be developed in our hearts? Truthfully does the Church, in her liturgy, cry to the Holy Ghost:

"If thou take Thy Grace away
Nothing pure in man will stay,
All his good is turned to ill."

—(Sequence of Pentecost.)

The Charity of God, that is, our power and disposition to love Him in return for His infinite love towards us, was first poured into our souls in holy Baptism, when we were "born again by water and the Holy Ghost." With that first grace we received the uncreated charity of God, the Holy Ghost, Who is the expression of the mutual love of Father and Son and the bond of the Ever Blessed Trinity. But He is also the bond that unites us with God. "The charity of God is poured forth into our hearts by the Holy Ghost Who is given to us." (Rom. 5.5) Even as the glorious sun sheds abroad upon all the earth heat and light and fertility and the power of abundant production, so does the Holy Spirit, shining into our hearts, produce there the light of grace, the warmth of love, the fruitfulness of good works. And if these holy results have been wanting in us who in Baptism had been made capable of producing them—if by sin we have deprived ourselves of all the benefits of our Redemption, it has been because we have shut out this divine radiance from our souls and have banished the Holy Ghost by Whom alone the merits of Christ can be made available to us. Let us not doubt this important truth. It is the first conviction necessary in leading us back to God when baptismal innocence has once been lost. It is most perilous, nay, fatal to all our spiritual hopes and prospects for us to forget how necessary to us is the Holy Ghost, by Whom alone we receive the graces of God and are linked with Him. Christ died for us, and all the treasures of His Redemption are open to us; but His Spirit must lead us to them. Whenever a soul is raised from sin to grace there is a renewal of the work of Redemption: but in this work the Holy Ghost is the means by which that soul is enriched with the merits gained by Christ, raised from the sad defilement of sin, and made but "little lower than the angels." To impress this great truth on our hearts, to convince us of the close relationship which the Holy Ghost bears to the work of redemption in our individual hearts, it may be well for us to recall how closely and intimately He was connected with the life and mission of Our Lord on earth. For thus we may realize His sacred and most necessary relationship to us in enjoying the fruits of that divine life and mission. To this thought, therefore, I invite your earnest and pious attention.

It is not difficult to prove the great truth which is the subject of our thoughts to-day—that, as shown by the life and mission of Christ on earth, there is a most intimate relationship between the Holy Spirit and the Incarnate Word. I recall to your minds the teachings of your faith, by which you know that the Three Persons of the Holy Trinity are one and inseparable, united from all eternity in a bond of union and oneness that surpasses our understanding here below. This same faith teaches us that all grace of God is given to us through the Holy Ghost. And so reason supplements the faith founded on divine authority and tells us that, though the Holy Ghost did not assume human form, He was most intimately united with the Eternal Son in His human life and its sacred mission. The object of this mission was the redemption and sanctification of men. Therefore, must the Holy Spirit have been specially interested and united with Christ in the work of our redemption and sanctification since the continuance and perfection of this work for all time, were to be specially the office and function of the Holy Spirit. In our previous considerations we noted, and found most fitting and proper, the work done by the Holy Spirit in preparing the world for the mystery of the Incarnation. Nor did He in His infinite mercy desert the human race when the day of its redemption had come. He Who had been from all eternity united with the Son of God, did not leave that Son when He became man. Nay, the object to be gained by the Incarnation, our redemption from sin, served as a new sacred bond between Him and the Eternal Word. Our Lord Himself declared of the Holy Spirit: "He shall glorify me; because He shall receive of mine, and shall shew it to you." (John 16.14)

I think there is no truth for which more striking testimonies may be selected from the Holy Scriptures than this relationship of the Holy Ghost to the life and mission of Christ. The Holy Spirit had prepared the way for the Eternal Word by which He came down from His royal throne of divinity to the lowliness of the stable of Bethlehem. But He had also prepared a holy welcome for the new-born Saviour, and the first adoring act of Mary as she sank upon her knees to worship her new born child as her God, was the work of the Holy Ghost in her heart. This Spirit of God drew the angelic hosts from Heaven in that solemn hour, and prompted them to break the silence of that midnight watch at Christ's birth with their adoring hymn "Glory to God in the Highest," Whom they truly worshipped also in the manger. This Spirit of God led the angels to the shepherds with the glad tidings that the Saviour was born, so that other worshippers might kneel before Him with Mary and Joseph. He led the wise men from afar by enlightening their minds on the great truth of the Redeemer's birth, and by filling their souls with the holy enthusiasm that brought them through long and perilous journeys to the crib at Bethlehem. Obedient to the law, Mary's first steps with her Divine Infant are directed to the Temple. And as the Lord of the Temple for the first time enters His shrine in visible form, the Holy Spirit had prepared for Him a humble but most earnest worshipper, who adoring Him as his Lord and God, proclaims His sacred character and mission aloud to all the world. Listen to the description of this first act of adoration in the Temple, and note how the Holy Spirit is again and again named as the prompter and inspirer of the venerable Simeon in the first public act of adoration: "This man was just and devout, waiting for the consolation of Israel, and the Holy Ghost was in him. And he had received an answer from the Holy Ghost that he should not see death before he had seen the Christ of the Lord. And he came by the Spirit into the temple." (Luke 2. 25 to 27).

Other Prophets had been inspired by the Holy Spirit to speak of the coming Christ, and their lips had overflowed with the sweetness and joy of His promises whispered into their hearts. But He gives a special preparation, a miraculous evidence to John the Baptist, the last of the Prophets and the immediate precursor of Christ, by manifesting Himself to the Baptist, by speaking openly to him and allowing him to witness His substantial presence and union with the Son. "And John gave testimony saying: I saw the Spirit coming down as a dove from Heaven, and he remained upon Him and I knew Him not; but He who sent me to baptize with water said to me: He upon whom thou shalt see the Spirit descending and remaining upon Him, He it is that baptizeth with the Holy Ghost. And I saw; and I gave testimony that this is the Son of God." (John 1. 32 to 34).

As we pass on to Christ's public mission, we can give but a passing thought of holy and deepest reverence to those years of the hidden life of Our Lord, which faith and love teach us were an uninterrupted communion with that Holy Spirit Who would one day glorify Him, when the fast approaching sorrows and humiliations of

His human life and the darkness of Calvary would have passed away
in the glory of the Ascension. Jesus begins His public mission by
receiving the ordinance of Baptism at the hands of St. John. To thousands of others had the Baptist imparted that sacred symbol of repentance in the Old Law. So numerous were the converts that the
Scripture says "All the people was baptised." But about this one
great Baptism the halo of God's glory is miraculously poured out,
and the Holy Ghost is the means and instrument by which all the
world may know that this supposed Son of Joseph was the very living
God. "Jesus also being baptized and praying, Heaven was opened.
And the Holy Ghost descending in a bodily shape as a dove upon
Him, and a voice came from Heaven, "Thou art my beloved Son,
in Thee I am well pleased." (Luke 3, 21 and 22). It was a glorious
scene, a divine testimony. Repeated on Thabor in Christ's Transfig-
uration, it sank deeply into the hearts of the Apostles, and was a powerful argument with them in preaching Christ crucified, but first
'glorified by the Holy Spirit' visibly coming to Him and remaining
with Him. It is the Holy Spirit that leads the Saviour of men to the
retreat of the desert for His final preparation for His mission, and for
that wondrous encountering of temptation by which He would teach
us how to conquer temptation. "Jesus being full of the Holy Ghost,
returned from the Jordan, and was led by the Spirit into the desert."
(Luke, 4. 1). As Christ comes into Galilee and begins His preaching,
we are told that "Jesus returned in the power of the Spirit." (Luke
4. 14). And so we follow Him to Nazareth and witness that sublime
scene, in which this Nazarene, sitting in the synagogue of Nazareth,
preaches His first great sermon of which we have any record, and
explains to His wondering hearers the magnificent prophecy of Isaiah. "And the book of Isaiah the prophet was delivered unto Him.
And as He unfolded the book, He found the place where it was written: The Spirit of the Lord is upon me, wherefore He hath anointed
me, to preach the Gospel to the poor, He hath sent me, to heal the
contrite of heart. . . . And when he had folded the book He restored
it to the minister, and sat down. And the eyes of all in the synagogue
were fixed on Him. And He began to say to them: 'This day is fulfilled this Scripture in your ears.' " (Luke 4. 17–21). He of Whom
Isaiah spoke is even here among you. My work it is "to heal the
contrite of heart, to preach deliverance to the captives, and sight to
the blind, to set at liberty them that are bruised, to preach the ac-

ceptable year of the Lord, and the day of reward.'' (Luke 4. 18–19). ''For this have I longed from eternity; for this came I into the world; to this work have I been anointed by the Spirit of the Lord, and fulfilling Isaiah's prophecy, this work I now gladly undertake because 'The Spirit of the Lord is upon me.' '' How wonderful and intimate this constant relationship between the Holy Ghost and Jesus Christ in all His life and mission on earth! They one day bring to Him a poor dumb man bodily possessed of the devil. In His Divine mercy He heals the victim. And deigning to reason with His followers and critics, and explain to them how He did this wondrous work, He assures them that ''I by the finger of God, cast out devils.'' (Luke 11. 20). And the liturgy of our Holy Church has taught us that the Holy Ghost is the ''Finger of God's right hand.'' Strengthened and encouraged by the ringing voice from Heaven, He boldly declares ''Now shall the prince of this world be cast out.'' (John 12. 31). And the prince of darkness was cast out from redeemed souls, banished by the outstretched arms of Jesus upon the cross, offering the great sacrifice by which our souls were redeemed from the power of evil. But the same Holy Spirit Who had prepared His way before His coming, Who had given repeated divine testimony that this was the Saviour, God, He also led Him up to that divine sacrifice for our souls. For St. Paul says: ''How much more shall the blood of Christ, Who by the Holy Ghost offered Himself unspotted unto God, cleanse our conscience from dead works, to serve the living God?'' (Heb. 9. 14).

But why shall I longer fix your attention on the testimony of Apostles and Prophets, since this same great truth is spoken to us so strongly and so repeatedly by the divine lips of Our Lord Himself? Throughout all His teachings we find the recurrence of this truth, the intimate relationship of the Holy Ghost to Christ's work of our redemption. And in the supreme moment of His leaving them, what does the Incarnate Word, speaking in human tongue, seek to impress upon His disciples more deeply than this His connection with the Holy Spirit, coupled with the promise that the coming of the Holy Paraclete would perfect and complete the work of Jesus' life! None of the Evangelists has written so fully and so glowingly of these promises of divine love—these consolations of the promised Paraclete, as the virginal disciple whose head was pillowed on the loving heart of Our Lord, and whose pen seems to glow with the very fire of the Holy Ghost.

The mission of the Eternal Word made man, was to be completed and perfected by the Holy Ghost. The Lord promised this; the Apostles expected this; all nations looked forward to this; the Fathers of the Church preached this; the symbols of faith all teach this; the Holy Church, guided by the Spirit of God, proclaims it throughout the world! The Saviour of the world had nearly accomplished His part of the work and was about to return to the Father who had sent Him. In view of this separation from those He loved He makes this solemn promise: "I will ask the Father, and He shall give you another Paraclete, that He may abide with you forever, the Spirit of Truth, Whom the world cannot receive." (John 14. 26). He Who is "the way and the truth and the life" is about to leave His Apostles, but He assures them that "The Paraclete, the Holy Ghost, Whom the Father will send in my name, He will teach you all things and bring all things to your mind, whatsoever I shall have said to you." (John 14. 26). It was the design of God's mercy that as in the Old Law certain individuals were gifted with the vision and the prophecy of the coming Saviour, so in the New Law, as St. Peter says in his great sermon on Pentecost, quoting the Prophet Joel, "In the last days, (saith the Lord) I will pour out of my Spirit upon all flesh." (Acts 2. 17). The fullness of God's Spirit was to be given to the Church of Jesus Christ that embraces all nations. And though the human hearts of the disciples were saddened at His leaving them, Our Lord cheers them by revealing to them the process and development of God's eternal decree, as He tells them: "It is expedient to you that I go; for if I go not, the Paraclete will not come to you; but if I go, I will send Him to you." (John 16. 7). For we are thus assured that it was God's design that as the Father had sent the Son, so the Father and the Son should send the Holy Spirit. St. John further assures us that "As yet the Spirit was not given, because Jesus was not yet glorified." (John 7. 39.) So that the coming of the Holy Ghost was the direct fruit and result of the life and mission of Our Lord on earth. "He shall glorify me," says Our Lord, "because He shall receive of Mine, and shall shew it to you." (John 16. 14). "When the Paraclete cometh, whom I will send you from the Father, He shall give testimony of Me; and you (under the influence and inspiration of Him whom you will then have received) shall give testimony, because you are with Me from the beginning." (John 15. 26–27). Before His suffering, Christ had ordained His Apostles to consecrate His sacred Body and Blood, doing even as he had then done. The institution of the Sacrament of Penance, by which men might be prepared for the Eucharistic gift, was reserved until the glory of His Resurrection had proved His Divine character and His power to entrust this sacred and wondrous office of forgiving sin to mortal man. Note the manner in which He gives this divine power to the Apostles, "He breathed on them, and He said to them, 'receive ye the Holy Ghost;' " (and by the power of Him you thus receive from Me) "Whose sins you shall forgive, they are forgiven them." (John 20. 22–23). The Acts of the Apostles expressly state His "giving commandments by the Holy Ghost to the Apostles whom He had chosen." (Acts 1. 2.) In the mystic days of His intercourse with them following His Resurrection, and while, so to speak, giving the finishing touches to their training and education as Apostles, He commands them "Stay you in the City, till you be endued with power from on High. And I send the promise of my Father upon you." (Luke 24. 49.) "You shall receive the power of the Holy Ghost coming upon you, and you shall be witness unto me in Jerusalem, and in all Judea, and Samaria, and even to the uttermost part of the earth." (Acts 1. 8.)

The Pontifical Mass of our redemption, celebrated by Him whom St. Peter terms the "Bishop of our souls," (1. Pet. 2.25.) at length came to its close, and upon the wings of the air He ascended to the right hand of His Father on High. So St. Paul quotes as the Psalmist foretold, "Ascending on high He led captivity captive; He gave gifts to men." (Eph. 4. 8). He sent that Holy Spirit Whom the Church so happily terms, "the Gift of the Most High." The Son, having been glorified in Heaven, sent the promised Spirit Who on earth would glorify Him forever more in the perpetuation of His work and by the santification of the souls of men.

Is it not true then that no Scriptural fact glows with more splendid evidences than this constant relationship of the Holy Spirit to the Incarnate Word, not only in Heaven but also here on earth? It is indicated in almost every word spoken by Our Lord, and His breathing of this Divine Spirit upon them, with the promise of His certain coming, is the last legacy He leaves as He ascends on high, it is the blessing that closes the solemn Mass of Christ's human life on earth. He had assured us that "The Son of man is not come to be ministered unto, but to minister and to give His life a redemption for many." (Mat. 20. 28.) How sacredly and touchingly does He carry out that assurance in the sending of the Holy Ghost, in the "ministration of the Spirit" as St. Paul terms it (II. Cor. 3. 8.) fulfilling all the work of the Incarnate Word, and continuing it even until He come again in glory "to judge the living and the dead."

These proofs of the inspired writers, nay of Jesus Christ Himself, are conclusive to our minds that the Holy Ghost in a special manner was connected with the life and mission of Our Lord and therefore is to-day intimately related to the work of our redemption. To gain the fruits of this redemption our souls must be sanctified, and the Holy Spirit is the Sanctifier of our souls. Realizing this, it is surely reasonable that we turn to Him with the best love and devotion of our souls, and treasure above all things His Divine presence in our hearts. Not to be in union with Him is the greatest of all evils, since the access to all spiritual good is thus closed to us. And now let us reflect how our past lives have shown us to be practically convinced of this important, essential truth. Ah, for most of us the retrospect is a most sad and unhappy one! It is but a poor excuse to say that our indifference to the Holy Ghost was the result of our thoughtlessness. Our eternal interests may suffer quite as much from our neglect of the truth, as from our positive turning to sin. Nay, our indifference to the Holy Ghost, our failure to realize how necessary He is to us in all spiritual things, has been the frequent cause of our falling into sin. From the moment when our first deliberate sin banished Him from our hearts that had become His temples in Baptism, through all our wanderings and indifference, He has hourly waited for us to re-admit Him to His chosen dwellingplace. To each of us He said "Behold I stand at the door and knock." We owed to Him our regeneration in Baptism, our dignity as children of God and co-heirs with Jesus Christ. Ungrateful as we showed ourselves to Him by committing sin, He raised us again and again from death to life. In every Sacrament we have ever received He again returned to our hearts, strengthening us in Confirmation, raising us from sin to grace in Penance, pouring out upon us the radiance of divine light and the fullness of grace in Holy Communion, through the living, most precious Body and Blood of Jesus, Our Lord! The fruits of Christ's life and death come to us through the Sacraments, and every one of these is the special work of the Holy Ghost in its application to us individually. Through them He has, all our life long, been pouring a stream of actual graces into our souls. Through them has He raised us from sin, given us grace that prevented our falling again, inspired us with holy thoughts and ambitions, freed us from our evil habits, sustained us in every weakness, sealed us unto Himself with the "seal of our God" as heirs of His kingdom. And all the while we perhaps have not even realized what He was doing for us. In our unhappy ignorance, we have been indifferent to Him "by Whom all things were made" in our spiritual lives. Even though we have led otherwise faithful, devout lives, the pall of this indifference has hung over us and has prevented us from bringing forth the hundred-fold fruit that might be expected from the many graces given to us. Worse than all, so often have we quenched His light, or like the foolish virgins, suffered it quite to die out by our neglect. By sin we have resisted Him, closed our eyes to His "most blessed light," turned a deaf ear to His pleadings by our conscience, met His love only with coldness and insults. Whenever we have fallen into sin we have nullified in our hearts the redemption of Christ, and placed ourselves as though Our Lord had not died for us. How many lives to-day are in this sin-laden condition; and all, because they will not allow Him to influence them and bring them back to the glory of divine pardon!

From this hour let us open our hearts to Him, beg Him to come and dwell with us, and work in us the work of the Most High which He alone can accomplish in us. In the past we have so often grieved Him by our many relapses, and by the want of earnestness and real sincerity in our lives. We have been insensible of His presence and work in us. We have made so many promises of amendment and yet have been so inconstant after he so often restored us. By our coldness, our self-love, our seeking to serve God and Mammon at the same time, we have given only a divided heart, an unloving, ungenerous heart to all His pleadings and warnings and graces and gifts. And yet He has not deserted us nor turned from us. If, then, to-day, as the result of this meditation on His infinite love for us, we turn to Him with repentance and love and great longing that He dwell with us and operate in us forever more, Oh, He will gladly come to us, with His seven-fold gifts and graces, making us His living temples here, and assuring for us the eternal enjoyment of Himself hereafter in Heaven.

THE RELATIONSHIP OF THE HOLY GHOST
TO THE INCARNATE WORD.

III.

In the Mystic Body of Christ, the Church.

"The Holy Ghost, whom the Father will send in my name, He will teach you all things, and bring all things to your mind whatsoever I shall have said to you." (*John, 14. 26.*).

Our previous reflections on the power and love of the Holy Ghost have shown us the wonderful relationship to Our Lord which He bore in preparing the world for the coming of the Redeemer, and in the life and mission of Our Lord Himself. It is my happiness and privilege to speak to-day of His relationship to the Church founded by Jesus Christ. That Church is the fruit of the Incarnation—the means for perpetuating the work of our redemption. The subject, therefore, is one that comes home closely to each one of us as children of the Church which Jesus established, enriched with His sacred blood, and, through the action of the Holy Ghost in that Church, made the means of our eternal salvation. The Holy Ghost, sent by the Father and the Son, mercifully took up the work which Christ had established on earth. The Church was the work of the Incarnate Word of God—a people gathered into one body from all nations. To build up the organism, to establish this Church with which He would abide until the very end of time, to unite it with Himself, "a glorious Church, having no spot or wrinkle," to make it an authority to which He might say before all the world, "He that heareth you, heareth Me; he that despiseth you, despiseth Me and Him that sent Me"—thus to make it a light for men in the deepest darkness of error or doubt or sin—a rock to which they might cling in fiercest storm of passion—this was the object of the life and teachings and sufferings and death of the Redeemer of the world. But this work of Christ was, according to Christ's own promise, not enlivened and made effective until on the great day of Pentecost, the Holy Ghost filled it with His visible presence, made it the dwelling place of His Divine Majesty, and the manifestation of His infinite power. The miracle by which

Christ's most sacred Body was formed in the womb of the Blessed Virgin when the Holy Ghost overshadowed her, was in some sense repeated in the quickening of this mystic body of Christ, the Church, when the Holy Ghost came upon it in visible form, and its first priests went out to their mission "endued with power from on high." (Luke 24. 49.) The Church, this mystic body of Christ, in all its life and strength and perfection, is the work of the Holy Ghost even as Christ's natural Body was formed and made perfect by the power of the Holy Ghost.

You, who are the children of the Church by the infinite mercy of that God Who chose you in preference to many others still sitting in darkness and error, have been made quite familiar with this title given to the Church, "The mystic body of Christ." Have you ever reflected how strong and manifold are the reasons for this title—how deeply it is founded in the testimony of the Holy Scriptures and in the writings of the Fathers from the earliest times? Let us glance at these for a moment. It is most important to realize this truth; for if the Church be Christ's body, then we, as members of the Church, are Christ's members—an inestimable privilege, a most sacred relationship.

St. Paul's speaking of the glory with which the Father had crowned the Eternal Son, returning from His great mission on earth, says: "He hath subjected all things under His feet, and hath made Him head over all the Church, which is His body, and the fulness of Him." (Eph. 1. 22. 23.) In his Epistle to the Ephesians the same inspired Apostle goes into full details of the creation and organization of this "one body and one Spirit." He speaks of the oneness of its faith, like the oneness of God, its Author. He pictures to us its organization, its officers, its functions, its object, "that henceforth we be no more children tossed to and fro, and carried about with every wind of doctrine by the wickedness of men." (Eph. 4. 14.) He presents to us its final aim: "For the perfecting of the saints, for the work of the ministry, for the edifying of the body of Christ, until we all meet into the unity of faith, and of the knowledge of the Son of God, unto a perfect man." (Eph. 4. 12. 13.) And having thus given us the details of this Church organization, he holds up the glorious promise and result: "Doing the truth in charity, we may in all things grow up in Him who is the head, even Christ, from whom the whole body, being compacted and fitly joined together, by what every joint supplieth, according to the operation in the measure of every part, maketh increase of the body." (Eph. 4. 15. 16.) Behold here the perfect body whose Head is Christ.

To the Romans he writes with equal point and directness: "For as in one body we have many members, but all the members have not the same office: so we being many, are one body in Christ, and every one members one of another." (Rom. 12. 4. 5.) With equal clearness he assures the Corinthians that though in this mystic body of Christ the various members are fitted for various functions, even as in our natural body, "all these things one and the same Spirit worketh. For as the body is one, and hath many members; and all the members of the body, whereas they are many, yet are one body, so also is Christ. For in one Spirit were we all baptized into one body, whether Jews or Gentiles, whether bond or free, and in one Spirit we have all been made to drink. . . . Now, you are the body of Christ, and members of member." (1 Cor. 12. 11–27.)

The words of the inspired writer seem so clear that they need no explanation. Yet I cannot forbear to repeat here the admirable comment of St. Augustine, which will also serve to present to us the opinions of the Fathers of the Church on this subject. In his sermon on Pentecost, adverting to St. Paul's words: "One body, one Spirit," he says: "The body is made up of many members, and one spirit quickens them all. By the spirit of man by which I myself am a man, I hold together all my members. I command them to move; I direct the eyes to see, the ears to hear, the tongue to speak, the hands to work, the feet to walk. The offices are divided, but one spirit holds all the members in one. Many are commanded and many things are done; but there is only one—the spirit—who commands and who is obeyed. What our spirit, that is our soul, is to the members of our body, that the Holy Ghost is to the members of Christ, to the body of Christ, which is the Church. Therefore the Apostle when he had spoken of this 'one body,' to convince us that it is not a lifeless body immediately adds the evidence of its life, and states, 'there is one Spirit.' " This mystic personality of the Church is further explained by the same St. Augustine when he says: "The head and the body are one man. Christ and the Church are one man, a perfect man. Of the two is made one person, Christ the head, the Church the body." St. Gregory the Great writes: "The holy universal Church is one body, constituted under Christ Jesus, its head."

Thus the Scriptures and the Fathers present to us the Church as the body, comprising all the elect of God in their several offices as Saints, Apostles, Pastors, Faithful—and all forming one perfect body with, because all united to the Head, glorified at the right hand of the Father, and Himself both God and man.

Now, upon this mystic body of Christ the Holy Ghost descended first on Pentecost, becoming its soul and life, and making it a living body, members united with the head and enlivened, perfected by the indwelling of God's Holy Spirit forevermore. This was the design of God; in the eternal decrees it was the economy of the God-head that the mystic body of Christ should awake to life and perfect activity, only by and through the action of the Holy Ghost. This had been the promise of Our Lord Himself, and everywhere He teaches His followers to look for the finishing of His work at the hands of the Holy Ghost. ''I will ask the Father, and He shall give you another Paraclete, that He may abide with you forever. . . . The Spirit of Truth. . . . You shall know Him; because He shall abide with you and shall be in you.'' (John 14. 16. 17.) ''The Paraclete, the Holy Ghost, whom the Father will send in My name, He will teach you all things, and bring all things to your mind, whatsoever I shall have said to you.'' (John 14. 26.) ''It is expedient to you that I go, for if I go not, the Paraclete will not come to you, but if I go, I will send Him to you.'' (John 16. 7.) So it is clear that our Lord's Ascension into Heaven, the return to His Eternal Throne of the Second Person of the Most Holy Trinity, was the very means decreed and ordained by God for the coming of the Third Person of that same Trinity, and for His constantly remaining with that body of which He should become the life and the soul. Nay, more, this coming of the Holy Ghost was, in the Divine Will, made the one and only means for bringing life and energy and perfect strength to Christ's mystic body. St. John records the glorious promises of mercy and love that fell from the lips of Our Lord on the great day of the Jewish feast of the Tabernacles—but they were promises, to be realized through the action of the Holy Ghost, and he distinctly adds, ''As yet the spirit was not given, because Jesus was not yet glorified.'' (John 7. 39) Closing a life whose every pulsation and thought had been to lead men to God—looking forward to the fruits His work would bear in the hearts of men, Our Lord says: ''When He, the Spirit of Truth, is come, He will teach you all truth, for He shall not speak of Himself;

but what things soever He shall hear, He shall speak. He shall glorify Me; because He shall receive of mine, and shall shew it to you. All things whatsoever the Father hath, are mine. Therefore I said He shall receive of mine and shew it to you." (John 16. 13–15.) And this divine prediction found its quick fulfillment, when ten days after the glorious Ascension of the Son, the Holy Ghost personally came to the infant Church, Christ's mystic body, and, filling her with His graces and gifts, began that union which Christ had promised should endure forever. A new dispensation was begun on that day, never more to end because it is perfect—the dispensation of the Holy Ghost. While the Eternal Son dwelt in visible, bodily form on earth, He was the Guide of the Church and the Centre of her unity. But He ascended to Heaven and sent the Holy Ghost, charged with the sacred office of putting into life and motion the means of our salvation founded by Christ. On that day, in the opening of this new dispensation of the Holy Ghost, He, becoming identified with the mystic body of Christ as its very life and essence, became forevermore to that Church the Centre of unity, the Unerring Guide, the Infallible Teacher of the truth of God. All that had gone before in the Old Law was type and figure. The ceremonies of the Law, the ritual of the Temple were but "a shadow of things to come, but the body is Christ's." (Col. 2. 17.) Even the work of Christ, the perfecting of His mystical body, was not complete until the coming of the Holy Ghost; for the perfect, living union of the head with the body was deferred until the Head was glorified in Heaven, and the Spirit was sent to glorify Him on earth. The second chapter of the Acts of the Apostles gives us the minute particulars of this great event. The Church was a new mystic Eve formed by Christ on earth, and He Himself, the glorified Author of the new spiritual order of things, breathed upon her from His Eternal Throne of glory His own Divine Spirit, and by that breath of divine life the Church became a living body, the mother of the living, the mystic body of Christ united to Him her Head. Thus vivified by and filled with the very Spirit of God, "who proceedeth from the Father and the Son," she, in the spiritual order and in a mystic sense, hears the renewal of the commission given in the first creation: "Increase and multiply, and fill the earth, and subdue it, and rule over . . . all living creatures that move upon the earth." (Gen. 1. 28) Oh, wondrous and lasting results of this quickening of Christ's mystic body by the Holy Spirit! St.

Paul exclaims: "If the ministration of death, engraven with letters upon stones, was glorious: . . . how shall not the ministration of the Spirit be rather in glory!" (2 Cor. 3. 7–8.) If the Jewish people were made the typical chosen inheritance of God, when amid the terrors of the aroused elements the old law of fear was announced from Sinai's heights, how much more tenderly and lovingly did the glowing tongues of Pentecost announce to a wondering world its reconciliation with God, the fulfillment of Joel's prophecy, the beginning of the law of love, the consecration of the Church of Christ, which becoming the tabernacle of the God of truth should never more be moved or shaken! Once the mysteries of God were fulfilled upon the head of the Nazarene when, at His baptism on Jordan's banks, "the Spirit of the Lord came upon Him, as a dove, anointing Him to preach the Gospel to the poor." The same Spirit also, coming in the form of fiery tongues, anointed the Church, Christ's mystic body, for the same work of the Gospel. The commission was heralded from Heaven on the wings of the rushing wind; it was executed throughout the world in the trumpet tones of the Apostles, and he of their number whom Jesus specially loved, reminding them how the Spirit given to them is their strength and authority beyond all dictates of men, boldly proclaims: "Let the unction, which you have received from Him, abide in you. And you have no need that any man teach you, but as His unction teacheth you of all things, and is truth, and is no lie." (1 John 2. 27.) "You have the unction from the Holy One and know all things." (1 John 2. 20.)

You, children of this Church in which the Holy Ghost dwells, members of Christ's mystic body and united to your head by the Spirit of God quickening all the body, you know, and knowing rejoice and thank God that the miracle of Pentecost is constantly continued in the Church—that He who came to the Church then, came to abide with her forever, and that the glorious sun of divine love and union which then rose upon the new Jerusalem, the Holy City of God, shall nevermore set. This constant presence in the Church forever of the very Spirit of Truth, makes her, as St. Paul says, "the very pillar and ground of truth." This His union with Christ's mystic body is something new and entirely different from the influence which the Holy Ghost had exercised from the dawn of creation and will exercise until the end of time in every individual, holy soul. That union between Him and our souls is a conditional one—we can break it if we so desire—it depends entirely on the correspondence and fidelity with which we receive Him and nourish His Divine presence—it depends, alas! upon our own frail and erring and changing will. But His union with the Church, the mystic body which He called into life, is not conditional but absolute. This body once alive in God can nevermore die. This union depends not upon the varying will of man, but on the eternal will of God, and changeless, perfect as God Himself, cannot be dissolved in all eternity. Remember that the head of this body is Christ, Who is God and man, and Who, as a Person of the Adorable Trinity, is perfectly and eternally united with the Holy Ghost. The head cannot be separated from the body, for he founded it to endure forever. The body cannot be united with its Head without eternally enjoying the divine life by which it is thus united, and this mystical body is imperishable because of this inseparable union with its Head and its Life. There can never, will never come a time when that life of the mystic body will be interrupted, for if that one moment should come, Christ's promise failed when He assured His Church that the Paraclete would abide with her forever. Individuals may fall away from the Church, and they perish even as members that are separated from the living body. But the Church lives forever by the life of God Himself. All her endowments are drawn from the Divine Person Who is her Head and from the Divine Spirit Who is her Life. You realize, therefore, how vastly this union of the Holy Spirit with the Church differs from His union with the sanctified soul of the individual just. St. Augustine says: "The Holy Ghost on Pentecost descended into the temple of the Apostles, prepared for Him, as a shower of sanctification. He came, no more as a transient visitor, but, as a perpetual Comforter and an eternal inhabitant . . . no longer only by the graces of His visitation and operation, but by the very presence of His Majesty."

Before the Incarnation, the Holy Ghost wrought invisibly. On Pentecost and daily since then, He manifests His presence and His operations by the visible Church of Christ, and the mystic body of Christ may truly be said to be the visible embodiment of the presence of the Holy Ghost.

The Church is indeed Christ's mystic body, but His union with the body was effected in a manner like to that other miracle of love by which the same Holy Ghost effected the union of the divine and the human nature of Christ in the one person of the Eternal Son. The

Church is Christ's mystic body, but by the Holy Spirit she is quickened, she is made perfect, she enriches all the human race with divine grace. St. Augustine says: "What did the coming of the Holy Ghost accomplish? How did he teach us His presence? How did He manifest it? They all spoke with the tongues of all nations. . . . One man spoke with the tongues of all nations. . . . Behold here the unity of the Catholic Church spread throughout the world, is declared." This mystic body remains unchanged amid all the world's changes, and is the daily fulfillment of St. Paul's words, "Therefore, receiving an immovable kingdom, we have grace," (Heb. 12. 28.) This mystic body of Christ stands amid all the darkness of error, the very pillar of truth, bright as the moon with the reflected brightness of the Sun of eternal justice; and even as did her Head and Founder on earth, so does she to-day proclaim to the princes of this world, and to all men, the eternal truth of God. For though her voice be spoken in feeblest tones, aye, by even unworthy lips, the word of her Head is fulfilled in her lowliest messenger, "It is not you that speak, but the Spirit of your Father that speaketh in you." (Matt. 10. 20.) Once men in their rage sought to lay hands upon the Head of this mystic body, that they might kill Him. "But He passing through the midst of them, went His way." (Luke 4. 30.) So have the clouds of hatred enveloped His Church in every age, and the storms of persecution and malice and misrepresentation have howled around her. The powers of the world have united against her, and those who knew her least have shrieked the loudest hate and rage. Yet has she ever moved on, unshaken by the tempests, firm in the truth and Spirit of God, and each new day has witnessed the enlarging of the camp, the spreading out of the "tents of Jacob," into which she gathers her children, not by arms, indeed, nor by worldly might, but by the unspeakable sweetness and mercy of her Divine Life and Soul, the Holy Spirit of God. For of her had Zacharias the Prophet written: "Not with an army, nor by might, but by my Spirit, saith the Lord of Hosts." (Zach. 4. 6.)

This mystic body in constant union with her Head and her Spirit is to-day, as ever, faithfully carrying out the work committed to her of enlightening and sanctifying souls, regenerating them to God in Baptism, strengthening them in Confirmation, nourishing them with food from Heaven, purifying them by the words of divine pardon, anointing them with the oil of salvation, transmitting her divine functions from age to age, ratifying, above, the contract of pure hearts here below, and doing all this work in the various sacraments by the power of that Spirit of God Whom Christ breathed upon her first ministers when commissioning them: "As the Father hath sent me, I also send you!" (John 20. 21.) The Church is the mystic body of Christ through which alone we can be united with God, for St. Augustine declares: "He cannot have God for his Father, who has not the Church for his Mother." And dwelling on this thought, he goes on to say: "What the soul is to the body of man, that the Holy Ghost is to the body of Christ, which is the Church. What the soul does in all the members of one body, that the Holy Ghost does in the whole Church. But see what you have to fear and guard against. In the body of a man it may happen that a member may be cut off, the head, the finger, the foot. Does the soul follow the severed member? While it was in the body, it was alive; once cut off, and its life is lost. So a man is a Christian and a Catholic while he is alive in the body of Christ; cut off, he becomes a heretic. The Holy Ghost does not follow that amputated limb. If, therefore, you would live by the Holy Ghost, hold fast to charity, love truth, desire unity, that you may attain a happy eternity." And you know that this golden eloquence of St. Augustine in the early days of the Church rings with equal force and truth in the so-called enlightenment and progress of these our days.

This is the Church of which, by God's great mercy, you have been made children—this the mystic body of Christ of which you are members—this the Spirit and life you enjoy as members of Christ's undivided, mystic body. Oh, the debt of gratitude we owe for all this to the Holy Ghost, a debt which has perhaps been accumulating through long years of indifference and neglect and forgetfulness of Him. This is the new spiritual creation in which you have shared, and of which David sang in prophecy: "By the word of the Lord the Heavens were established; and all the power of them by the Spirit of His mouth." (Ps. 32. 6.) And now remember the sacred obligations which this great blessing brings with it. The first and greatest fruit of that life which we enjoy by the Holy Ghost in the Church, is full and perfect union with our Head, showing itself in our increased knowledge and love of the Eternal Son, Our Lord and Savior, Jesus Christ. In the human body we know the intimate connection between the head and the heart. Then if, as we have seen, Christ is the Head of the Church, the Holy Ghost is most certainly and truly the Heart and Soul of the Church. St. Thomas says: "The head enjoys a certain pre-eminence over the members of the body, but the heart has its hidden influence. And therefore is the Holy Ghost compared with the heart, because invisibly, He vivifies and unites the entire body of the Church." The fruit of this hidden influence is to bind us more and more closely to our Divine Lord in love, the more we allow ourselves to be influenced by the Holy Ghost. It was on the occasion of the visible descent of the Holy Ghost as a dove, that Peter throbbing with the revelation of the Father in holy enthusiasm exclaimed: "Thou art Christ, the Son of the living God." St. Paul was but the organ, the mouthpiece of the Holy Ghost, when he so tenderly wrote to the Ephesians praying: "That he would grant you, according to the riches of His glory, to be strengthened by His Spirit with might unto the inward man. That Christ may dwell by faith in your hearts, that rooted and founded in charity, you may be able to comprehend with all the saints what is the breadth, and length, and height, and depth; to know also the charity of Christ." (Eph. 3. 16–19.) That disciple whom Jesus loved declares that the fruit of the Holy Spirit in us consists, above all, in bringing man, and the whole world to a true—a living faith in God's Incarnate Word. "By this is the Spirit of God known. Every Spirit which confesseth that Jesus Christ is come in the flesh, is of God." (1 John 4. 2.) These are our models, my brethren, these the fruits the Holy Ghost must produce in us as the evidence of His presence in our hearts. This is the main object of all devotion to the Holy Ghost, increased knowledge of, earnest longing and deepest love for Jesus our Redeemer, in Whom alone is our hope of salvation. Not without reason has the Church in our day sought so earnestly to win our hearts to the twin-devotions to the Holy Ghost and to the Sacred Heart of Jesus; and not without deep significance does her ritual cause the festivals of the Blessed Sacrament and of the Sacred Heart of Jesus to follow, very closely, the festival of the Holy Ghost. She presents to us the loving Heart of Jesus and the Eternal Soul of the Church, "one heart and one soul." The evil days have come upon us. The spirit of Antichrist is abroad in the world. By slander, by calumny, by basest misrepresentation, by open denial and by cunning sarcasm, by bold opposition and by quiet indifference, this evil spirit is laboring, however, fruitlessly, to destroy the divine union existing between the person and the doctrine of Christ, the dogmas and the miracles of Christ, the work of Christ and the operation of His Church, the salvation in Christ and the world's true and only progress, which is to know Him and love Him. Only the grace of the Holy Spirit can enable us to stand firm in all these dangers, and in His Divine strength and boldness alone can we proclaim to an infidel, scoffing, unbelieving world, ''Every Spirit that dissolveth Jesus, is not of God, and this is Antichrist, of whom ye have heard that he cometh, and he is now already in the world.'' (1 John 4. 3.) The world is indeed overwhelmed in malice, but our duty is not the less clearly marked out. To strengthen us for just such conflicts as those of our day against revealed religion, the Holy Ghost was given to us; and we, remaining in firm and unhesitating union with the Church in which He dwells forever, will be strengthened with His strength to overcome every foe. Our Lord foresaw these trials and conflicts. It was His will that we encounter them and by our valor show our true appreciation of His Divine gifts and graces. His prayer to His Eternal Father for each of us, still rings in our ears; ''I pray not that Thou shouldst take them out of the world, but that Thou shouldst keep them from evil,'' (John 17. 15)—not that we be spared the shock of the conflict, but that we gain the crown of victory, being strengthened in the faith by Him who is the Life of that body of which we are members. If we fail to avail ourselves of that Life and Strength we are lost, we shall go down in the conflict. If the Spirit of God dwell not with us, if for a moment we die the spiritual death of separation from Him, the wicked spirit of the world will sweep like a simoon over the soil of our hearts, destroying every vestige of virtue and holiness, and sinking us into that dread night of sin and indifference from which only a miracle of God's mercy can ever again rescue us!

The further fruit of these thoughts, if taken deeply into our hearts will be an eternal gratitude to God, because in His infinite mercy, and by the merit of ours, He has given us the gift of His faith, and has made us members of the living, mystic body of Christ, the Catholic Church. There is a special significance in the words of the Apostles' Creed in which, from our infant days until now, we have declared, ''I believe in the Holy Ghost,'' and in the same breath, ''in the Holy Catholic Church.'' These two mysteries of grace and mercy are inseparably united. On Pentecost the Holy Ghost became the Life and Soul of the Church, the constant Guide, and the unerring Teacher of her faithful children. This His sacred office has continued uninterrupted in the Church to this hour; it will continue forever. To-day, as on that birth day of the Holy Catholic Church, He is her Guide and Teacher. He is her Divine Authority; He speaks to us through the Church, to-day, as in the first days. Her ministers teaching the truth the Church receives from Him, worthily declare, "It hath seemed good to the Holy Ghost and to us." (Acts 15. 28) He, as a Divine Person, is as truly present in the Church, as our Divine Lord was present in His Church before His Ascension into Heaven. Every act of the Holy Church is influenced and dictated by Him. Her great Councils are assembled in His Name, and their first act is to offer to the Majesty of God the Mass of the Holy Ghost imploring His light. The official opening cry of these Councils, twice repeated, is, "Come, Oh Holy Spirit, our Creator. We are present here, specially gathered in Thy name." And as in the great General Councils so does this solemn invocation witness the formal opening of every National or Provincial Council, and of every Diocesan Synod. And, in virtue of this abiding presence and guidance of the Holy Ghost, the voice of the Church declaring the "truth that is in Jesus Christ," is really and truly the unerring, undeceiving, authoritative voice of God the Holy Ghost. The preaching of the Apostles of Christ, the teachings of the first Pentecost Sunday, the utterances of the Church to-day, are all equally the voice of the same Divine Spirit Who spoke in the beginning in a tongue understood by all nations, and Who speaks to-day similarly to all peoples of the earth. So will it be until the end of time; so will it continue throughout the glories of eternity, for the mystical body of Christ, His Church, will never cease to be, since her life is infinite and eternal. Now we behold her in her three great classes, triumphant in Heaven, in her faithful children crowned—militant on earth, in her obedient children still bearing the brunt of the conflict—suffering in purgatory, in her loving children awaiting the day of their final deliverance. But the curtain of time will soon be drawn aside and will open up to us the boundless visits of eternity. Then the whole Church reigning with Christ in Heaven will be united with Him its Head, and its eternal life in the Holy Ghost will continue in the perfect number of the blessed. There we "shall see Him face to face," and shall also know each other in Him, our Head. Through all the orders of Angels and Saints, there will be preserved our strict, personal identity, our perfect mutual recognition, our complete union with our Head and Spirit in one Eternal Body and Soul.

Oh, the wondrous mercy of God that has deigned to make us members of this body of Christ! Oh, the infinite value of being members of His Church! Oh, the sad blindness that could cause us for one moment to forget or undervalue the priceless gift of our faith! On our knees, and with deepest gratitude let us daily thank God for His inestimable mercy in making us members of the Church whose very soul and life is the Holy Ghost! Guard this treasure as sacred beyond all else! Others have lost it, are daily losing it, and in pitiable blindness, make light of this saddest, greatest loss. Multitudes have fallen away from this Church—provinces, whole nations have lost their faith. Who has suffered? Not the living mystic body of Christ, Whose life remains eternal in the Holy Ghost and cannot be dissolved, Whose work goes on evermore the same, though individuals, congregations, nations fall away from her and die, as must all members separated from the living body.

Guard against the least weakening of your faith—against the first approach of danger. Never before, perhaps, did so many dread dangers assail this our priceless inheritance of faith. Perhaps the greatest of all dangers is the indifference characteristic of our times, which would sink religion below notice, which boldly proclaims it immaterial what men believe, what the Holy Ghost teaches us, or whether or not we follow His guidance.

To each of us the tender words of St. John have a deep significance, a fearful warning of surrounding dangers: "Little children, it is the last hour, and as you have heard that Antichrist cometh; even now there are become many Antichrists, whereby we know that it is the last hour. They went out from us; but they were not of us." (1. John 2. 18–19.)

It is the last hour, yet a little more courage, yet a little longer struggle, and the crown will be gained. Over the battle field rings the voice of your Divine Head. "Know you not that you are the temple of God, and that the Spirit of God dwelleth in you?" (1 Cor. 3, 16) Yet a little longer walking in humble, unquestioning faith under the guidance of that Church to whom Christ said: "He that heareth you heareth me," strong in the certainty that her life and soul is the Infallible Spirit of the Eternal God. Then time shall be swallowed up in eternity. We, members of Christ's mystic body, shall enter upon the eternal life of that body in Heaven, where, as the reward of our faith here, "we shall all meet into the unity of faith and of the knowledge of the Son of God." (Eph. 4. 13.)

THIRD SERIES.

THE RELATIONSHIP OF THE HOLY GHOST
TO THE WRITTEN WORD OF GOD.

I.

He is the Author of the Scriptures.

"But to us God hath revealed them, by his Spirit." (I Cor. 2. 10.)

The series of meditations on the Holy Ghost which we begin today, refers to His sacred and divine office as the Author and Interpreter of the Sacred Scriptures, and as our Teacher and Guide in the use of God's Written Word. I recall to your minds, first of all, the details and circumstances of His visible coming to those Apostles some of whom, with their immediate disciples and successors, subsequently wrote the various books of the New Testament. Their Lord and Master was about to leave them. He with Whom they had walked so long in familiar, daily intercourse, from Whose divine lips they had learned the eternal truths which they were about to preach to mankind, He was about to ascend to the glory of the Father Who had sent Him. But His leaving them was not to break the holy bonds that tied them to Him, they were not to be left orphans, but "eating together with them, He commanded them, that they should not depart from Jerusalem, but should wait for the promise of the Father, which you have heard (saith He) by my mouth. For John indeed baptized with water, but you shall be baptized with the Holy Ghost not many days hence." (Acts 1, 4–5.)

And indeed not many days did they wait for the glorious fulfillment of this His promise. The great void which His leaving them had brought to the hearts of the Apostles, the days of their seeming orphanage and of the longing desires of their souls, were of brief duration. They engaged in the devotions of their holy Novena, that first, most solemn, most fruitful type of all the Novenas that have ever since been celebrated by the children of the Church. And then, as they sat together in continued prayer with Mary, the Mother of Jesus, in that city which had been the scene of Christ's ignominious death, in that upper room where they gathered in great fear of their persecutors, "These days of Pentecost were accomplished and suddenly there came a sound from Heaven, as of a mighty wind coming; and it filled the whole house . . . Parted tongues as it were of fire, sat upon every one of them, and they were will filled with the Holy Ghost." (Acts 2. 1–2–3–4.) And so the Church of Christ sprang into glorious life and strength. This is her certificate of divine incorporation, this the secret of her joy and the warrant of her mission from that day to this, this the motive of the chant she has evermore sung with Mary; "My soul doth magnify the Lord, and my Spirit hath rejoiced in God my Saviour . . . Because He that is mighty hath done great things to me, and holy is His name." (Luke 1. 46–49.)

Christ having ascended into Heaven, sent from the throne of His Divine Majesty that Holy Spirit Whom He had promised, that "other Paraclete, the Spirit of Truth." From this Divine Spirit did the Church learn all truth. By Him were the teachings of Christ amplified and deeply engraved in the Apostles' hearts to be preserved forever. He, dwelling in that Church forever made her truly and absolutely the depository of truth, beyond all danger of error. He speaking by that Church, made her the infallible teacher of God's truth to men. For surely it would be but an imperfect, a useless work of the Holy Ghost to teach truth to the Church unless He also guided and directed her in giving to the world, not error, not even doubt, but that absolute and certain truth of which He assures her by His constant presence. He came to glorify the Son, to make the work of redemption and sanctification fruitful among men. He came to direct the lips and enlighten the minds of those from whom men were to learn the truth of God. And whether this truth of God was to be imparted by the living voice of the preacher, or by the pen of the writer speaking to multitudes of all the centuries, it was equally the office of the Holy Ghost to illumine the mind and guide the tongue of the Apostle or the pen of the Evangelist. Therefore, as the Holy Ghost inspired the early teachers in the Church in every word they uttered in the discharge of their sacred mission, so, necessarily, did He inspire them in every word they wrote in the discharge of their divine work. And if, as we are expressly told, it was not they that spoke, but the Spirit of God who spoke in them, it follows most logically and necessarily that when many truths of salvation were imparted in writing, they were reduced from spoken to written form, He taught them the truths they wrote, and He is the Author of those Sacred Writings as fully as He was of their utterance by the tongues of the Apostles. As we proceed with these thoughts we shall see how this writing of God's Word, this recording of the faith that had already been preached by the Apostles under the inspiration of the Holy Ghost, was a secondary, a supplementary means adopted for spreading among men the "truth as it is in Jesus." But having been determined upon, the Sacred Scriptures, in the recording of those truths committed to their pages, were most properly the work of that Holy Spirit through Whom we were to learn all truth, whether it be imparted by the living voice alone, or jointly by the voice and the written page. And so by means of the Apostles and the Evangelists, the inspired speakers and writers of God's inspired word, did the Holy Ghost prepare for and transmit to future generations the mystery of God's love as told by the Prophets of the Old Law and witnessed by the Prophets of the New Testament. There is the pen-picture of the life and work of the Word that "was made flesh and dwelled among us;" there the records, not indeed of all, but of many of the truths He announced to the world—of that revelation which Christ had written upon the hearts of His disciples and which the Holy Ghost completed and perfected. In the enumeration of the "wonderful works of God" for which we are indebted to the Holy Spirit, we can never forget, and the Church ever remembers with most joyful gratitude, the Written Word of God, the various books of the Sacred Scripture both of the Old and of the New Law, which "The holy men of God" penned by the light from above, illuminated, aided, directed, strengthened against error by the Spirit of Truth, the Holy Ghost. Not in criticism, and in the earnest desire to give no pain to any one, I dare assert that whatever true reverence still remains in the world for the Sacred Scriptures as God's Written Word, untouched by human frailty, uncontaminated by the possibility of human error, pure and true and reliable as they came to us from God's Holy Spirit, can be found only in the Catholic Church, who alone reveres and guards the Scriptures not as mere historic documents upon which every one may exercise and express his own judgment, but as in very truth, the inspired Word of God. And this deep reverence, this holy love of the Church for God's Written Word, is the necessary outcome of that wonderful relationship we have already seen to exist for ever between her and the Holy Spirit. The Written Word is to her the "Word of life," for it is the Word of Him who is her Life and Soul. And even as she is intimately united with the Holy Ghost by His constant dwelling with her, so does she revere and love and treasure as her great trust, that inspired Word of which the Holy Ghost is the Author.

For a proper understanding of this important subject and of the position of the Catholic Church regarding the Bible, it seems necessary that we glance for a moment at the claims of those outside of the Catholic Church, note with how much or how little consistency these have been maintained, and what is the value of the many difficulties, which, in our days, are raised against the inspiration of the Scriptures, and therefore against the truth that the Holy Ghost is their Author. The great religious convulsions of the sixteenth century by which so many souls were unhappily separated from the unity of the faith, seem to have established for them one great principle, that the Bible alone is the absolute rule of faith. The Protestant Reformation from which practically all our dissenting Christian brethren date their origin, some three hundred years ago, staked its existence on the Bible. If then there be at work in their midst any principle subversive of this great cardinal principle of their existence and life—if this corner-stone of all their structure be attacked and weakened, the fact that such undermining is going on is vital to the good of their life and religion. To say nothing of the various forms into which the Protestantism of the sixteenth century has since subdivided itself, the organization which seemed, among Protestants, most anxious to guard the Holy Scriptures and maintain their inspired character has certainly been the Church of England. Even in her first separation from the Church, and though she rejected certain books of the Scriptures, the traditional teaching of the Catholic Church on the inspiration of the retained books was not disputed but was readily accepted. Her earliest writers accepted and adopted all the forms of expression on the inspiration and truth of the Sacred Scriptures which had until then been current among Catholic writers and speakers. Thus Hooker, an early writer in the Church of England, says: "God so employed the Prophets in this heavenly work that they neither spake nor wrote a word of their own, but uttered, syllable by syllable, as the Spirit put into their mouths." (Hooker's Works, Vol. 3, P. 62.) For a century after the Reformation this was the general tone of Protestant writers, and in all the best years of the Reformation this seems to have been the opinion of those Anglican Divines whose true learning and sound judgment have made them eminent. Let us look at some more modern testimony from the same source. A member of the University of Oxford writes: "The Bible is none other than the voice of Him that sitteth upon the Throne. Every book of it, every chapter of it, every verse of it, every word of it, every syllable of it, every letter of it, is the direct utterance of the Most High." (Burgon, Insp. and Interp. of Scrip., p. 89.) A member of Trinity College, Dublin, writes: "The Holy Spirit, as the productive principle, embraces the entire activity of those whom He inspires, rendering their language the Word of God. The entire substance and form of Scripture, whether resulting from revelation or natural knowledge, are thus blended together into one harmonious whole." (Lee, on the Insp. of Holy Scrip., p. 32, 33.)

Now, it is not for us here to say what is the authoritative doctrine of the Church of England to-day. But it is quite certain that the doctrine of its great writers as quoted above, is not the doctrine taught to-day. The vast preponderance of its authors now doubt, hesitate, or quite deny the absolute inspiration of the Scriptures. I quote one recent writer with whom the great majority agree, and who in startling contrast to the opinions we have just heard, clearly states: "There is no appearance in their writings that the Evangelists or the Apostles, had any inward gift, or were subject to any power external to them different from that of preaching or teaching which they daily exercised; nor do they anywhere lead us to suppose that they were free from error or infirmity." (Jowett on the Interp. of Scrip. Essays and Reviews, p. 345.) I repeat that I cannot give the official teaching of the Anglican Church on the points thus asserted and denied at the pleasure of the writers. Unfortunately, it is difficult to fix the fact that there is any teaching authority which can enforce obedience and respect in that organization. But it is a significant fact that recently its highest ecclesiastical tribunal declares that these latter views on inspiration are not inconsistent with the Anglican formularies, and admits the liberty of its ministers individually to examine and determine certain verses or parts of Scripture, though it "could not be permitted to a clergyman to reject the whole of one of the books of Scripture.'' (Judgment Bishop of Salisbury vs. Williams, p. 16.)

And remember that this laxness of judgment, this ruinous freedom of opinion, is not merely with regard to the disputed question whether this or that book is to be regarded as a portion of God's Word or not, but affects, questions, denies the inspiration of those books which are admitted to be truly a part of the Scriptures.

In view of these facts, where now is the corner-stone upon which the whole work of the Reformation was made to rest—where the consistency with which that vital principle of existence has been preserved and guarded—where the comparison between the tottering structure with whose avowed foundation work every one is allowed to toy and trifle, and that Church builded upon the rock against which Christ promised that no error should prevail?

These sad facts should startle those whose whole religious system depends upon the Bible alone. The defection of the Church of England on this point is perhaps one of the saddest elements in this complication, for she, until recently, seemed to stand as the only barrier, outside of the Catholic Church, to the ever advancing tide of Rationalism that has devastated so many portions of Protestant Europe and has made all divine revelation a mockery and a jest. The Catholic Church alone has the proper reverence and appreciation for the Holy Scriptures. Hitherto the skepticism and unbelief of the rationalistic world at large had worked outside of the Church of England and had found her a firm opponent. If to-day these new views are put forth in that Church and by men highly respectable and cultivated, men whose eminence and personal excellence and mental culture enable them to wield a powerful influence in that Church, what is this but the withdrawal of the last opponent to Rationalism, and the demonstration to all the world that the Catholic Church alone holds, believes, defends the inspiration of the Written Word of God?

Now as to the value of the many objections against the inspiration of the Holy Scriptures raised either indirectly by the manner in which men use the Bible, or directly by open accusation and defiance, remember that they are not new. Like certain bodily epidemics, they come in waves, sometimes subsiding for a time, only again to rush in with new violence, but ever remaining the same in composition and character. In every age has the Catholic Church fought the fight which she to-day wages against those who would deprave

God's Holy Word. Glance for a moment at the history of this subject. In the very lifetime of St. John a sect called the Cerinthians, rejected all the New Testament except the Gospel of St. Matthew and the Book of the Acts. In the second century the Carpocratians rejected the entire Old Testament; others acknowledged only the Gospel of St. Luke and St. Paul's Epistles to Timothy and Titus. In the third century the Archontici rejected the Old Testament, and numerous other sects rejected most of the Old and of the New Testament. In the fourth century, the Gnostics, the Manichaeans and others threw aside the greater part of the Old and of the New Testament. The writings of St. Ambrose and of St. Augustine in the fourth and fifth centuries teem with answers to objections on the reliability of the Scriptures, which are repeated as new in our day. The eighth and ninth and succeeding centuries witnessed a repetition in new mouths, and from new pens of errors spoken and refuted in the early days of the Church. In the fifteenth century, and again in the sixteenth, Herman Rissuich and David Georgius rejected the whole Scripture as imperfect and useless. Luther and his followers threw aside the Epistle of St. James, of St. Paul to the Hebrews, the First Epistle of St. John, the Second Epistle of St. Peter, and the entire Apocalypse. Others with increased license held all the Scriptures to be mere fables, like the Libertini of the sixteenth century, and the Ambrosians of the same date, who despising both the Old and the New Testaments, claimed that they themselves enjoyed divine revelations. Remember that all these various views had their numerous and enthusiastic adherents, and note how strangely familiar they sound in our modern ears. The seventeenth century witnessed the introduction of the system of modern infidelity, which is termed Rationalism, which may be defined as the abnormal and illegitimate use of reason. Its stronghold has always been, as it now is, in the Protestant portions of Germany, and it is safe to say that in the eighteenth and the nineteenth centuries, there was no book of the Old or the New Testament which had not been rejected by some of these modern critics. Doubtless the best representative of them all is Spinoza, and many are those who follow his views on the inspiration of the Scriptures. He may be termed the father of modern skeptical criticism, not indeed because he brought forward any new or unanswered objections, but rather because he reduced most of the old objections to system and method and form. This Rationalism, as it is termed, has at intervals spread throughout Europe, has taken noxious root even in this, our fair land, and, as we have seen, threatens now to disarm the only champion who outside of the Catholic Church has hitherto stood up boldly in defense of the inspired character of the Sacred Writings. These historical details, I know, are very dull and prosy. I could not venture to claim your notice for them but that they prove my statement, that the opposition to the Sacred Scriptures in these our days is not a new thing, but has been renewed in every age from the days of St. John the Evangelist to the Tom Paines of the last generation and the Ingersolls of our present day. Who has stemmed this ever-surging tide of opposition to the Bible as God's Word? What power has preserved, amid this ever-raging conflict, that Sacred Volume which in whole or in part has been repudiated by some in every age of Christianity? The Catholic Church alone has thrown the aegis of her protecting arm around this treasure, recognizing it as her divine inheritance, and in the strength of the Holy Spirit from Whom she received it, she alone has preserved it pure and uncontaminated from all error, as the very truth of God.

Let us now see what is the teaching of the Catholic Church on the subject of the divine character of the Holy Scriptures. Briefly, it is as follows: The writings of the Prophets and of the Apostles are Holy Scripture. These certain Sacred Books contain the truth and the discipline of Christ, not in their entirety, but in connection with the authorized traditions by which the fullness of faith has been preserved and handed down in the Church. God is the Author of these Sacred Books. They, as well as the spoken utterances which are called the traditions of the Church, are given by the Holy Ghost's guidance, and He, therefore, is the Author of all such books and traditions, both of the Old and of the New Testament. These Sacred Books are specified in number and by name. This catalogue of the books comprised in the Sacred Scriptures is called the Canon of the Scriptures. In its fourth session, the great Council of Trent fully and distinctly recites the books that form the Canon of the Old and New Testament. But in doing so, that Council only repeated the decisions of the Council of Florence in the fourteenth century, of Constantinople in the sixth, of Carthage in the fourth, and of the Pontifical declarations of the early Popes, St. Innocent and St. Gelasius. The Church holds that "these entire books with all their parts" are to be held as sacred, that is, inspired, and to have God for their Author.

No part of these books is of merely human authorship, and therefore in no part of them can error or falsehood be found, for they are, in all their parts, of divine authority. The Church further declares that that special Latin version of the Holy Scriptures known as the Vulgate, is to be accepted as authentic. This is Catholic faith, readily and fully accepted by every child of the Church, and he who rejects this doctrine thereby separates himself from the living body of Christ. It is not necessary for us to enter here into the various discussions of the Doctors and Theologians of the Church, some of whom, like the earliest writers, maintain that every particle and word of the canonical books were written by the dictation of the Holy Ghost, so that not only the substance, but even the composition and style of the language are to be ascribed to Him. Other scholastic writers hold that the whole matter of the Holy Scriptures was written by the aid of the Holy Ghost, but that He did not necessarily dictate the entire form, nor every particular word or letter. But while this latter is perhaps the most generally accepted view in the Church, the essence of the matter is entirely covered by the teachings of the Church which I have named above. Should varying views at any time cast a doubt or uncertainty, or in any manner imperil the great deposit of faith which the Holy Church guards with divine authority, then will her authoritative voice ring over the world, as we have heard it in our day in the dogmas of the Immaculate Conception of Mary, and of the Infallibility of the visible head of the Church on earth.

From what I have stated as the doctrine of the Catholic Church on the Holy Scriptures, you will note the vast divergence between her teachings and those of our Protestant brethren, so far as these latter can be definitely determined. To them the Bible is the immediate and only rule of faith. The human judgment of each individual is lawfully exercised to determine what the Holy Ghost does or does not teach in the Sacred Volume. The practical results of this system are everywhere around us, by which there are not only as many varying views as there are churches, but by which the whole teaching office of the Church is abolished, the object for which the Holy Ghost came to dwell with us forever is nullified, and each individual becomes a supreme authority to himself in fixing the truth of God. Against this, it is the doctrine of our Holy Church that Sacred Scripture is the partial and therefore the remote rule of our faith. The main ground of our faith is the constant presence of the Holy Ghost in the teaching Church, His uninterrupted, divine illumination by which from the day of Pentecost He has made her the depository of truth, and has preserved this truth full and entire. True in the course of time portions of this truth were committed to writing by the sacred authors, and as they wrote, He, the Holy Spirit of Truth, enlightened their minds and guided their pens. But all the truths which He had taught the Church were not necessarily written. St. John closes his Gospel with the distinct statement that: ''there are also many other things which Jesus did, which if they were written every one, the world itself, I think would not be able to contain the books that should be written.'' (John 21. 25.) So that the Written Word is but a partial record of that truth which in its fullness was committed to the Church. Though no line had ever been written, though not a book of the New Testament had ever come into existence, yet the word of Christ would have remained divinely true, ''He, the Paraclete, will teach you all things, and bring all things to your mind, whatsoever I shall have said to you.'' (John 14. 26.) The office of the Church as the divine depository of truth and as the teacher of men would have been carried out fully, entirely, completely, though no writing, no means but the living voice of the Church had been used for preaching God's revelation to the world. The immediate rule of our faith, and the reason of our obedience to the Church as to an infallible guide, is not the written pages alone, but the commission solemnly given by the Church's Divine Founder, ''Go ye into the whole world and preach the Gospel to every creature.'' (Mark 16. 15.) The Apostles were sent to preach, not to write, and though under the dictates of the Holy Spirit some of them subsequently used the pen also to aid them in their mission, their Apostolic work did not depend on such writing, writing was not the essence of the commission they received from Christ, and hence the books they wrote, being but partial records of the truths they preached, can never be said to contain all the deposit of faith, nor to be the complete and only rule of our faith. Our faith was in the world before a line of the New Testament was written. It would continue the clear and absolute truth of God and as such would be preached and preserved by the Church even though by some calamity every copy of the Sacred Scriptures were to-day destroyed throughout the world, and men suddenly forgot that such books had ever existed. For our faith and the functions of the Church as the preserver and dispenser of God's truth and graces, rest upon an order of divine facts quite independent of the Written Word, aye which has already filled the world ere the Sacred Volumes made their first appearance. This is meant when we speak of the authorized traditions of the Church, traditions not, as in a human sense, liable to the changes of time and the variations of repetition, but firm as God Himself because taught by Him and by Him preserved forevermore in the Church as the means of grace and salvation.

With the doctrine of the Church thus clearly before us, recognizing the fact that not the Holy Scriptures alone, but these, with the authorized traditions of the Church, are the rule and ground-work of our faith, you will now realize how great is the love and reverence of the Church for the Holy Scriptures. She holds that the infallible Spirit of God effected and guided their writing, even as He did the spoken utterances of the Church from the beginning. She holds that the books of the New Testament are the wondrous fulfillment of those of the Old Law which also had been penned under the inspiration of the Holy Ghost. Remember Our Lord's words: "I am not come to destroy the law or the prophets . . . but to fulfil. For Amen I say unto you, till Heaven and earth pass, one jot, or one title shall not pass of the law, till all be fulfilled." (Matt. 5. 17–18.) Throughout the world every child of the Catholic Church touches with awe the sacred records of God's mercies to men, venerates with deepest reverence the mysteries of God's Holy Word. Why? Because he knows and believes that their Author is "that Spirit who searcheth all things, yea, the deep things of God," and in the words of my text he glories in the assurance that "to us God hath revealed them by His Spirit." (1 Cor. 2. 10.) And this our reverence for the Holy Scriptures as the work of the Holy Ghost is well founded. St. Peter declares that "the holy men of God spoke, inspired by the Holy Ghost." (2nd Pet. 1. 21.) He declares that the Prophets of the Old Law "prophesied of the grace to come in you, searching what, or what manner of time, the Spirit of Christ in them did signify . . . the Holy Ghost being sent down from Heaven." (1. Pet. 1. 10–12.) The same Apostle discharging his first function as head of the Apostolic College states: "The Scripture must needs be fulfilled, which the Holy Ghost spoke before by the mouth of David." (Acts 1. 16.) Indeed the Scriptures themselves are filled with evidence that the Holy Ghost specially is the Author of the Sacred Text. This seems to be His special work by "appropriation," as in the sanctification of our souls. Whenever there is any reference to inspiration it is specially attributed to the Holy Spirit. Our Lord Himself attributes to the Holy Spirit the prophetic gift by which David called Him Lord who in the order of nature was his descendant. "How then doth David in Spirit call Him Lord?" (Matt. 22. 43.) The absolute truth of the inspiration of the Sacred Scriptures has been taught and defended by the Doctors of the Church in every age. St. Irenaeus says: "The Scriptures are perfect, being dictated by the word of God, and by His Spirit." St. Chrysostom says: "All that is in Scripture we must thoroughly examine for all is dictated by the Holy Ghost . . . The mouth of the Prophet is the mouth of God." St. Gregory of Nyssa writes: "Whatever the Sacred Scriptures declare are the utterances of the Holy Ghost. Therefore the Holy Prophets filled by God are inspired by the power of the Holy Ghost and the whole of Scripture is therefore said to be divinely inspired." Listen to St. Augustine: "In the Sacred Scriptures God Himself speaks . . . These are the handwriting of God . . . the adorable style and pen of the Spirit of God . . . The faith wavers if the authority of the Divine Scriptures is shaken . . . In Scripture there is no place for either correction or doubt." St. Ambrose declares: "They wrote not by art, but by grace. For they wrote those things which the Holy Ghost gave them to speak." St. Gregory the Great says: "The Author of the Book is the Holy Ghost. He wrote the things Who dictated them to be written. He Himself wrote Who inspired the writers in the act of writing. Whatsoever the Fathers declare in the Sacred Oracles they declare not from themselves, but they received them from God." But why multiply evidences of a truth so apparent to every child of the Church? The Books of Holy Writ, since they have the Holy Ghost for their Author, are to the Church an object of deepest veneration and most guarded carefulness—not to be touched, nor handled, nor spoken, nor read, save with that reverence and devotion which are due to the very handiwork of God the Holy Ghost. In our own day her authoritative voice has spoken this same truth which she has defended in every age, and amid all the jarring dissonances, the utterly reckless liberalism and the shocking blasphemies of our times, the great Vatican Council has solemnly proclaimed the great truth, old, yet ever new, "The Sacred Scriptures have God for their Author, since they are inspired by the Holy Ghost." (Sess. IV.)

Take to your hearts most earnestly these teachings of our Holy

Church concerning the Sacred Scriptures. The more you realize them and are impressed by them, the greater also will be your reverence and love for the great treasure that has thus been left in the keeping of our Mother for our spiritual benefit. This solemn conviction that the Holy Ghost is the Author of the Sacred Books, must necessarily surround them with the halo of divinity and must present them to the true Catholic in a light in which none outside of the Church can ever regard them. Others may treat them lightly and with unconscious profanity may make them the sport of the hour and the pretended authority for each new "wind of doctrine." The Church alone has shielded them from the corruptions and profanations of men, for she holds them of priceless value, a great treasure which she received from the Holy Ghost. Under her guidance let us open the Sacred Pages and drink from the fountain of divine truth there unsealed for us. And even as we read the Sacred Text, let our hearts be poured out in new and great gratitude to that Holy Spirit Whose mercy created and opened for us this abundant source of light and grace, the Inspired Word of God.

THIRD SERIES.

THE RELATIONSHIP OF THE HOLY GHOST
TO THE WRITTEN WORD OF GOD.

II.

He is the Interpreter of the Scriptures.

"Thinkest thou that thou understandest what thou readest." *(Acts 8. 30.).*

In our previous discourse we considered how the Holy Scriptures are to the Catholic Church an inestimable, a truly divine treasure, since their Author is none other than God, the Holy Ghost. They are the Testament of the Most High, the gift which, through the operation of the Holy Ghost, Jesus Christ left to His Church as a perpetual inheritance for her children. Plainly it is of vital importance that we properly understand them, that in reading them we may be sure that we enjoy the proper interpretation of the will of Him by

Whom they were given to us. And this leads us naturally to the point of our reflections to-day. It is Catholic faith that, as the Holy Ghost is the Author of the Scriptures, so, speaking by the living voice of that mystic body of Christ of which He is the Spirit, He is the infallible Interpreter of the Sacred Writings.

The common jurisprudence of men daily confirms the statement of St. Paul, ''Where there is a testament, the death of the testator must of necessity come in. For a testament is of force, after men are dead; otherwise, it is as yet of no strength, while the testator liveth.'' (Heb. 9. 16–17.) When death has carried away the maker of a will or testament, then are its seals broken, its contents published to all those interested. Those who are named as executors enter upon the discharge of their trust. Should there be any question or doubt as to the true meaning of the said will, the settlement of such doubts and the proper interpretation of the will are not left to the conflicting and diverging opinions of the heirs, but the matter is carried before a legitimate tribunal, authorized to act in such cases, and the decisions of that tribunal are the final solution of the whole meaning of the will—are accepted as the proper interpretation of the mind of him who was the author of the testament. The records of our courts are evidence of the many, many instances of disputed wills. And yet it is sadly true that never was a testament given to men concerning which there have been so many diverging views, so many bitter contests among the heirs, as in the case of this Testament of God which He has given to us by His Holy Spirit. What is the natural and proper method of conciliating and uniting so many opponents? Experience among those outside of the Church has proved that the constant and repeated assertion of individual opinion on the subject has led only to greater and wider division among men. Certainly reason would dictate the acceptance of the interpretation of the Holy Scriptures given by that tribunal which alone is of competent authority. We have already seen how the Holy Ghost was given to Christ's Church, to remain with her forever, to teach her all truth, to guide and direct her in her divine commission of ''preaching the Gospel to every creature.'' Therefore she who is in constant union with the Holy Ghost, she whose very life and soul He is, she is the tribunal divinely established, who alone can authoritatively dispel such doubts as may arise as to the true sense of the Scriptures. And as the Holy Ghost lives and dwells forever with the Church of Christ, her voice is His voice, and, by her mouth, God's Holy Spirit becomes the unerring and final interpreter of God's Word.

It would seem reasonable—to us, as children of the Church and members of Christ's living, mystical body, it does seem most reasonable to expect that so plain a truth should be accepted readily, and should unite all the children of our Heavenly Father in the unity of His faith and the acceptance of His will. But alas, it is not so. From the beginning, there have always been some who have ignored the authoritative interpretation of God's Word, and, so far as in them lay, have sought to break His will and make it ineffectual. In proof of this turn to the fourth chapter of St. Luke's Gospel. We read that on a certain Sabbath day Our Divine Lord went, as usual, to the synagogue. God's sun probably smiled upon the people as they assembled on that holy day, and smiled all the more gladly because for them types and figures had given way to the real presence of the Messiah, and He Whom they expected as the Promised One, at last had come to them indeed. On that day Our Lord filled the office of Public Reader. He opened the Holy Scriptures at that page where Isaiah the Prophet had written so warmly of His coming, and had named so many signs by which men might recognize Him, when He at length came among them. Our Lord, in His very Divine Person stood there among them, gifted with all the power and truth of His Divinity, and became for them the living Interpreter of the Scripture, which He had read for them. "This day these words are fulfilled in your ears," fulfilled right there and then in His Divine Person and presence. They had this text before them. Like the other portions of the Old Testament, the synagogue had for ages been most zealous in guarding the fullness and purity of every chapter and book of the Sacred Volume. And yet with these very Scriptures in their hands, they failed to recognize Him of Whom the Scriptures spoke. He came, filled with the Spirit of God, to do all the work Isaiah had indicated as the work of the Messiah, and they thought Him a mere illiterate carpenter, the son of Joseph of whom probably little was known in the higher social circles of the synagogue. He, the very Son of God, the Divine Teacher of Truth, spoke to them—and they thought it the voice of a perhaps rather presumptuous youth. He stood there interpreting for them with divine unerringness the mystic words of the Prophet, and they, with the Books of the Law in their hands, rejected Him the Lawgiver—rejected His interpretation, and read the Book as it pleased them—rejected that living voice of a Divine Teacher and turned to the written page as they in their human comments chose to interpret it. As St. Augustine says: "They were the guardians of the letter, but they knew not the spirit of the Sacred Scriptures." And of them and all who are like them does St. Paul declare: "The letter killeth; but the Spirit quickeneth," that is, giveth life. (2 Cor. 3. 6.)

You say this was a most deplorable blindness, a most ruinous perversity. It was so, indeed. But was that the only instance? Is it not most unhappily repeated, daily, hourly around us? Christ, the Second Person of the Holy Trinity, stood then among men, and they refused to accept His interpretation of God's Word. The Holy Ghost, the Third Person of the God-head, is just as really present to the Church to-day as Christ was present before His Ascension. Unless all Christ's promises have failed, and such failure has destroyed the very possibility of His Divine character then the Holy Spirit Who came to Christ's Church to teach her all truth and to abide with her forever, is actually and substantially present in and with that Church to-day, and, therefore, speaking by her voice, is the infallible interpreter of Holy Scripture. And yet men refuse to accept His interpretation of God's Word. Men do not recognize the personal presence and influence of the Holy Ghost to-day, and so refuse to hear Him. The Jews did not recognize the Messiah Who stood in their midst. So the blindness and perversity of our day are at least as deplorable as were those of the Jews. How far this blindness rendered the Jews excusable in their rejection of Christ—how far men's similar blindness of to-day may render them excusable in their rejection of the Holy Ghost, this is a mystery hidden with the God who will one day judge all men. But, at least, the blindness is most deplorable, and the responsibility assumed is a fearful one.

What has been the result? Until the unity of faith was broken, men believed and accepted that one infallible voice of the Holy Ghost speaking by the Church with which He dwells forever—that voice which with divine authority has interpreted God's Word, whether written or unwritten, in all ages and in every land. This one great principle was rejected, and, alas, to-day so many reject Christianity altogether. Many who term themselves Christians deny the inspiration of much if not all of Scripture. So wildly has this flood rushed on, that, could the authors of the "Reformation" re-visit the world to-day even they would not be able to recognize their work as projected by them. The laxness of views introduced by Protestantism has undermined all the barriers raised against doubt and infidelity. Doubt upon every doctrine of Christianity and upon every book of Holy Writ fills the air around us, and is almost insensibly inhaled, a poisonous miasma into the hearts of men, until it has sadly infected the minds not only of the irreverent and the scoffers at all religion, but even of well intentioned, though misguided Christians. There is but one barrier to stem this flood. Children of the Catholic Church, I beg you to realize this and find in it a strengthening of the bonds that unite you with your Mother. The Catholic Church alone, in entire faith in God's constant presence and guidance forever, stands out as the one, only, consistent, inflexible keeper and defender of the Holy Scriptures as God's true Word. And by the light and direction of the everpresent Holy Ghost, she alone declares to men both the letter and the sense of the Sacred Writings. To her whether preaching the unwritten or interpreting the Written Word of God, has the divine assurance been given, "He that heareth you, heareth Me. He that despiseth you, despiseth Me and Him that sent Me." Therefore as you reverence the Holy Scriptures as God's inspired Word, and as you hope to inherit the mercies and treasures there bequeathed to your souls, cling with strongest faith to that rock on which alone you can remain safe and unshaken while the storms of doubt and unbelief and infidelity rage all around us, and countless numbers who have left this safe anchorage are wildly, madly "tossed about by every wind of doctrine."

The lengthened experience of those who separated from the Church, and thereby rejected the voice of the Holy Ghost as the Interpreter of Holy Writ, teaches us the effect of that rejection in the countless opinions of the sects and of their individual adherents. Contrast with these the peace, the security, the unity, and the certainty enjoyed by all those who as dutiful children of the Church hear the voice of the Holy Ghost speaking by her mouth. We know that she is divinely guided in her interpretation of the Scriptures. Before the New Testament was written, the Church of Christ, as the organ of the Divine Voice, had spread the Gospel of Christ and the revelation of God over the known world. She continues this office today, and her authority and full reliability rest upon the command of her Divine Head, and upon the everpresent guidance of the Holy Ghost. If, as we have seen, she is Christ's mystical body, enlivened by the Spirit of God, is not her infallibility a necessary consequence? Can we suppose that she, who by the indwelling of God's Spirit is constantly united with her Divine Head, Christ Jesus, is nevertheless daily going through the world teaching error and falsehood in His Divine Name? The Holy Ghost was promised, to teach her all truth. Can we believe that she is blind to the truth which radiates brilliantly from His constant presence with her? Nay, is not her infallibility practically admitted at least in part by those who reject her as the interpreter of the Scriptures? For what guarantee of the genuineness of such books as they retain have they, save that which is impressed on them by the Church from whom they originally received them? And if she once erred in incorporating as God's inspired Word certain books which, as her opponents claim, were not so inspired, if she at any time erred in the interpretation of the Sacred Text, what assurance have they that the books they retained were not equally the effect of error and corruption on her part? Trace the question back to its simplest, first principles, and is it not evident that all authority for the Scriptures emanates from and is centered in the Catholic Church? To-day the world is filled with editions of the Holy Scriptures, partial or complete, in every known tongue. The art of printing has multiplied and scattered them everywhere, and the stream of their supply seems now to be at its widest. As we go backward in history this stream narrows more and more, as printed books were yet more or less scarce, until we reach the period when there were only manuscript copies—very numerous indeed, but also very few as compared with the present abundance. These ancient manuscripts, executed by the children of the Church under her supervision and scrutiny, are to-day the criterion by which the authenticity of the present text is determined. So farther and farther back, while always and ever it is the voice of the Catholic Church that determines what books form the Sacred Scriptures—the Council of Trent in the sixteenth century re-echoing the voice of that of Florence in the fourteenth, that of Constantinople in the sixth, that of Carthage in the fourth century, and there we reach the period of the earliest authentic manuscripts of the Scriptures, for none are now known to exist of an earlier date than the fourth century, representing the great and divine original. That original copy, like the body of Moses, has been withdrawn from the keeping of men. Whose authority extends beyond that period and fixes the authenticity of any of the Sacred Writings?

Only that of the Church who preserved their contents as part of the revelation received from God. To hear some men talk, one might believe that their printed Bibles are attested fac-similes of the original, that they are stereotyped or photographed copies of the original manuscripts of the Evangelists and other inspired writers. They forget the long lapse of time during which they must of necessity depend on authority for the very existence of the Written Word and for its authenticity. They forget that that authority is only and absolutely that Church whom they to-day charge with corrupting the Scriptures, and the voice of whose Life and Spirit they refuse to hear in the interpretation of the Sacred Text. She alone knows their authenticity by virtue of the operation of the Holy Ghost teaching her all truth, and therefore also such portions of it as are contained in the Sacred Writings. She alone attests their authenticity with that certainty and infallibility which necessarily result from the fact that the Spirit of God dwells with her forever! The custody of the Holy Scriptures was but a supplementary part of her divine commission. The faith, the worship, the sacraments of the Church were spread throughout the world before the books of the New Testament were written. Her office had gone on, the preaching of the Gospel to every creature had been done for many years before the books forming the New Testament had all been written and gathered into form. The first Gospel, that of St. Matthew, was not written even in the original Hebrew for five years after our Lord's Ascension, and was not translated into its present Greek form for five or six years more. St. Mark's Gospel was written about the same time; that of St. Luke about twenty four years later; that of St. John not until about sixty years after the Ascension. The earliest of the Epistles were written about fifteen years, and the latest more than thirty years after the Ascension of Christ. Even then they were often of a local, and even of a personal character, and for generations were known only to those parts of the Church to which they had been specially addressed. These various writings were not gathered into one volume, the "New Testament," as we term it, had no existence as such for nearly a hundred years after Our Lord sent His Holy Spirit to His Church. Yet the divine work of the Church had gone steadily on, and she had faithfully and effectively discharged her sacred mission during all that time. How? Was it by the distribution of the Bible? Did the work to which the Holy Spirit inspired the Apostles on Pentecost consist in their going through the crowds gathered around them, supplying each one with a copy of the Scriptures with the admonition to read, and await the issue in his heart? Or did Peter and the others stand up with the Sacred Text before them, and venture to suggest that thus and so might be the probable meaning of the text, advancing even this qualified opinion with a certain amount of deference to the judgment of their hearers whose opinions, by private interpretation, were quite as good as that of the preacher? It surely needed not the coming, the guidance, the light of the Holy Ghost merely for such work as this! And we know from the Acts of the Apostles that in fact their work was widely different from this, as they boldly faced the angry multitudes, preaching Christ crucified, and at length bringing them down upon their knees with the repentant cry: "What shall we do, men and brethren"—(Acts 2. 37)—what shall we do to be saved? These facts are given in proof of the great truth that the commission and divine character of the Church depend not on the Scriptures, but antedate them. The Scriptures depend on the Church, not the Church on the Scriptures, and her work of attesting and explaining them is but a part and incident of her divine commission. Where is the consistency in holding that the Church, thus divinely commissioned, could then preach the truth of God to men, and today cannot infallibly interpret God's Written Word to men, though the Holy Spirit Who then enlivened her, dwells with her the same, yesterday, to-day and forever! She who for many years before the issuance of the Holy Scriptures had brought to God countless martyrs, confessors, penitents and saints, she who had by her labors for men swelled the great army of the saved around the eternal throne, she whose arms even then touched the sunrise and the sunset, she who by the presence of the Holy Ghost was then as she is to-day the divine and perpetual teacher of God's truth, is she not to be heard and believed when by the Holy Spirit she presents to us as authentic that portion of her treasure which is written, and when she declares to us the sense and meaning of God's Holy Testament! For a moment lay aside, if you will, her divine authority and consider the matter in a purely human light. In human affairs the most certain rules for interpreting obscure passages are the opinions of learned men, the precedents established by the rulings of competent tribunals, and the exposition in which contemporaneous writers agree. Now taking it even on this low ground, are not all these authorities found in the Catholic Church, as she interprets the Scriptures? You have the opinions of the learned Doctors and Saints in every age. You have the multiplied decisions of her many Councils in all the centuries. You have the same unanimous, present exposition of the Sacred Text in accordance with the divine fact of her mission, her faith, her sacraments that existed before the Scriptures, and of which these are only a partial record. Her enemies dispute her claims as the infallible interpreter of the Scriptures; and yet, virtually, each sect, each individual, sets up the same claim for himself, for he is sure that he is right in his interpretation. And thus Churches and men who admit that they are not infallible, yet never err in their own judgment! They say that the Scriptures are so clear that the humblest mind can grasp their sense. If this be so, why do they fail to grasp it, and wander off into endless contradictory opinions? Are they a better authority than the Church whose children of all ages and of every race have read the Scriptures in the sense of the Church guided by the Spirit of Eternal Truth? Reason is said to be all-sufficient for understanding the Scriptures, Why does not reason lead them to the truth, which is and can be but one? And if reason be sufficient, are we to despise the reasonings on this subject of the countless numbers of Saints and Doctors of the Church, nay the reason of the united Church of all ages and all people? They tell us that all who prayerfully search the Scriptures will be there led to the truth. Yet truth is one, cannot contradict itself. Then why are they, though acting in best faith, led, not to one truth, but to endless contradictions? And granting, as we earnestly do, that prayer should accompany our reading of the Scriptures, did not St. Augustine, St. Ambrose, St. Chrysostom, St. Cyril, St. Charles—a host of Saints in every age, read the Scriptures with earnest prayer to God for rightly understanding them? These all agree to the least particulars in their understanding of the Scriptures. Divine aid, which it is presumed is given to each individual, was surely given to them also. Their unanimous consent is the sense and voice of God in the Church. They as individuals certainly enjoyed the guidance of the Holy Spirit claimed by the individual interpreter of to-day for himself. Much more did they enjoy it collectively, and when standing all together. Infinitely more is it enjoyed by the whole Church united, whose illumination and guidance are the direct fruit and result of the perpetual presence of the Holy Spirit of Truth.

The sad experiences of men outside of the Catholic Church

daily prove the truth of St. Peter's words: "Understanding this first, that no prophecy of Scripture is made by private interpretation. For prophecy came not by the will of man at any time, but the holy men of God spoke, inspired by the Holy Ghost." (2 Pet. 1. 20–21) Therefore the Scriptures are to be read, not by private interpretation, but their mysteries are to be unveiled by that Church directed and guided by the Author of the Scriptures. St. Peter knew that such adverse claims would be made. In his own day some men drifted away from the teaching authority and disputed the meaning of his great fellow-worker in God's vineyard, St. Paul. And so the chief of the Apostles writes in his second Epistle: "Our most dear brother Paul, according to the wisdom given him, hath written to you: as also in all his Epistles, speaking in them of these things; in which are certain things hard to be understood, which the unlearned and unstable wrest, as they do also the other Scriptures, to their own destruction." (2 Pet. 3. 15–16.)

Recall that wondrous scene written in the eighth chapter of the Book of Acts, and from which my text is taken, so clearly teaching us the need of an interpreter of the Scriptures. "A man of Ethiopia, an eunuch, of great authority under Candace the Queen of the Ethiopians," was returning from a devotional pilgrimage to Jerusalem. He sat reading the Scriptures—the prophecy of Isaiah. God's Spirit said to Philip, one of the Apostles who had received the Holy Ghost on Pentecost, "Go near and join thyself to this chariot." The Apostle did so, and boldly asked, "Thinkest thou that thou understandest what thou readest?" The man's prayer at Jerusalem had doubtless been a true and sincere one. Did it bring to him a private, or a personal power of understanding the Sacred Text? He himself tells us the contrary by his reply to the Apostle: "How can I understand unless some man shew me." And doubtless recognizing, as the fruit of his prayer, that from Philip's lips he might learn the truth hidden as yet from his interpretation, he begs the Apostle to sit down and instruct him. And so by the mouth of Philip was the Spirit of Truth shed into that heart, and the great gift of faith and conversion crowned the prayer and the searchings of the eunuch. He was a type and model for all coming generations, and the whole scene, if it teaches anything, teaches us to depend not upon our own interpretation of God's Word but upon the interpretation of that Church through whom the Holy Ghost speaks to our hearts and of which Philip was only the minister. Had the eunuch, like the men of modern times, refused the interpretation of the Church, and held to his own private opinion, would he ever have received the grace of faith and the knowledge of the "truth as it is in Christ Jesus"? The Word of God, hidden often from our unaided human intellect, can never be fathomed by even the greatest wisdom of man. "For who hath known the mind of the Lord? Or who hath been His counsellor?" (Rom. 11. 34.)

The Scripture is the Word of God given by the Holy Ghost through the Prophets and Apostles. But, St. Paul says: "The things also that are of God no man knoweth, but the Spirit of God. Now we have received. . . . the Spirit that is of God, that we may know the things that are given us from God." (1 Cor. 2. 11–12.) Where have we received, where are we to-day to find that Spirit of God, save in that divine organization whose life He is, and with whom He dwells forever? The Holy Ghost guided the minds and the pens of the holy men whom He inspired to write God's Word. Until the end of time, and while one soul remains to be saved, He will speak to the world in perfect interpretation of the Holy Scriptures. But those who would hear His teachings must draw near to Him and gather around His pulpit. The truth of God often veiled in mystery will be disclosed by Him only to those who kneel before His sanctuary. The Written Word of God is holy, unmixed with error, infallible. But they who unfortunately separate themselves from the body of which He is the Spirit lose the true Word of God. The Scriptures separated from the Church perish. Their proper interpretation is lost in the conflicting opinions and dissensions of men. And when their right sense is lost, the true Scriptures are lost, just as a man's will is his will only in the sense in which he intended it to be read, and in no other. It ceases to be his will when it is interpreted in any sense against his intention. St. Jerome says: "The Gospel truly consists not in the writings but in their sense, not on the surface, but in the marrow, not in the foliage of words, but in the root of truth. The Divine Scriptures when misinterpreted by men, become human." St. Augustine says that the texts of Scripture which men misinterpret are the *"pluvia laqueorum,"*—the shower of snares of which David speaks in the tenth Psalm. All faith in God's Word is soon lost in the fog of doubt and uncertainty as to its true meaning, and from this corrupt parentage of doubt the world to-day is filled with the more unworthy offspring of unbelief, atheism, and infidelity. "Their speech spreadeth like a canker," says St. Paul, (2 Tim. 2. 17.) The only safeguard against the ever-increasing evil of the misuse and abuse of the Holy Scriptures is firm, faithful, unwavering love for and adherence to that Church in whose keeping, guided by the Holy Spirit, God has placed their true interpretation. "Guard against these proud thoughts," says St. Augustine, "and remember that even the great Apostle, St. Paul, when struck down, enlightened and converted by a voice from Heaven, yet was sent to the ministers of the Holy Church to receive the sacraments and to be received within her portals. Remember that the Centurion, Cornelius, though assured by an angel from Heaven that his prayer had been heard and his alms had been accepted in the sight of God, yet was directed to send for Peter, that at his hands he might not only receive the sacraments, but might also be instructed in the faith and learn what to believe, what to hope for, what to love." St. Irenaeus declares: "Where the divine treasures have been stored up, there must we learn the truth—from those whose succession is traced back to the Apostles. For they guard the faith, they expound the Scriptures without danger of error."

From all this it must be clear to you how dearly the Catholic Church loves, how sacredly she venerates the Holy Scriptures. We hear the constant cry, "The Bible, the Bible, and nothing but the Bible." Her voice also is raised, not in vague generalities, but proclaiming to the world the Word of God in all its fullness and truth. She alone is the Scriptural Church. Is it Scriptural when those who have separated from her declare, "This is my body," means "This is not my body,"—"Whosesoever sins ye forgive," does not convey the power of forgiving sin;—"Thou art Peter, and upon this rock I will build my Church," does not mean that Peter is the rock on which Christ's Church is built;—"They shall anoint him with oil," does not mean that the sick are to be anointed? Why, the Catholic Church alone by her life and practice proves that she does accept the Holy Scriptures as the Word of the living God. The words, "He that loveth father or mother more than me, is not worthy of me," have led thousands of her children to lives of heroic sacrifice. The words, "Whosoever shall lose his life for my sake, shall find it," have created a whole army of martyrs. The words, "If thou wilt be perfect, go sell all thou hast and give it to the poor,'' have nerved countless numbers to lives of active charity and self-sacrifice which the world can never understand. ''What doth it profit a man if he gain the whole world and lose his own soul?''—these words have raised the hearts and minds of myriads of her children from the too eager pursuit of this world's goods to the coming treasures that shall never fail! All her public services are composed of the very texts of Holy Writ. Her Masses, her Breviary, all her Ritual have the Sacred Scriptures for their groundwork. The Sacred Volume is put into the hands of her deacons at ordination that it may be the guide of their life and the burden of their preaching. The same Volume is laid upon the shoulders of her bishops in their consecration that it may be the yoke under which they will labor and the glad burden of their office. One of the many whom God's great mercy brought from the darkness of error into the light of her truth, beautifully says: ''Every doctrine of the faith, every sacrament, every festival is exhibited in the very words of the inspired books. Every doctrine and sacrament becomes the centre around which the prophecies, the types and the fulfillments, recorded in Holy Scripture are gathered. They who by the grace of God have come from the wilderness into the true fold, can perhaps alone fully appreciate the change from the level and dim surface of the Sacred Text as read outside of the Church, to the luminous distinctness, the splendor and the beauty of the very same words when they are proclaimed by the voice of the Church in the acts of its public worship. From every page of Scripture words hitherto passed over seem to rise up as prophets, seers and evangelists, and to speak with accurate and living voice of the presence and power of the Kingdom of God. It is as if David and Isaiah and the Beloved Disciple and the Apostle of the Gentiles were speaking to us and worshipping with us.'' (Card. Manning.)

In this reverential spirit of the Church did St. Paulinus act when he laid the Holy Scriptures in a tabernacle side by side with the tabernacle of the Blessed Sacrament. St. Edward kissed the sacred page both before and after reading it, as the priest does every day in the Holy Mass as he ends the reading of the Gospel. St. Charles always read it with uncovered head and on bended knees. Let us then imbibe this spirit and follow this example of the Church who reverences every jot and tittle, every portion of the Holy Scriptures as ''the message of the King,'' and guards them as a trust dearer than life itself.

So shall we also love and reverence the Written Word of God, interpreted for us by the Holy Spirit. Pray that the many whose spiritual lives are made desolate by the clouds of doubt and the storms of dissenting opinions, may learn and accept the will of our Father in its true, divine interpretation, and that thus all God's children may be re-united in His faith and in carrying out His will. So shall we enjoy its full and true beauties in the light of divine interpretation. So will it be the joy and comfort of our lives here, until the clouds through which we now see their Divine Author and Interpreter shall pass away—faith shall be crowned with the glory of His vision, and, all the veils withdrawn, we shall "see Him face to face."

THIRD SERIES.

THE RELATIONSHIP OF THE HOLY GHOST
TO THE WRITTEN WORD OF GOD.

III.

He is Our Teacher and Guide in the Use of the Scriptures.

"Thou hast hid these things from the wise and prudent, and hast revealed them to little ones." (Matt. 11. 25.)

To-day we end the holy exercises of the Novena which during nine Sundays we have endeavored to present to the Divine Majesty of the Holy Ghost as the tribute of our reverence and love. To-day we close the series of meditations on His great mercies which the Holy Spirit has permitted us to make together. The thoughts that come to us to-day are but the necessary results of those reflections, in which we have recognized the Holy Ghost as the Divine Author and the unerring Interpreter of the Holy Scriptures. Recalling the words of St. Peter, "The holy men of God spoke, inspired by the Holy Ghost," (2 Pet. 1. 21) we know that He Who inspired them, whether teaching by word or by writing, is truly the Author of all they thus impart to us. And with the admonition of the same Apostle clearly before us, "No prophecy of Scripture is made by private interpretation," (2 Pet. 1. 20) we have been led to the inevitable conclusion that He, the Spirit of God in the Church, speaking by her mouth, and He alone, is the authentic and infallible Interpreter of the Holy Scriptures. And recognizing these great facts, that the Sacred Writings are God's very Word, and that their true signification is given to us by the very Spirit of God Who dwells with the Church forever—to-day, the same as twenty centuries ago surely we prostrate ourselves in great gratitude to God Who has given us so divine a treasure. We know that God Who does nothing uselessly, earnestly desires that our individual souls gain the full fruit open to us in His Sacred Word. We know, too, that this fruit can be enjoyed only by the proper use of the Scriptures. And therefore reason builds up for us the conclusion that if we would benefit properly by them, if the sacred pages shall be to us indeed the "word of life," we must use them under the guidance and instructions of their Author and Interpreter, God's Holy Spirit. His Divine arms are opened wide to receive us and lead us in the way of truth. It is His merciful office to-day to radiate throughout the world the brilliancy of the Pentecostal fires of divine light—His to enlighten and teach us—His to open the treasures of the Scriptures for our souls. He, by His grace, His unction, His consolations, His varied and most salutary operations will break this super-substantial bread of life to all who ask it in truth. He will give this "milk of the strong" to all who truly desire it. He will open up to our thirsting souls the waters bubbling forth to eternal life from the unsealed fountain of the Holy Books.

But, oh, my brethren, remember how greatly we need His guidance and instruction in this work which may, at our hands, become either so salutary or so disastrous to our souls! The Jews also had the inspired books of the Old Law. But their eyes were blinded, they failed to use the Scriptures properly, and so they groped in darkness, in the very shining of "the life that was the light of men," Who was "the true light, which enlighteneth every man." (John 1. 4–9.) St. Augustine declares: "The Jew carries the text by which the Christian believes." The possession of the true Scriptures was of no benefit to them. The variations and dissensions that fill the Christian world to-day are the outcome of a similar unwise use of the Scriptures. We, children of the Church, members of the body whose Life is the Holy Ghost possess this Heavenly treasure. For us its mystic seals have been broken; it is open to the eyes of our souls in all its beauty and power and truth, and an infallible voice guides us through its every page and sentence. And yet, alas, so many of us also call forth the wail of the Prophet, "The heart of this people is blinded." So many of us neglect this great gift of God and rarely open His Sacred Word which should be to us, as it was to the Prophet, "our meditation, day and night."

Now let us begin this day to remedy this great fault, and let these our final reflections to-day teach us how to avail ourselves fully and profitably of this great treasure. It seems hardly necessary to state that in using them, we must use the true Scriptures; not a partial or garbled version compiled by human authority no matter how eminent or how learned, but only that version which the Church has, under the inspiration of the Holy Ghost, stamped with her attest of its genuineness, and which bears her infallible interpretation of all obscure passages. The cry of modern life outside of the Church, is "The Bible without note or comment." And we see all around us the sad results of this principle. God the Holy Ghost, inspiring the Church, and speaking by her, has given us "notes and comments" on Holy Scripture which no man dare ignore or exclude, save at his peril. "He that will not hear the Church let him be to thee as a heathen and a publican."

Then, further, it is necessary that we read the Scriptures with hearts open to the guidance and teachings of the Holy Spirit. He is veiled often in the Sacred Text, but he is clear to our hearts in His inspired teachings by the Church. He creates a spiritual sense of hearing as we listen to His Word. He opens the eyes of our souls, and as He is the Author of the spoken and the written truth, He also becomes the Guide and Teacher of our intellects, our minds and our hearts. As He, "the finger of God's right hand," wrote those pages by human hands which he guided, so by His grace does He open the eyes of our human understanding and the portals of our human hearts to their divine wealth and beauty. He is the sound from Heaven, Who, like the zephyr vibrating the strings of the harp, ravishes our souls with the divine harmonies of Holy Writ, subduing our rebellious minds, and filling our desolate hearts with the music of His truth. He sheds the light of His Divinity upon the darkest passages; He, from the Written Word, kindles in our hearts the fire of His love. This will be the fruit of His teaching, for St. Paul assures us that "All Scripture, inspired of God, is profitable to teach, to reprove, to correct, to instruct in justice, that the man of God may be perfect, furnished to every good work." (2 Tim. 3. 16–17.) The true Scripture is that which "came not by the will of man at any time," (2 Pet. 1. 21)—that which is not "made by private interpretation." (2 Pet. 1. 20.) Laid open to us by the teaching and guidance of the Holy Ghost in the Church, the dead letter becomes alive by the Spirit of God. Its Spirit "which giveth life" is breathed into the soul and quickens it with great desire of the truth. Thus Holy Writ becomes the remedy for our spiritual wounds, the light that guides us to God, and like the manna of the Old Law and the Eucharist of our altars, it is a "food containing all sweetness."

Let me earnestly impress this great truth upon your hearts, that you cultivate the pious habit of thus reverently reading and treasuring God's Holy Word. Read it frequently; read it with earnest reflection; above all, read it with fervent prayer to the Holy Ghost for His guidance while you read. Learn to hunger for its hidden plenties, and you will be permitted to eat. The Prophet Ezechiel tells us of a mysterious vision given to him. "And I looked, and behold, a hand was sent to me, wherein was a book rolled up; and he spread it before me, and it was written within and without . . . And he said to me: Son of man, eat all that thou shalt find; eat this book." (Ezech. 2.9–3. 1.) So shall our spiritual hunger also be satisfied by the plenty of God's Word. The Holy Scripture may be said to be like the great seven-fold treasures of the New Law, the Sacraments. For, like them, it is in itself efficacious and powerful for conferring heavenly grace, but for its full effect it requires of us the removal of all obstacles; and the more worthy our dispositions in approaching it, the more abundant will be our measure of grace and sanctification. It contains in its sacred folds the light, the heat, the virtue that shine forth from the seven-branched candlestick of the Holy Sacraments. It teaches us of our regeneration in Baptism, of our strengthening in Confirmation, of our great food in the Holy Eucharist, of our cleansing in Penance, of our anointing in Extreme Unction, of the divine blessing given in Matrimony, of the power and dignity of the Holy Orders. The Church makes it the model and rule of life of her priests and bishops. In the ordination of her priests, she implores Almighty God "that they show themselves well grounded in the lessons St. Paul gave to Timothy and to Titus—so that, meditating on Thy Law day and night, they may believe what they read, teach what they believe, and practice what they teach." (Pontif. Rom.) In the consecration of her bishops she lays the Sacred Book with full weight upon their shoulders, with the solemn commission, "Receive the Gospel. Go and preach it to the people committed to thee." (Ibid.) Not less solicitous is she that all her children should drink freely of this fountain of divine truth, and we never come nearer to her ardent wishes than when we have learned to read God's Word frequently, reverently, with great desire to learn its truths, with a spiritual hunger and thirst for its inspired wisdom. You recall the loving visit made by our Lord after His Resurrection to the two disciples who in sadness at His death were walking from Jerusalem to Emmaus. He answered their prayer and went in with them at the end of their journey. They knew Him not until He broke the bread. Then they knew the Lord. But subsequently recalling the incidents of His visit, "they said one to another: Was not our heart burning within us, whilst he spoke in the way, and opened to us the Scriptures!" (Luke 24. 32.) That was the effect of His teaching. And if our hearts be prepared as theirs were, that will be the effect of the Holy Ghost opening the Scriptures to us. Our hearts will burn with divine love, if we but approach the sacred flame hidden in the Text. Again and again like the invalid whom Christ healed, must we descend into the deep well where lies the truth of God's Written Word, until at length the angel of His mercy come and set into motion for our healing those waters of eternal life. Like the blind man by the wayside we must cry out again and again for His grace. Like the woman in the Gospel we must seek to touch the hem of His garment with which He has clothed Himself in the Sacred Text. Then will our eyes also be opened, and from His vesture there will flow to us a divine virtue that will heal us and save us.

From those who do not know the Catholic Church, we frequently hear the statement that she does not encourage her children to use the Scriptures, or that she largely substitutes other devotions in place of the reading of the Scriptures. From what has been said in this and in former discourses, the first accusation is unmeaning and untrue. For all her devotions, her Masses, her Vespers, the official prayers of the Breviary daily offered by her ministers—her entire Ritual is very largely composed of the very words of the Sacred Text, and in the language of the people these are in the hands of all her children. As to the second objection, her great reverence for God's Word causes her indeed to see to it that her children use it properly. But examine the books of devotion and prayer whose use she authorizes. You find the Sacred Volume in every well-regulated Catholic family. The prayer-books of the people all have for their basis the truths of Sacred Scripture—the Creed, which is the compendium of the truths there written—the Law of the Ten Commandments and their perfecting by the Gospel—the mysteries of the Holy Trinity, the Incarnation, the Passion of Christ—the grace of the Seven Sacraments as taught in Scripture—the counsels of Penance, Piety, Charity and all other virtues. We have, indeed, already seen that great as is the treasure of the Holy Scriptures, these are not the Church's greatest possession. They are the "letters of the King," but lo, the King Himself dwells on her altars! Her solemn public devotions have in them something more than only the reading of God's Word, for they comprise the renewal of the great sacrifice of Calvary, the bodily presence of the Eternal Son of God, and her adoration and worship of Him truly present. Henry III of England was once asked by Louis, King of France, why he went so often to Mass and so seldom to the sermon, and he answered: "Because I had rather speak face to face with my friend than hear about him." The presence of Jesus in the tabernacle draws to that point all eyes and all hearts when Catholics assemble for divine worship. We read the letters of a friend when he is absent; but when he is with us we turn to him and converse with him direct. The perpetual, daily, hourly worship of God dwelling really with us, fills the hearts of all the children of the Church, and the reality of His presence gives a secondary importance to His Word, as dearly loved and sacredly honored as it is by all true Catholics. And thus the public worship of the Catholic Church has in it a divine character which cannot be understood by those outside of the fold. But next to the adoration of the Eternal Son constantly present on our altars, and next to the methods and greatness of that worship, and the treasuring of the sacramental graces that flow from the tabernacle, the Church has no dearer, no more valued gift of God than His Holy Word. That her children may know not "to wrest them to their own destruction," but to find them indeed the words of truth and of life, she supplies vast numbers of books of devotion and meditation which, from first to last, are the text of Holy Scriptures explained and applied. All the numerous expositions and commentaries, the many volumes of meditation for every day in the year, what are these, but the Holy Scripture brought home to the people, identified with their daily lives, in the most accurate and prac-

tical manner? Why, such works hardly exist outside of the Church.
The few that have appeared from time to time have quickly fallen
into general disuse. It is a significant fact that such few devotional
books as are found in Protestant hands are, to a very great extent,
translations or adaptations of Catholic works. But even these do not
approach the bountiful supply of such works in the Church—so
abundant that no earnest, thoughtful Catholic is without some book
of devout meditation on the Holy Scriptures.

But always and ever she warns her children to read the Scriptures with the reverence and devotion taught us by their Author, the
Holy Ghost, that under His guidance we may treat holy things in a
holy manner and run no risk of profaning the treasury of God. She
holds up to us the warning of Jeremias: "Cursed be he that doth the
work of the Lord deceitfully." (Jer. 48. 10.) The reverent reading
of the Scriptures under the guidance of the Holy Ghost was the life
work of every Saint in her calendar to whom that treasure was ac-
cessible in life. Read the Scriptures; but let it be with that humble
and docile heart that is suited to the creature conversing with his Creator, for He that "hath scattered the proud in the conceit of their
heart, He that hath put down the mighty from their seat * * hath exalted the humble and hath filled the hungry with good things." (Luke
1. 51–53). Read the Scriptures; but let it be in true appreciation of
our own weakness and blindness, and with earnest prayer that the
Holy Ghost be our Teacher and Guide; for St. James admonishes us:
"If any of you want wisdom, let him ask God, Who giveth to all
men abundantly, and upbraideth not; and it shall be given him."
(James 1. 5). God hears the prayers of the humble. "Thou hast hid
these things from the wise and prudent (in their own conceit) and hast
revealed them to little ones." (Matt. 11. 25.) Those who ask not for
His light in humility, be they never so rich in their own imaginings
"He hath sent away hungry," and those who would irreverently
search His Majesty shall be overwhelmed by it. We need His guidance in His paths, in which poor reason alone cannot lead us.
"Honor the veiled mystery in the Scriptures," says St. Augustine,
"and honor it the more deeply the more the veils hang heavy. They
but guard the honor of the secret. But for those who reverence them
all veils shall be lifted." He further declares that man is more wise
or is wanting in true wisdom just in proportion as he is more or less
deeply acquainted with the Holy Scriptures. Read the Scriptures; but

let it be with the discernment given from God by which this great spiritual food will be thoroughly digested and will diffuse its life and strength through all your spiritual system. So will their words, made clear to your hearts by the light of the Holy Ghost, enable you to wing your flight heavenward like the eagle, and to become in the daily struggles of human life valiant soldiers of Christ, having taken "unto you the helmet of salvation; and the sword of the Spirit, which is the word of God." (Eph. 6. 17.) The Scriptures are a fountain from which the revelation of the Most High flows into our souls. The Spirit of God will move their waters for those who reverently descend to their hidden depths, and the erring will come forth regenerated by a spiritual baptism to a new life, more devout, more heavenly, more God-like.

To-day, as from the beginning, the Holy Scriptures are the powerful weapons wielded by Doctors and Saints against the noxious spirit of the world. Their truths uttered by St. Paul, he declares, "mighty to God unto the pulling down of fortifications, destroying counsels, and every height that exciteth itself against the knowledge of God, and bringing into captivity every understanding unto the obedience of Christ." (2 Cor. 10. 4–5.) The Gospel has been preached, is to-day proclaimed throughout the world by the ministers of the Church, but their minds become learned and the zeal of their holy mission is great in proportion as they have deeply and reverently studied the Scriptures under the guidance of the Holy Spirit. Their work is effective in bringing souls to God, in proportion as St. Paul's words are verified in them: "My speech and my preaching was not in the showing of the Spirit." (1 Cor. 2. 4.) And what is thus true of the ministers of God is, in some sense, true of each one of you also. For you also are to engage in the work of the Lord. It is your duty to be able "to give a reason for the faith that is in you," and to defend it against the many onslaughts daily made. Above all, it is your duty "to let your light shine before men," and to show forth in your daily lives the fruit and effects of the truths God gives to you in the Holy Scriptures. For St. Peter assures you: "You are a chosen generation, a kingly priesthood." (1 Pet. 2. 9.) Therefore I say, as docile children of your Divine Teacher and Guide, read the Scriptures. Let them be to you your remedy and unction in all the dangers and cares of your lives. But remember that like Magdalen you must break the vase, that is, the mere letter of the Scriptures, so that the sweet odor of the ointment of the Spirit may be diffused around you. Let God's Word be your joy and strength in all the distractions and labors of life. But, under the guidance of the Holy Ghost, break the shell which is the mere letter that you may enjoy the sweetness of the kernel which is the spirit, and in the wisdom of the Holy Ghost you will realize that "her conversation hath no bitterness, nor her company any tediousness, but joy and gladness." (Wisdom 8. 16.) St. Paul says: "Meditate upon these things, be wholly in these things, that thy profiting may be manifest to all * * * For in doing this thou shalt both save thyself and them that hear thee." (1 Tim. 4. 15–16.) Read the Scriptures, and let their fruit so abound in you that your daily lives may be the evidence of God's power and love. Thus led by His Spirit, enlightened by His grace, directed by the "Finger of God's right hand," preserved from all error, avoiding all sin, your lives will become witnesses unto God, daily "testifying the Gospel of God's grace."

Oh, how much of this work is open to us to-day, this hour! Never were Our Lord's words more applicable than to-day and in this great land: "Behold, I say to you, lift up your eyes, and see the countries, for they are white already to harvest." (John 4. 35.) "He that reapeth receiveth wages, and gathereth fruit unto life everlasting; that both he that soweth, and he that reapeth, may rejoice together." (John 4. 36.) So many souls there are around us who see not the light shining so brightly. So many there are who indeed read the Scriptures, yet having no Divine Guide are not filled, yet cry aloud hungering for the truth. Do we owe no duty to them? Are we not all of us, bound to lead them to the waters, which, set into motion by the Holy Spirit, will give them health and light and life? Dare we answer of our brothers as Cain did of his: "I know not. Am I my brother's keeper?" (Gen. 4. 9.) No, my brethren, it is our duty and our happy privilege to seek to procure for others the light given to us and to bring every understanding, be it brilliant as that of Athens, or Corinth, or Rome, when St. Paul preached, or subtile and indifferent as our modern enlightenment, "unto the obedience of Christ." This great work which should come home to every child of the Catholic Church, is to be done, not by wrangling argument or heated discussion. It is to be accomplished first of all by thoroughly informing yourselves on the truths and doctrines really taught by the Church. For it is a sad fact that the ignorance of many Catholics serves as a barrier to keep others out of the Church. This work is to be done by prayer, by constant supplication to the Holy Ghost that He would fill the hearts of all men, and by restoring the unity of faith, would indeed renew the face of the earth. This work is to be done by our individual example, which is so much more powerful than any words. Our lives must show the effects of our faith and of our study of the Holy Scriptures, by being the daily, logical, consistent results of the teachings of the Holy Ghost in our hearts. The Sermon of our Lord upon the Mount is addressed to each of us to-day also: "So let your light shine before men, that they may see your good works, and glorify your Father who is in heaven." (Matt. 5. 16.) So shall we gain for our own souls, and it may be for many others also, the full and divine benefits offered to us by the use of the Scriptures under the guidance of the Holy Ghost.

And now but a few words, as we close the series of our meditations on the Holy Ghost. It has been the mercy and grace of the Holy Spirit that has enabled us to make them. We have recognized His many claims on our devotion and love—the wonderful importance of His work in our salvation from the beginning, now and throughout eternity in heaven. We cannot but admit that hitherto our lives have not shown us to be deeply impressed by the great truths which these reflections have brought home to us. We have been so cold, so indifferent to Him, while He thought of us from all eternity, guided every step of our lives, and opened for us the many and abundant means by which we may lead holy lives. Oh, may He by Whose grace we have been permitted thus to meditate on His Divine Goodness, also make these thoughts fruitful in our hearts. May the closing to-day of our Novena in His honor, produce results like those of that first Novena by which the Apostles prepared for His coming. They were entirely changed. From shrinking, timid, doubting disciples they were transformed into heroes whose entire lives from that hour were given to God's work, and whose work ended only when the Martyr's crown floated down to them from the hand of God. So may it be with us also. As we go forth now, at the close of this Novena, let it be as new men, who have laid aside their old carelessness and indifference. Realizing how closely we are related to the Holy Ghost—how essential He is to us in gaining our salvation—how greatly we need Him, and how strong are His claims on our love, let us be renewed in His spirit to-day, and may our lives henceforth be all guided by Him, and His devotion become the characteristic of our souls. We owe Him our best homage for so many reasons. First, for the glory of His Divine Person, for He is God, co-eternal, co-infinite, consubstantial with the Father and the Son. We owe Him special adoration for His work for us and in us, His work in the first creation, but, above all, in the second creation when our souls were redeemed, and we who had been enemies became the children of God through Him. For through all our lives has He been renewing for us the most benefits and graces of our Redemption in Christ. Again and again we have died the death of the soul by sin, and ever again by leading us to repentance and absolution, He has restored us to life in God. In every Sacrament, and above all in the Holy Eucharist has He constantly enriched us with the boundless graces of Christ's Sacred Blood. His light has been ever on our path teaching us our duty, sustaining us in our weakness, sealing us with the very seal of our God. And we have so often quenched that light by sin—have resisted the good impulses and holy thoughts He inspired, and when He had again and again enlightened our hearts with His light and led us back to God, we have again and again by carelessness, like the foolish virgins, allowed the light to die out. We have so often grieved Him by our relapses, by our coldness, by our indifference while He sought to lavish upon us His Divine virtues and His seven-fold gifts. And all this is to be remedied. The fruit of these our reflections and meditations must be atonement for the past, and new, better lives for the future. Our debt to Him is a great one and we must no longer delay its payment. We owe Him daily praise, adoration, worship, as the very God Whom we need not seek abroad, but Whose altar is created in our hearts and Who dwells there until our sins drive Him from us. We owe Him reparation, which will consist in rooting out of our hearts the special sins by which we have grieved Him—sins against the light He gave us, sins against His whisperings in our conscience, sins of worldliness by which we have failed to remember that He dwells with us, sins of indifference by which we have ignored His presence and His work in us.

Let us make it a rule to ourselves from this time never to allow one day to pass without some special prayer and act of devotion to the Holy Ghost. Let us give our whole heart to Him with all love and trust. Let us beg Him, our Sanctifier, to make us holy. He will hear our prayer, for He is loving and tender and generous in all His works.

He will make our sinful wills yield and blend themselves into His Divine Will which is our sanctification. He will demand of us no work or effort without also supplying us with the divine strength by which we can accomplish it.

O, God the Holy Ghost, Whom from my first use of reason in childhood until now I have grieved and slighted and forgotten and resisted! Behold, now my heart is ready, create a new heart within me, a heart alive to Thy great mercies and inflamed with Thy love. After my long wanderings receive me back to Thy grace. Come to me with Thy seven-fold gifts—the spirit of Wisdom and of Understanding, of Counsel and of Fortitude, of Knowledge and of Piety, and of the true Fear of the Lord which is the beginning of all Wisdom. Kindle in my heart the fire of Thy love and it will consume all dross of sin. Place me in the crucible of true sorrow and penance that I may offer to Thee the pure gold of my earnest love and constant devotion.

"Per Te sciamus da Patrem, Noscamus atque Filium, Teque utriusque Spiritum, Credamus omni tempore."

Oh, may Thy grace on us bestow
The Father and the Son to know,
And Thee, through endless times confessed
Of both, the Eternal Spirit blest!

And to Thee, O Holy Spirit, Who with the Father and the Son
    livest and reignest in the unity of the Godhead, shall be
    all honor and glory, for eternity.—Amen.

INDEX TO PREFACE AND INTRODUCTION

INDEX TO TEXTS

Other Volumes in This Series